Texts in Philosophy
Volume 28

Quantum Heresies

Volume 19
History and Philosophy of Physics in South Cone
Roberto A. Martins, Guillermo Boido, and Víctor Rodríguez, eds.

Volume 20
History and Philosophy of Life Sciences in South Cone
Pablo Lorenzano, Lilian Al-Chueyr Pereira Martins, and Anna Carolina K. P. Regner, eds.

Volume 21
The Road Not Taken. On Husserl's Philosophy of Logic and Mathematics
Claire Ortiz Hill and Jairo José da Silva

Volume 22
The Good, the Right & the Fair – an introduction to ethics
Mickey Gjerris, Morten Ebbe Juul Nielsen, and Peter Sandøe

Volume 23
The Normative Structure of Responsibility. Law, Language, Ethics
Federico Faroldi

Volume 24
Karl Popper. A Centenary Assessment. Volume I. Life and Times, and Values in a World of Facts
Ian Jarvie, Karl Milford and David Miller, eds

Volume 25
Karl Popper. A Centenary Assessment. Volume II. Metaphysics and Epistemology
Ian Jarvie, Karl Milford and David Miller, eds

Volume 26
Karl Popper. A Centenary Assessment. Volume III Science
Ian Jarvie, Karl Milford and David Miller, eds

Volume 27
Unorthodox Analytic Philosophy
Guillermo E. Rosado Haddock

Volume 28
Quantum Heresies.
Kent A. Peacock, with a foreword by James Robert Brown


Texts in Philosophy Series Editors
Vincent F. Hendriks                    vincent@hum.ku.dk
John Symons                            jsymons@utep.edu
Dov Gabbay                             dov.gabbay@kcl.ac.uk

# Quantum Heresies

Kent A. Peacock

With a foreword by
James Robert Brown

© Individual authors and College Publications 2018.
All rights reserved.

ISBN 978-1-84890-241-1

College Publications
Scientific Director: Dov Gabbay
Managing Director: Jane Spurr

http://www.collegepublications.co.uk

Cover art and figures in Chapters 4 and 10 by Evan Peacock
Original cover design by Laraine Welch

Printed by Lightning Source, Milton Keynes, UK

---

All rights reserved. No part of this publication may be reproduced, stored in a retrieval system or transmitted in any form, or by any means, electronic, mechanical, photocopying, recording or otherwise without prior permission, in writing, from the publisher.

For Sharon—fellow heretic.

# Foreword

## James Robert Brown

Quantum mechanics has been an irritating puzzle since its founding almost a century ago. The work of Heisenberg, Born, Pauli, Bohr, de Broglie, Schrödinger, Dirac, and others was a stunning achievement, but utterly perplexing. Einstein hated it. He famously remarked 'God does not play dice,' but he could probably endure the indeterminism. What really troubled him was the anti-realism, 'Does the moon exist only when we look at it?' and the 'spooky action at a distance,' which flies in the face of Special Relativity (SR). How, we all wonder, could a theory that is so empirically successful be so unintelligible? Why can't we understand it?

Kent Peacock and all those who try to make sense of QM enter current debates at the point of mystification. An interpretation of QM is an attempt to take the mystery out and to say how the world works so that the quantum theory is a success. When we measure, do we discover the result or do we create it? When we get correlated results in distant measurements, is the outcome due to a common cause or does one measurement somehow influence the other? If one side of an apparatus does influence the other side, it would seem to require faster than light signals in violation of SR's insistence that $c$ is a maximum. Is there any way of saving both QM and SR, or must one give away? Various interpretations have tried and largely failed to cope with these questions.

*Quantum Heresies* is at once a perfect title and a misleading one. A heresy is a break with orthodoxy, the dominant consensus view. But there is no consensus. Long ago the Copenhagen interpretation was the orthodox account, but it has since given up that title. Now no view is even close to dominant. If heresy is any view other than orthodoxy, then almost all views today are heretical. But Kent especially merits the heretic label, because of his particular view about QM and superluminal connections, especially in connection with so-called peaceful coexistence, and also because of his new take on central properties of time. We should not, he thinks, be trying to reconcile QM and SR. The tension is widely recognized, but few are quite so ready to embrace and explore the nonlocal world as is Kent.

One of the most impressive things in Kent's past work on the foundations of physics is the examination of so-called no-signalling theorems in QM that are alleged to show superluminal connections will not alter the measurement statistics. These 'theorems' are a central part of the attempt to have quantum non-locality be compatible with special relativity. What Kent has done is to show that these, in their various different ways, are actually circular arguments. For example, in quantum field theory certain operators are thought to commute because special relativity guarantees there will be no causal interference outside the light cone. The no-signalling theorems use these commuting operators to then 'prove' that distant measurements won't affect one another; i.e., that no signal can be sent between them. This is a question-begging assumption when SR itself is at issue. Kent's work on exposing these problems is exceptional and of the highest importance, and it should have a major (negative) impact on 'peaceful co-existence' between SR and standard QM.

There are many foundational issues explored with rare insight in this exceptional volume. But as well as content, style matters. Einstein, right about so much, was wrong in asserting: 'If you are out to describe the truth, leave elegance to the tailor.' Rubbish. Plodding prose might not be hazardous to one's health, but it dullens the spirit. Readers of these very fine chapters will be treated not only to some remarkable insights in philosophy and physics, but they will also enjoy Kent's sparkling style. Those who enjoy this book will also enjoy his very accessible history, *The Quantum Revolution* [165]. Kent is one of the finest philosophical writers anywhere on any topic, something to be promoted and cherished. Read, learn, enjoy.

# Preface

This book is a collection of my papers on quantum nonlocality and related problems such as the nature of time and simultaneity, originally published from 1992 to 2014. It was John Woods who suggested that I resurrect these writings and who generously recommended my proposal to College Publications. John is also my co-author on one paper included here; Brian Hepburn is co-author on another.

A word on the title. A 'heretic' is one who chooses, not necessarily one who dissents from orthodoxy. But heretics often end up as dissenters anyway, because orthodoxy so often turns out to be wrong when viewed with a fresh eye. I must confess, though, that from the outset I went into this particular corner with my elbows up, because I suspected that certain questions (to be explored below) had been dismissed far too quickly.

Quantum nonlocality is just about the hardest intellectual problem in the world, and arguably one of the most important. No one should think that they have the last word on it, least of all this general issue philosopher of science. However, I am confident that I am raising questions that have not been given the attention they deserve, even if the answers I sketch for them turn out to be utterly mistaken. Think of this anthology not as a retrospective but as a report on work in progress.

# Contents

**Foreword**
    JAMES ROBERT BROWN     vii

**Preface**     ix

**Introduction**     1

**1 What Was it That Was to Have Been Proven?**     12

**2 A New Look at Simultaneity**     15
    2.1 Statement of the Problem . . . . . . . . . . . . . . . . . . . . 16
    2.2 Heinlein on Time and Simultaneity . . . . . . . . . . . . . . 17
    2.3 The Mathematical Problem . . . . . . . . . . . . . . . . . . . 19
    2.4 Intrinsic Simultaneity as Equality of Action . . . . . . . . . . 23
    2.5 Conclusions . . . . . . . . . . . . . . . . . . . . . . . . . . . . 25

**3 On the Edge of a Paradigm Shift**     27
    3.1 Introduction: A Call For a Fresh Approach . . . . . . . . . . 28
    3.2 Some Basics . . . . . . . . . . . . . . . . . . . . . . . . . . . . 29
    3.3 Is there a Bell Telephone? . . . . . . . . . . . . . . . . . . . . 31
    3.4 A Fiendish Device . . . . . . . . . . . . . . . . . . . . . . . . 32
    3.5 But Why Can There Not Be a Common Cause? . . . . . . . . 35
    3.6 Information and the Locality of Particle Dynamics . . . . . . 37
    3.7 Could Relativity Really Be a Principle Theory? . . . . . . . . 42
    3.8 Nonlocal Hidden Variables? . . . . . . . . . . . . . . . . . . . 46
    3.9 Two Alternate Approaches . . . . . . . . . . . . . . . . . . . 47
    3.10 On the Edge of a Paradigm Shift . . . . . . . . . . . . . . . . 49

**4 An Adventure Outside the Light Cone**     50
    4.1 Motivation for this Study . . . . . . . . . . . . . . . . . . . . 50
    4.2 Derivation of Superluminal Transformations . . . . . . . . . 51
    4.3 A Problem for Space Travellers . . . . . . . . . . . . . . . . . 56
    4.4 Causal Paradoxes . . . . . . . . . . . . . . . . . . . . . . . . . 56

| 5 | To Understand Anything We Have to Understand Everything | 58 |
|---|---|---|
| | 5.1 Isms and Schisms | 60 |
| | 5.2 Science and Subjectivity | 64 |
| | 5.3 Experimental Metaphysics | 68 |
| | 5.4 Theories of Everything | 72 |

| 6 | Bub and the Barriers to Quantum Ontology | 77 |
|---|---|---|

| 7 | Quantum Logic and the Unity of Science<br>JOHN WOODS & KENT A. PEACOCK | 83 |
|---|---|---|
| | 7.1 Motivating Quantum Logic | 83 |
| | 7.2 Feynman's Problem | 86 |
| | 7.3 Lattice Theory: A mined-out vein? | 89 |
| | 7.4 Discrediting or Underdetermining? | 91 |
| | 7.5 The breakdown of bivalence; or *ex superpondendo quolibet*? | 95 |
| | 7.6 The Unity of Science, Again | 111 |

| 8 | Temporal Presentness and the Dynamics of Spacetime | 113 |
|---|---|---|
| | 8.1 Probabilism and Spacetime Structure | 114 |
| | 8.2 Generalizing Simultaneity | 116 |
| | 8.3 Telepathic Twins? | 117 |
| | 8.4 Invariant Simultaneity as Equality of Action | 118 |
| | 8.5 Conflicts with Relativity? | 119 |
| | 8.6 Covariant State Reduction Based on Phase Invariance | 122 |
| | 8.7 Quantum Mechanics and the Ontology of the Future | 123 |

| 9 | A Nitpicking Distinction | 126 |
|---|---|---|
| | 9.1 An Occasion for Pain? | 126 |
| | 9.2 The Problem | 127 |
| | 9.3 The 'Proofs' | 129 |
| | 9.4 Where the Investigation of Signalling Might Go | 133 |
| | 9.5 Causal Paradoxes and the 'Spirit of Relativity' | 134 |
| | 9.6 The Limits of the Possible | 135 |

| 10 | Superluminal Influences | 137 |
|---|---|---|
| | 10.1 Alleged troubles with superluminal effects and influences | 137 |
| | 10.2 Is there a distinguished frame? | 141 |
| | 10.3 Absolute motion? | 144 |
| | 10.4 Conflict with Einstein's relativity of simultaneity? | 147 |
| | 10.5 Alternative concepts of simultaneity | 149 |
| | 10.6 'Causal' accounts of quantum mechanics | 154 |
| | 10.7 Summary—and what must lie ahead | 157 |

## 11 The Truth is (Still) Out There
### KENT A. PEACOCK & BRIAN S. HEPBURN — 159
- 11.1 Introduction ........ 160
- 11.2 Can We Explain the Correlations? ........ 161
- 11.3 Causal Interpretations of QM ........ 163
- 11.4 Bohm and Hiley on Signalling ........ 164
- 11.5 Nonlocality of Multiparticle Dynamics ........ 168
- 11.6 Symmetrization and Nonlocality ........ 170
- 11.7 The Hamiltonian for Entangled Particles Cannot Be Additive ........ 171
- 11.8 Nonlocal Energy: It's Everywhere ........ 174

## Envoi: The Work To Be Done — 176

## Acknowledgements — 182

## Bibliography — 184

## Index — 201

# Introduction

The burden of the investigation reported in this book is to question the received view that quantum mechanics and Einsteinian relativity stand in a relationship of 'peaceful coexistence'. I also sketch some elements of an alternative to that view, and take some side-forays into scientific realism, quantum logic, and the metaphysics of time. I am well aware that it is a risky business to challenge scientific orthodoxy, especially on such a central point—one might simply turn out to have wasted a great deal of time and energy on a mistake (and in the process misdirected the time and energy of others as well). The history of science shows that the community of competent observers can indeed be wrong about important matters. However, the history of science also shows that this is rare. If you really do think that the received scientific view of a key question is wrong then you had better be prepared to present a very good argument for your case, and you had best make sure that you understand exactly why the orthodoxy is accepted by those who ought to know. I have worked hard in order to try to meet these standards; the reader will have to judge whether I have succeeded.

What do I mean here by 'wrong'? I mean that the scientific community failed to arrive at a conclusion that was not only readily available from but demanded by the evidence in hand at the time. A good example of science coming to its senses after having been wrong for a long time was the sudden acceptance by Earth scientists of the concept of continental drift, after decades of what *in retrospect* looks like obstinate refusal to see the obvious [105, 106]. A mistaken consensus can change rapidly when scientists are presented with a critical mass of evidence and a believable alternative theory. The evident *fact* of continental drift was not accepted until the *theory* of plate tectonics was developed to the point at which what had looked like a random coincidence (the jigsaw-puzzle match of the continental shelves and rock strata of South American and Africa) came suddenly to be seen as a natural consequence of underlying structure and dynamics.

Another good example of a similar 'paradigm shift' was the acceptance (not as fast as in the case of plate tectonics) of the theory of serial endosymbiosis in cell biology. This is the notion that eucaryotic (nucleated) cells are obligate symbiotic associations of procaryotes (bacteria). The eventual acceptance of the symbiotic view of cellular structure is due in important part to the imagination and intellectual courage of Lynn Margulis, a scientist whom I particularly admire [134, 135]. In both cases, a view that was for decades regarded as far-fetched speculation has become dogma taught to first-year students.

With regard to the challenge of quantum nonlocality I believe that we are very close to the point at which a critical mass of evidence will catalyze a similar 'paradigm shift'. The challenge, again, is to grasp underlying dynamics—and also (and much more than in the earth science and cell biology examples) to be willing to *give up* certain conceptions which for a long time have been taken as beyond reasonable question.

Let me be clear: I am not anti-scientific—far from it, for I think that science (broadly understood) is as essential for survival to humans as eyesight is to birds of prey. In most respects my considered scientific opinions are reasonably orthodox. I think that anthropogenic global warming is one of the two defining challenges of our time [167] (our destruction of biodiversity being the other). I know that vaccines have saved millions of lives, possibly including my own (since I was among the first cohorts of children to receive the polio vaccine). I think that Darwin's picture of how evolution works is essentially correct (though following Margulis and others I think that symbiosis plays a larger role in evolution and ecology than most experts are prepared to accept [166]). I think that the broad picture of the universe that modern science has painstakingly built up is more or less right *as far as it goes*, though I am readier than many would be to point to the significant omissions, gaps, and contradictions in that picture. So I am, I very much hope, not entirely a crank or contrarian. It is just that I think the arguments that have been presented in favour of 'peaceful coexistence' do not begin to hold water, for reasons that I attempt to explain in this book. I'm not sure why brilliant minds from Einstein down have made these mistakes, except that they seem to have been misled by some very deep-seated philosophical prejudices against the possibility of nonlocality. I hope that my work will help to dispel these prejudices, though I am not sure that this modest volume will be sufficient to do the job on its own.

But I am getting ahead of myself. I should first say a little about what led me to become obsessed with a problem that most people think (or hope) was settled a long time ago. Then I'll try to summarize where I think matters now stand (I'm writing in June, 2018).

I grew up in a middle-class family near Toronto, Ontario; my father was a sculptor, classical pianist, and professional architect. An uncle and a grandfather were also multi-talented architects. In my parent's household it was axiomatic that creativity was the most valuable human capacity, and that authority exists to be questioned. As a teenager I was enthralled with science fiction the way that many young people are enthralled by video games today. But I read widely in science and philosophy as well and I realized that what drew me to science fiction above all else were its sweeping visions of the universe and humanity's possible place in that universe (or universes!). I was talented in both writing and mathematics but utterly lacking in personal discipline. My first foray into academia, in the old math, physics and chemistry program at the University of Toronto, was (to put it gently) not entirely successful. I worked in the so-called 'real world' for several years, including a stint as a construction labourer in the employ of a survivor of the Battle of Stalingrad. Eventually, I decided that I should aim for graduate school in philosophy since I realized that the *way* I think about things is almost compulsively philosophical, and since philosophy would give me the best chance to find a professional milieu where I could explore my too-diverse intellectual interests.

I was finally admitted to graduate studies in philosophy at the University of Toronto in 1986. In graduate school I at last felt at home academically, and I wondered why I had not gone there a long time before. Under the genial but exacting guidance of Jim Brown I completed a PhD in 1991 on the tensions between quantum nonlocality and relativity. As a PhD student I also taught a course on environmental philosophy, which reawakened a long-standing interest in ecology, the environment, and climate. My first book was a text on environmental philosophy, adapted from the course notes for my environmental philosophy courses at Toronto and the University of Western Ontario [162]. Recently, I've devoted much attention to the network of urgent problems surrounding global warming, sustainability, and energy. I've also ended up teaching a lot of logic, so much so that I sometimes describe logic as my 'day job'. But despite the distractions of a busy academic career I've never stopped thinking about the mysteries of the quantum world and the ways in which it must supersede the classical worldview.

By the time I started grad studies I had already given a lot of study and thought to the special theory of relativity and its possible limitations. I was fascinated by the question of whether or not the theory really does prohibit faster-than-light motion. Even then, it seemed to me that there was something arbitrary and hasty about the conventional reasoning that dismissed that possibility, and I was not alone in that thought, for from the 1960s onward a large literature had sprung up exploring the possibility of 'tachyons' (faster-than-light particles) and so-called 'extended relativity'. This literature was of uneven scientific quality, but it was animated by a very cogent observation: it could well be that orthodox special relativity does not allow for superluminal motion not because such motion is impossible, but because the theory simply has not been correctly formulated for the superluminal case.

My interest in this problem quite likely was triggered by over-exposure to science fiction, where it is usually taken that superluminal space travel is simply a technological problem that will be solved sometime in the indefinite future. But I was also becoming increasingly aware of ecological questions, and I realized that it is very important to know, sooner or later, whether the human species must remain forever confined to the planet of its birth or whether we can spread to other worlds. Some of my colleagues in philosophy do not think that this question is worthy of serious discussion; I disagree (though I am well aware that other challenges, such as global warming and economic inequality, are far more immediate). The most important issue, though, is not whether various speculative possibilities such as warp drive spaceships, traversable wormholes, or tractor beams could be made to work. The deep issue is that despite all the scientific advances that have been made, we still cannot answer many of the most basic questions about the nature and operations of the physical world (where like the ancient Greeks I take 'the physical' to be synonomous with 'the natural'). Many years of study and thought convince me that Carlo Rovelli is right when he observes,

> I believe that we are going through a period of profound confusion, in which we lack a general coherent picture of the physical world capable of embracing what, or at least most of what, we have learned about it. The 'fundamental scientific view of the world' of the present time is characterized by an astonishing amount of perplexity, and disagreement, about what time, space, matter, and causality are... I think it is fair to say that today we do not have a consistent picture of the physical world at all. [189, pp. 180–181]

Why should anyone care about such arcane questions? In simple terms, because it is exceedingly *dangerous* for our species to be so ignorant of the forces and factors upon which our precarious survival depends. Yes, there are more immediate problems, but in the longer run we cannot afford the *risk* of not being able to solve the measurement problem of quantum mechanics, or of not understanding the nature of time. Science and philosophy exist in part to satisfy our insatiable curiosity and our spiritual yearning for comprehension, but they are also survival tools—for humans, among our most essential. We ignore fundamental conceptual problems at our peril. Hence, it is not foolish to probe the chinks in the walls of scientific orthodoxy, even at the risk of scientific error.

During my grad school days I explored various mathematical options for extending special relativity to the superluminal case. (Some of this work is reported in 'An Adventure Outside the Light Cone', in this volume, Chapter 4.) Then I became aware of the existence of something called Bell's Theorem, and I quickly came to agree with H.P. Stapp's estimation that Bell's result is 'the most profound discovery of science' [212, p. 270].

One of the most intriguing questions that was widely discussed from the 1970s onward is whether there could be a 'Bell telephone', some means of exploiting quantum nonlocality so as to send controllable messages faster than light. This might seem to be just another science fictional speculation, but quite a lot turns on the question, for if a Bell telephone could be built then that would constitute, *prima facie*, a flagrant violation of special relativity as it is usually understood. Numerous authors, both physicists and philosophers of physics, hastened to publish technical proofs that a Bell telephone is impossible. Abner Shimony, who had made an important contribution to the field by helping to formulate a version of Bell's Inequalilty that was amenable to testing [96], was among those who produced a no-controllable signalling proof (which Brian Hepburn and I have criticized; see §11). Although (in my opinion) Shimony's no-signalling proof does not accomplish what he thought it accomplished, he made a valuable distinction (following Jon Jarrett [119]) between *controllable* and *uncontrollable* nonlocality. Perhaps, Shimony suggested, we should think of nonlocality as involving not action at a distance, but what he picturesquely called *passion at a distance*. It would only be the ability to control nonlocal interactions by local means, he argued, that would threaten relativistic causality. The no-signalling arguments would therefore underpin what he ironically termed *peaceful coexistence* between relativity and quantum mechanics [201]; the two theories go to different churches, but (if no-signalling is correct) they do not produce conflicting predictions that would bear on what Shimony took to be the well-established relativistic picture of causation.

As I started my PhD studies I began to read the no-signalling literature, and at first I took it that these authors must obviously be right; after all, their work had been published in refereed journals with high standards and some of the proofs were technically very impressive. But as I studied the no-signalling proofs more closely, doubts began to nag.

Some philosophers have more imagination or more technical knowledge than others, but most of us by training develop an acute sensitivity to the structure of an argument, what is supposed to follow from what. It is not good enough to accept an argument merely because you like the conclusion. It became apparent to me that the no-signalling arguments I studied at that time (some of which are cited at various points in this volume) relied on very strong locality assumptions in order to derive their conclusion that quantum nonlocality cannot be controlled by local means. In simple terms, these proofs *assume from the outset* that there is no causal or dynamic interaction of any sort between the distant particles in an entangled state, and then show on the basis of this assumption that there is no controllable interaction. (There are several technical ways to carry this out.) No interaction at all unsurprisingly implies no controllable interaction. As my student and co-author Brian Hepburn later put it, the no-signalling arguments seem merely to demonstrate the trivial result that an operator that does not affect a wavefunction does not change the wavefunction—or more precisely, an operator that is assumed to not affect a subspace does not change the statistics on that subspace.

From this critical point of view, the no-signalling arguments are a typical illustration of the tendency of a body of scientific or philosophical thought to become self-confirming in such a way as to define embarrassing problems out of existence. It is always easier to add epicycles than to find new laws of motion, and, indeed, often the conservative approach does turn out to be the correct approach. But not always!

A detailed critique of peaceful coexistence between quantum mechanics and relativity formed a large part of my PhD dissertation of 1991. The gist of the critique was published in 1992 in *Physical Review Letters* (and is reproduced in this volume, Chapter 1). I later learned that essentially the same view had been developed independently by P.J. Bussey [45], J.B. Kennedy, Jr. [121], and P. Mittelstaedt [147]. Kennedy's paper of 1995 in particular is an exceptionally clear and comprehensive review of the signalling problem.

When I studied the relationship between quantum mechanics and relativity in my PhD years, I thought it was obvious that the problem was to challenge relativity. To my Young-Turkish eye, the orthodox arguments for peaceful coexistence were a tissue of question-begging. But whether or not an argument is circular depends in part on what is at stake. The orthodox view sees the matter from a different perspective; Shimony and many other defenders of peaceful coexistence thought it was obvious that relativity should be on an equal logical footing with quantum mechanics or even have logical priority over quantum mechanics. Bussey had stated with devastating accuracy,

> non-communication in EPR experiments in standard formulations of quantum theory is obtained trivially by means of ... *ad hoc* assumptions about the behaviour of multiparticle amplitudes, rather than as a consequence of basic physical principles. [45]

However, the defenders of peaceful coexistence thought that they were justified in imposing such assumptions because they thought that if quantum mechanics conflicts with relativity, quantum mechanics must be wrong.

As Kennedy pointed out, whether or not relativity or quantum mechanics comes first is ultimately an empirical question. But at least we need to get clear on what the theories actually say. As noted above, it is by no means a given that the basic postulates of special relativity do, in fact, prohibit superluminal transmission of matter or information. However, it is also not clear that the basic principles of quantum mechanics themselves have been applied correctly to entangled multiparticle states, and this is the question that I am emphasizing in my current explorations. My view now is that it is unproductive to bicker about whether or not the argument for peaceful coexistence is circular; that argument has been made as clearly as it can be made without further insights into the dynamics of entangled states. *That* is the interesting and useful problem to solve right now, for there is increasingly strong evidence that the standard no-signalling arguments simply *do not apply* to entangled states. For more on this, see §11.7 in this volume.

The critiques of the no-signalling proposition that I and others have advanced have made some people very angry. I don't want to engage in polemics here; rather, I will simply note that the negative responses I have encountered often demonstrate a lack of understanding of what it is for an argument structure to be circular. This is not surprising; circularity is an occupational hazard of the theorist (in both science and philosophy), and it has to be constantly guarded against—even to the point of playing the 'devil's advocate' or 'tenth person'[1] in response to items of conventional wisdom that no sensible practitioner would think of questioning but where much is at stake. In this spirit, the most fruitful way to advance the discussion of nonlocality now is to do a job that should and could have been done as far back as the 1930s, which is to get absolutely clear on the correct description of the dynamics of entangled states—in a way that depends upon *no* presumptions about whether or not quantum mechanics 'should' be consistent with orthodox classical relativity or classical conceptions of separability and causality.

My early work on foundations of physics was far from being purely critical. Once one can get past the taboo against thinking that Einstein's reading of relativity could be open to revision or even replacement, the problem becomes to envision a physical worldview in which nonlocality has a natural place, perhaps even a central place. An important part of this large project must be to rethink and generalize our notions of simultaneity. The orthodox interpretation of relativity says that there is no invariant notion of distant simultaneity, because the only kind of distant simultaneity that orthodoxy recognizes is simultaneity with respect to a time coordinate, and that is always frame-dependent. Quantum nonlocality, especially as it is manifested in entangled states, forces us to reconsider this narrow view, for entangled particles seem to act as a single entity even when separated arbitrarily far apart in space and time. The Latin word for simultaneity, *simul*, has two meanings: at the same time, and in joint process. These two senses of simultaneity are often equivocated in today's normal usage; this makes sense in Newton's universe (where there is absolute time) but not in an Einsteinian universe (where time coordinates are functions of states of relative motion). The holism of quantum processes suggests that it would be useful to resurrect the second sense of simultaneity, especially in a universe in which distant events which are part of the same process in an invariant way are not necessarily going to be at the same time coordinate in all frames of reference.

If this notion of simultaneity as joint process can be made to work without being entirely divorced from modern physics, it needs to be definable in terms of relativistically invariant quantities (or, at least, that is the first thing

---

[1] As Warmbrunn, the fictional Mossad agent in Marc Forster's 2013 movie *World War Z* put it, 'It is the duty of the tenth man to disagree. No matter how improbable it may seem, the tenth man has to start digging under the assumption that the other nine are wrong ... Since everyone assumed that this talk of zombies was cover for something else, I began my investigation on the assumption that when they said zombies, they meant zombies'. Similarly, some technically competent person must investigate the foundations of quantum mechanics on the basis of the working hypothesis that when Nature seems to be saying spooky action at a distance, She means spooky action at a distance.

that one should try). In my 'New Look at Simultaneity' (Chapter 2) I expanded on a science fictional scenario found in Robert A. Heinlein's *Time for the Stars* [107]. Heinlein presents an ingenious twist on the twin paradox: Tom and Pat are identical twins capable of telepathy. Tom goes on a relativistic journey, but he and Pat remain in contact by 'mental radio', which is hypothesized to be instantaneous in their initial shared rest frame back on Earth. (Why this frame would be picked out is a question that Heinlein does not directly address. That question leads to a large discussion of whether such a frame would be 'preferred' in a way that contradicts the Principle of Relativity, or merely defined for essentially cosmological reasons. I hold to the latter view.) At what points on their worldlines are the twins 'present' to each other? There is a sensible answer to this question: given certain reasonable initial conditions, the twins' mutual specious present is at world-points of constant *action*.

It's only science fiction, but it offers a toy model suggesting how one could construct an invariant notion of joint process. I hold no particular brief for the reality or otherwise of mental telepathy; rather, the point of Heinlein's story was to ask a hypothetical question: what *would* it be like if two consciousnesses could be, in effect, present to each other? They would *not* be present to each other across a hypersurface of constant time coordinate, and so the usual relativity of simultaneity is simply *irrelevant* to the question of whether there could be some sort of joint presentness that could live within relativistic spacetime. Of course, the fictional telepathy of Heinlein's story is a stand-in for the 'telepathy' exhibited by the correlated particles of quantum mechanics, which is not fictional at all.

The Heinlein thought experiment also bears on whether or not there is a *block universe*. Loosely speaking, this is the view that past, present, and future are all on the same ontological footing, so that there is no invariant or global distinction between what has happened and what will happen. As Hermann Weyl famously put it, 'the objective world just *is*, it does not *happen*' [233]. The block universe is still very popular with philosophers of physics, but personally I find it to be deeply implausible. One of the standard arguments often given in favour of the block view is that because of the relativity of time-coordinate simultaneity, there is no objective meaning to the notion of distant presentness. If, however, there are notions of simultaneity based on invariant quantities such as action or phase, as I have suggested, then the standard argument is simply a *non sequitur*.

Like Aristotle, I see the natural universe as dynamic in its every fibre. However, as as Lee Smolin points out [211], it is difficult to capture the notion of dynamism in a mathematical formalism. One possibility is that one can approach this problem indirectly, by showing that an unchanging picture is inconsistent with quantum physics. What needs to be done, in effect, is to construct a Bell's Theorem for the whole universe. Tim Maudlin defines the block view as the claim that there is 'a single unique determinate four-dimensional whole of physical events that serves as the truthmaker' for all possible claims about past, present, and future [139, p. 1808]. However, *prima facie*, because of the Bell-Kochen-Specker no-go results, there are innumerable statements about possible experimental outcomes that cannot *have* truthmakers before the experiments are performed. So perhaps quantum mechanics itself can unblock the universe. This is another large project in progress; see Chapter 8 for more detail.

During my grad school years I also gave much thought to the problem of finding a covariant description of wave function collapse. There is a large literature on this problem, but virtually all of it takes for granted that state collapse or reduction would occur over hypersurfaces of constant time. Since those structures are frame-dependent, one concludes that there can be no covariant picture of state collapse. It puzzles me that anyone acquainted with relativity theory would have imagined for a moment that state reduction should be keyed to the time coordinate. One would naturally seek to describe state reduction in terms of a frame-independent quantity, with phase being the obvious candidate. I have published this suggestion in a number of places, but it, too, needs further development.

I will try to summarize where I think we stand today, recognizing that every one of the following points demands further analysis and debate, and that some are more conjectural than others:

1. The standard no-signalling 'proofs' merely demonstrate no-controllable signalling for product states and (while they are technically valid in that their conclusions follow from their premises) they are thus irrelevant to the question of whether controllable signalling is possible with *entangled* states.

2. Very likely the only way to explain the violation of locality conditions such as Bell's Inequalities is in terms of some sort of nonlocal dynamics (which will look superluminal in some frames of reference, and instantaneous in others).

3. Whether or not entangled states do manifest nonlocal dynamics, and whether such nonlocal dynamics are controllable by local means, are distinct questions.

4. The fact that we do not presently know how to control nonlocality by local means does not mean that it is impossible to do so.

5. The existence of nonlocal dynamics does not violate the Principle of Relativity or general covariance because if nonlocal interactions or processes are instantaneous in some particular state of motion, that state is picked out for reasons of cosmological history, not fundamental law. If there is a universal hypersurface in which wave functions collapse, that would

no more violate the Principle of Relativity than does the existence of the Cosmic Microwave Background Radiation rest frame, which, although invariantly specifiable, is an accident of cosmological history.

6. We need more useful and expressive language with which to speak of quantum nonlocality; that is why I have explored alternative notions of simultaneity as explained in this volume. My proposals may in the end not be the best way to go; I encourage innovation in this direction.

7. If there is any threat to the Principle of Relativity, broadly construed, in modern physics, it lies in the existence of singularities in classical relativistic theories—in gravitational collapse (widely discussed), and in the singularity at $v = c$ in Lorentz-invariant theories (not widely enough discussed). A singularity is not a 'thing' but a point or region in which a theory breaks down; it indicates the inapplicability of a theory in such regions, and thus the necessity of going beyond that theory.

What I have been trying to do in foundations of physics for over twenty five years is best expressed by the title of one of the papers in this volume, 'On the Edge of a Paradigm Shift'. Despite all the evidence in favour of nonlocality, physics is still locked into a paradigm (or Gestalt) in which locality is virtually definitive of physics, and any indication of nonlocality is an aberration, a pathology, to be resected from the corpus of physical theory by any means possible. The weight of evidence is moving us toward a new paradigm in which it may seem obvious that physics is fundamentally nonlocal (or, more properly, *a*local), and locality will be seen as an emergent limit case.[2] Of course, I could be wrong about this. Clever people continue to produce theories which they hope will explain away all of the nonlocal effects of entanglement or entanglement itself, and as of this writing, such theories cannot be positively ruled out. However, I think there is another approach that could be much more fruitful: instead of trying to define nonlocality out of existence, let's work as hard as possible at trying to see how to adapt our thinking to it as if it were real. Could we use nonlocality as a tool? If the arguments against what Shimony called controllable locality fail, then maybe (whisper it) it is controllable! Physicists have for the most part refused to think about this since it seems so far-fetched. However, in a time when humanity desperately needs methods of producing, manipulating, transmitting, and storing energy that do not threaten to destroy our planetary environment, all avenues should be explored. We've known about quantum mechanics for over a hundred years now and nonlocality almost as long. We have always thought that nonlocality must be a mistake, but perhaps it is not; perhaps it is just the way things are.

---

[2] For a forceful statement of the possibility that relativity is emergent, see Nobelist Robert B. Laughlin [127, Chap. 10].

Accepting that fact, if fact it is, could make a lot of difference to the chances of success for the human project in this strange and complicated universe.

## On the Organization of this Book

I had considered dividing this book into parts (dealing with, for instance, the critique of peaceful coexistence, simultaneity, scientific realism, and special relativity). However, so many of the papers overlap in theme or topic that in the end it was more natural simply to present them in the order of their original publication. Apart from a few reviews, these comprise my published papers on foundations of physics and the philosophy of spacetime from 1991 to 2014, together with one paper not previously published ('A Nitpicking Distinction'). I thought it would be useful to organize all of the citations into one unified bibliography. I have taken the liberty of making a few minor corrections and updates where necessary; otherwise, apart from the citation method, these papers are as first published. (Except for the paper written in collaboration with Brian Hepburn, the final two sections of which have been brought up to date.) Would I express some of these ideas differently now? Of course; but I'll let the record stand as it is.

# Chapter 1

# What Was It That Was to Have Been Proven?[1]

In Ref. [193], Roy and Singh take the novel step of expressing the postulate of signal locality (i.e., no faster-than-light signalling) as a set of inequalities, and they make the important observation that these inequalities are open to experimental test. As Roy and Singh point out, numerous authors (including themselves [192]) have demonstrated that nonrelativistic quantum mechanics (NRQM) and local quantum field theory (LQFT) do not allow superluminal signalling. (For review, see Refs. [71, 159].) Roy and Singh further say that 'A violation of the [Roy-Singh inequalities]...would also imply a violation of quantum theory which respects signal locality' [192, p. 2762]. However, all of the various no-signaling proofs can be seen to depend upon locality assumptions which could be construed as extraneous to the formalism of quantum mechanics proper.

Proofs within the context of LQFT depend either upon assumptions about the localizability of the interaction Hamiltonian between measuring apparatus and system [71], or upon the postulate of microcausality [192, 71, 70, 57], which states that observables at a spacelike separation always commute. Neither of these approaches really addresses the question of signal locality; the locality of the system-apparatus interaction is exactly what one has to establish in the general case, while microcausality was introduced to the general formalism of QM as an additional restrictive postulate specifically in order to *ensure* conformity of LQFT with relativity [157, 200]. No-signalling proofs within the framework of NRQM also depend upon the assumption that the effects of measurement are fully localizable. This assumption can be expressed in various ways: for instance, by using the reduced density matrix to compute

---

[1]This was first published as, 'Comment on "Tests of Signal Locality and Einstein-Bell Locality for Multiparticle Systems",' *Physical Review Letters* 69(18), 2 November 1992, 2733. I am grateful to the American Physical Society for permission to reproduce this paper in *Quantum Heresies*.

probabilities and expectation values in spacelike separate subsystems [19]; by allowing observables acting on spacelike separate subsystems to commute [93]; by allowing joint probabilities to be defined for spacelike separate observables [120]; or by directly working out the consequences of a local system-apparatus interaction Hamiltonian [202].

These arguments make it clear that one cannot exploit nonlocal correlations by means of purely dynamically localizable measurements in order to violate signal locality, in spite of some early suggestions that this might be possible [109]. (That, in effect, would amount to a violation of the second law of thermodynamics.) However, they leave entirely open the possibility that some hypothetical apparatus might have nonlocal effects upon the multiparticle system; as far as we know, this is not generally prohibited within QM. It is true that any procedure carried out by humans must involve steps (such as flicking a switch) that are manifestly local; however, it does not follow that these purely local operations cannot be coupled to nonlocal processes in such a way as to produce a violation of relativity.

Should such hypothetical nonlocal observables happen to commute in their action on the global system, then the proofs cited above that rely upon commutativity (such as [70]) show that there would be no signalling. However, we do not know what would happen in the case of noncommuting nonlocal operators. Whether there are such remains to be determined by further experimental and theoretical analysis. In this context, it obviously would be question begging to rule them out simply because they might violate relativity. Indeed, with the clarification afforded by the above-mentioned proofs we can now say that the problem is just to examine this possibility.[2]

**Twenty-Five Years Later**

In a brief response [191], Roy and Singh stated that they agreed with me that 'a generalized quantum theory which does not obey microcausality need not obey our signal locality inequalities... The nonconventional possibilities raised by Peacock can be quite stimulating, particularly if concrete models and their violation of signal locality inequalities are demonstrated'. Of course, the final remark was a polite way of saying, 'put up or shut up'. From one point of view, that is a fair response. On the other hand, a criticism may still be sound even if the critics who offer it are unable to offer a superior position to replace the one they are criticizing. I suspect, though I cannot prove, that one of the reasons that the critiques of peaceful coexistence that has been presented by myself, J.B. Kennedy [121], and others have not been taken very seriously is that there still is no clear alternative to a hobbled theory of quantum fields with

---

[2] This work was supported by doctoral and postdoctoral fellowships from the the Social Sciences and Humanities Research Council of Canada. Thanks to J.R. Brown, P.H. Eberhard, I. Pitowsky, A.J. Stacey, W. Seager, and A.I. Urquhart for useful discussions.

locality restrictions written in by hand. So Roy and Singh's remark, made in 1992, points toward an important job that still remains to be done.

There is one thing that I would now put differently. I spoke of operations by experimenters such as flicking a switch or adjusting a control knob as 'manifestly' local. The notion I was trying to get across is that there is no general reason why we cannot think of relatively localized operations as *coupled to* nonlocal systems, opening up the possibility of localized control of such nonlocal systems. I would still say that there is absolutely nothing in quantum theory *in general* that rules out this possibility. However, I would now say that the locality of an operation even as mundane as flicking a switch is not necessarily as obvious as it might appear. The wave packet associated with Alice flicking a switch at her end of an EPR device may have a tail extending throughout the universe. What we can say is that there are some operations that are localized to a sufficient approximation, which means merely that their nonlocal aspects may be ignored for most practical purposes. But that is all we can say in general: whether or not a process is localized is a practical question, not a matter of principle.

# Chapter 2

# A New Look at Simultaneity[1]

In recent years there has been renewed discussion of the problem of temporal becoming [140, 141, 64, 215]. The theme of this paper is that these discussions, timely and interesting as they are, do not go deeply enough into the question. I would like to suggest that a certain way of thinking about simultaneity, which as far as I know was first sketched in Robert A. Heinlein's 1956 science fiction novel *Time for the Stars* [107], opens up a set of possibilities that deserve serious consideration.

More precisely, I will address the following question: is there anything in the formal structure of Minkowski spacetime which corresponds to our intuitive albeit imprecise notion of a global 'present'? It is generally assumed that because of the relativity of optical simultaneity the answer to this question is, resoundingly, no.[2] I wish to suggest that this familiar argument is a *non sequitur*. The inference from the relativity of simultaneity in terms of equality of time coordinates to the non-availability in Minkowski spacetime of invariant structures that could represent an intuitively plausible 'Now' does not follow, since equal-time hyperplanes are not be the most natural way to represent this intuitive notion. My suggestion for an alternative—which is due to the science fiction writer Robert Heinlein—is tentative; it has the drawback of a slight degree of arbitrariness, but the advantages of simplicity, mathematical elegance, and psychological naturalness. It may not be right, but if it is found to be wrong, it will be wrong, I believe, for an interesting reason. At any rate, Heinlein's ingenious hypothesis deserves to be better known, and it cannot be

---

[1]This was first published as, 'A New Look at Simultaneity,' in D. Hull, M. Forbes, and K. Okruhlik (eds.), *PSA 1992: Proceedings of the 1992 Biennial Meeting of the Philosophy of Science Association, Volume One*. East Lansing, Michigan: Philosophy of Science Association, 1992, pp. 542–552. Many thanks to the Philosophy of Science Association and the University of Chicago Press for permission to reproduce this paper in *Quantum Heresies*.

[2]By *optical simultaneity* I mean equality of coordinate times as defined by Einstein's synchronization procedure. This useful term is due to Brent Mundy [151]. For a very clear description of how spacetime coordinates are constructed in special relativity, see Taylor and Wheeler [217].

denied that some new ideas are desperately needed if there is to be any hope of moving this inquiry forward.

## 2.1 Statement of the Problem

To help put my present discussion in perspective, it will be useful to compare it with the approach taken in a paper by Howard Stein [215]. In this paper Stein restates and clarifies his objections [214] to what he believes to be a serious and persistent misinterpretation of Minkowski geometry appearing in various guises in the works of N. Maxwell [140, 141], H. Putnam [177] and C. W. Rietdijk [185]. Stein's major purpose is to evaluate Maxwell's claim that special relativity is incompatible with what Maxwell calls probabilism, the thesis that there is objective becoming. Stein says,

> The issue is whether a notion of 'real becoming' can be coherently formulated in terms of the structure of Einstein-Minkowski space-time. Now, such a notion requires that one distinguish 'stages' of becoming, in such a way that, at each such stage, the entire history of the world is separated into a part that 'has already become...' and a part that 'is not yet settled...' In order to make a decisive attack upon this issue, it is necessary to agree on some general principles that the answers to these questions should be required to satisfy. I believe the following are uncontroversial: (i) The fundamental entity, relative to which the distinction of the 'already definite' from the 'still unsettled' is to be made, is...the *here and now* [Stein's emphasis]; that is, the space-time point...[215, p. 148]

The gist of Stein's reply to Maxwell is that an objective notion of becoming can indeed be defined in Minkowski spacetime but only relative to individual spacetime worldpoints. All and only the points in the past cone of a given point can be said to be definite with respect to that point, while (if I understand Stein correctly) all points in the future cone and sidecone of the given point are 'unsettled' with respect to, or as of, the given point. Maxwell's fundamental error, in Stein's view, is to speak carelessly of an objective notion of a global present and to try to separate the unsettled from the definite in spacetime analogously to the way this would be done in a Newtonian universe, where the ontologically unsettled part of the world would be thought of as the locus of all points forward in time from some sort of hyperplane or hypersurface of absolute (invariant) simultaneity. Since there can be no invariant concept of simultaneity in special relativity, Stein reminds us, there can be no global distinction of settled and unsettled points even though there is a perfectly sensible distinction relative to every given worldpoint. There is no invariant way to partition all of spacetime into two disjoint regions by means of a spacelike hypersurface or thin region bounded by two spacelike hypersurfaces such that one region would be agreed by all observers to be 'still unsettled'.

## 2.2. Heinlein on Time and Simultaneity

Stein states the orthodox view with vigour and clarity and indeed hints [215, p. 152] that suggestions that relativity theory allows a notion of 'present (spatially distant) actualities' are so transparently fallacious that they should probably not 'find continued publication'. He suggests that our persistent intuition that there is a global present is merely an illusion or sheer mistake, akin to an untutored person's sense that it is paradoxical to think of the Earth as floating freely and unsupported in space.

My object in this paper is to draw Stein's 'uncontroversial' point (i) into question, and thus in effect to claim that there might, after all, be a sensible way within relativity theory to define present distant actualities. This is, obviously, a risky position to take; I entirely agree that if it is true that present actualities must necessarily be at the same time coordinate then making such a claim would be evidence of a simple failure to do necessary physics homework. If one could somehow succeed in doing this, however, then there might be room after all for the sort of global notion of becoming that Maxwell is interested in. However, I will not attempt to decide the question of becoming itself here, only suggest that there could be grounds upon which it could be decided other than those which Stein considers.

### 2.2 Heinlein on Time and Simultaneity

Robert A. Heinlein (1907–1988) was a best-selling American science fiction author whose novels and short stories contain wide-ranging speculations that have fascinated and delighted millions of readers—and at times infuriated not a few of them as well. He is best known for his novel, *Stranger in a Strange Land* [108], which, somewhat to Heinlein's own amazement, became a cult favourite of the 'hippy' generation. Heinlein's stories are generally fast-paced adventure yarns, focussed on human interest. But Heinlein clearly had thought deeply and sometimes most originally about the scientific, political and philosophical concepts that he sketched in a misleadingly casual way as background to his stories.

In particular, he obviously had done a great deal of thinking about the apparent and real contradictions between relativity theory and our intuitions of real global simultaneity and the real passage of time. Heinlein attempts to resolve or at least reconcile himself to these incongruities in many of his writings, but, I think, he comes closest to the heart of the problem in his novel, *Time for the Stars* [107]. The premise of this novel is that there may be another relevant notion of simultaneity than the usual sense of equality of time coordinates, an invariant notion of simultaneity which is not expressed in terms of equality of time coordinates but in terms of some history-dependent relation between the proper times associated with spatially distant events.

I'll summarize Heinlein's story, leaving out the melodrama. We imagine a time in the not-too-distant future, in which the far-seeing Long Range Foundation has launched a program of interstellar exploration. The goal: *Lebensraum* for Earth's teeming billions of talking hominids. A very efficient rocket drive has been developed, based upon direct conversion of mass to energy. (Sadly, Heinlein omits to tell us the precise reaction sequences, containment methods, and other key details of the workings of his 'torch'.) It is now possible for a large spacecraft to be accelerated to nearly the speed of light. Several arcs are to be sent out in various directions, to search for habitable planets. There is a problem, however: an effective means of communication between the ships and home base must be found.

Fortunately, the LRF has also been sponsoring research aimed at enhancing the latent telepathic abilities possessed by identical twins. Heinlein was, of course, trading on the familiar folklore surrounding identicals; I don't know whether he actually believed that identical twins are or could be really telepathic. It turns out that with appropriate coaching some young identical twins can be trained to enhance their telepathic abilities to the point that they can literally converse mind-to-mind at will. What is most interesting and important is that the mind-to-mind interaction is instantaneous in a frame of reference in which the twins are mutually at rest; it is also completely undiminished and unaffected by distance, so that Heinlein's highly trained telepathic twins literally have a direct window into each other's minds regardless of where they are.

Heinlein's novel is a classic example of a 'what-if' story: *what would happen if the twins in the infamous twin scenario could directly read each other's minds? Would the twin who had been accelerated actually perceive his brother's co-moving clock to run fast?* The fact that Heinlein may have been pulling our legs is not important; what makes his story so interesting is the brilliant and consistent way he plays out the implications of this fictional thought experiment.

Two teen-aged twin brothers, Tom and Pat, are recruited into the program; Tom embarks on an interstellar torch-ship while Pat remains at home on Earth. As the ship accelerates away from Earth they remain in mind-to-mind contact, and an amazing thing becomes apparent; Tom begins to perceive Pat's thoughts to be running fast in comparison with his own, while Pat, of course, perceives Tom's thoughts as correspondingly slow. They get so out of synchrony that Pat has a birthday days before Tom; then, as the ship approaches peak velocity (as close to $c$ as they can push it) the disparity between mental rates becomes so severe that for weeks of Tom's time they cannot communicate at all. When the ship decelerates in its approach to a distant star enough that the boys can again contact each other, Tom discovers that years have passed for Pat, and when he finally returns home to Earth after many adventures, but having aged only two or three years, he finds brother Pat a cranky octogenarian in a wheelchair. Tom marries his grandniece and gets on with his life. (I have omitted many twists and turns of Heinlein's clever and well-written story; I highly recommend it.)

One might well ask what can be hoped to follow from a science fiction story which presumes and in fact crucially depends upon something—mental telepathy—which almost certainly does not exist. Let me make it crystal clear that I do not think that there is the slightest evidence for direct mind-to-mind contact beyond the kind of anecdotes and folklore that one hears around the campfire. However, there is no harm and sometimes much good in thinking hypothetically. The point is that Heinlein's story can give us some feel for what it would be like to talk about a distant event—a thought in my telepathic twin's mind—which was present to my mind in the way that my own immediate thoughts and sensations are. Howard Stein correctly points out that

> ... the fact that there is no experience of the presentness of remote events was one of Einstein's basic starting points. [214, p. 16], quoted in [215, p. 155]

However, Heinlein lets us see what might follow if there *could* be experience of the presentness of remote events. We have always automatically assumed that the Now as defined by sets of such events would be attached to common time slices; Heinlein gives us good reason to think that this unquestioned assumption deserves examination. The point of recounting the Heinlein story—and indeed the major point of this paper—is to make it plausible that the notion of the Now or specious present is not necessarily tied to equal time slices in spacetime, and that in fact there is a much more natural, and mathematically coherent, choice of spacetime structure to correspond to our psychological intuition of a 'present'.

## 2.3 The Mathematical Problem

Heinlein's story therefore leaves us with an interesting mathematical puzzle: given the initial conditions of the story, is there any way of identifying the particular proper time on Pat's worldline which is 'present to' a given proper time on Tom's worldline? Heinlein does not give an explicit general definition of his notion of invariant simultaneity. Unlike most science fictional speculations, however, it is clearly enough sketched that we need do very little additional work to state it, and to some degree justify it, explicitly.

At one point in the story, Heinlein suggestively speaks of two spacelike separate events happening 'at the same apparent instant by adjusted times' (p. 89). Adjusted how? Earlier in the narrative (pp. 77–83) he tells us enough to let us fill in the gaps. He recounts an experiment that Tom and Pat participate in, the purpose of which is to test the instantaneity of their mind-to-mind link.

Pat, on Earth, is asked to listen to a highly accurate metronome and 'tick' in step with it via mindlink to his brother Tom on the ship (which by now has attained a high enough velocity with respect to Earth that relativistic effects should become apparent). Tom sounds off Pat's ticks as he perceives them; later, Tom sends metronome ticks back to his brother. (The shipboard metronome was synchronized with the Earthbound metronome before the voyage began.) Sure enough, we find that the metronome aboard the spaceship is running more slowly in direct comparison to the Earthbound metronome. We can obtain a direct measurement of the difference in elapsed proper times between shipboard and Earthbound metronomes. How could we calculate this discrepancy, knowing the initial conditions and the acceleration schedule of the ship?

Another way of putting the problem is this: relativity as presently understood says that there is no invariant way of comparing the rate of time flow of the two twins while they are in flight and spatially distant from one another. In any given frame one can define a rate of change of Tom's proper time with respect to Pat's, but this quantity is frame dependent since the two proper times—i.e., clock readings—must be taken or measured at some particular times in some given frame of reference. One can only compare their proper times in an invariant way at the beginning and end of the journey, when they are coincident. However, if we grant for the sake of argument the science fictional hypothesis of telepathy, then there is a means of directly comparing clock readings at all points on the two worldlines; it would be as if Tom's clock and Pat's clock were effectively coincident even though they were far apart in space. If Tom and Pat really are telepathic in the sense that each can have direct experience of certain conscious thoughts and perceptions of the other, then Tom's local clock light years from Earth can be 'present to' Pat back home; Pat can experience what Tom experiences. We can therefore again restate the problem: if Pat's proper time—the reading of his local co-moving clock—is $\tau$, what particular reading $\tau'$ of Tom's clock will he (Pat) have direct experience of? That is, to use Heinlein's terms, how do we 'adjust' their proper times to find their common 'apparent instants'?

We can get an answer to this question if we make the assumption that each twin's mental processes keep in step with their local co-moving standard clocks, so that their thoughts and perceptions speed up or slow down in step with their clocks. This is not at all unreasonable if we grant that mental processes are linked to or dependent upon or even identical to certain kinds of physiological processes, since physiological processes would certainly keep step with the advance of proper time.[3] Then Pat has an unmediated window onto Tom's clock. What time will he read on it?

The suggestion implicit in Heinlein's story (although not stated exactly as I do here) is that we should answer this question in the simplest and most

---

[3] There does not seem to be any *a priori* reason why a person's consciousness should keep right in step with their physiological clock, although anyone for whom this was not true would be very unusual indeed. For an idea of what might happen if there could be such a person, see Philip K. Dick's novel *The World Jones Made* [61]. Jones is a man whose specious present is about three days ahead of everyone else's. Jones has enormous difficulties adjusting to day-to-day life, since he has to teach himself to respond to three-day-old memories rather than direct perceptions. However, he possesses extraordinary powers of prediction—until three days before his own death...

## 2.3. The Mathematical Problem

natural way:

$$\tau' = \sqrt{1-\beta^2}\,\tau, \tag{2.1}$$

(where $\beta \equiv v/c$ is the relative velocity of the twins, where we assume that their clocks were synchronized and initialized to zero at the beginning of the journey, and where we assume for simplicity that Tom was given only a very short burst of high acceleration and then allowed to coast freely. If you like, assume that Tom jumped from Earth onto a spaceship passing at relative velocity $\beta$.)

How do we justify this formula? It would be perhaps safest to regard it merely as an hypothesis or as a definition of what we shall mean by 'same apparent instant', since there might be a danger of falling into circularity (and in effect falling into the very trap that Stein warns us against) if we try to justify this formula by appealing to some notion of global simultaneity. It would indeed be the simplest hypothesis (and in fact the only possible non-arbitrary hypothesis) because the proper time $\tau'$ given by this formula is the only proper time along Tom's worldline that we have any particular basis for picking out, given the conditions of the problem. However, it is an hypothesis. Nevertheless, I think we can go some way toward making it plausible. We know that this formula would give us Tom's local clock reading if Tom has been somehow deflected elastically in mid-course and brought back to coincidence with Pat at Pat's local time r. But that is almost what having telepathy amounts to; in effect, it is as if the two clock readings could be brought into coincidence at any point in their journeys even though they are far apart in space. Equation (2.1) is exactly the relationship we should expect to find between their readings whenever this could be done. (In a more realistic case Tom's elapsed proper time would be given by a line integral expressing the accelerations he was subjected to in his journey, but the principle is the same.)

If Pat—the Earth-bound twin—wants to know what proper time is 'Now' for his brother (i.e., what time his brother will tell him it is if they become telepathically linked at Pat's proper time $\tau$), all he has to do is look at his own elapsed proper time and apply this formula. His brother, in turn, can apply the inverse of the above formula to find the corresponding time for the Earth-bound twin. Of course, the effect is not symmetrical, since only one twin underwent acceleration. This may seem suspicious to those of us who (perhaps like Herbert Dingle; cited in [133]) believe that all velocity-dependent effects in relativity should be entirely symmetrical between the co-moving observers. But we are not dealing here with a purely velocity-dependent effect, but a path- or history-dependent effect, which certainly can be unsymmetrical between different observers depending upon what has happened to them in their pasts.[4]

---

[4]There has been a long and wearisome controversy over whether the claim that the twins should be found to have aged differently when they are brought into coincidence marks an inconsistency within relativity. This debate is summarized engagingly by L. Marder [133]. It seems

I will run through the argument once more in a slightly different way. Given the initial condition that the twins start out with synchronized standard clocks initialized to zero, if the twins had always remained relatively at rest their clocks would have continued to run at the same rate in all frames and their elapsed proper times would be equal whenever the clocks were brought into coincidence. In fact, their local clock readings would always agree with the global time coordinate in the inertial frame in which they were both at rest. Their mutually experienced present—if we allow them to be telepathic— would be comprised of events which would be simultaneous in this Lorentz frame. Now suppose that after initialization they undergo relative motion, and suppose—as it would seem most natural to do—that each twin's mental processes remains synchronous with his local co-moving clock. Then, to find the proper times which they would experience together in one apparent instant we would have to correct for their motion histories. That is, we would correct not for their relative motion but in terms of the line integral giving their elapsed proper times from their common initial point as a function of the accelerations they had experienced. Since the only relevant difference between the two twins is the difference in accelerations (or gravitational fields) they had experienced, it can only be this which would determine the difference in their proper times in their mutually experienced present.

In summary: the events that are invariantly simultaneous or belong to the same apparent instant are not those which are at the same time coordinate in some inertial frame or other but which (given suitable initial conditions) have proper times which differ only through adjustments due to acceleration history. Since Pat and Tom would experience the same proper times on their local clocks (synchronized when initially coincident) if it were not for the relative motions they had undergone, the simplest hypothesis is that the only difference in proper times they will note will be that due to their motion histories, calculable as if their two clocks could be brought into spatial coincidence.

It is important to emphasize that there is a degree of arbitrariness in this way of identifying the proper times which correspond to the supposed apparent present of the twins; I only claim that the way of doing it suggested here is very simple and natural. Since we obviously don't really know what telepathy would be like, we have to guess a little bit; I am trying to come as close as possible to work out what it would be like for one twin to simply be able to directly experience distant events experienced by the other. Even if I have in fact inadvertently imported some prior notion of global presentness or absolute time—and I do not feel entirely secure that I have not—I think that the model we have arrived at here is interesting enough to deserve study on its

---

clear that Dingle and other like-minded authors have simply failed to grasp the basic distinction in relativity between relative-velocity dependent quantities such as apparent time rates and path-dependent quantities such as elapsed proper time. See [217] for a very clear exposition of the relevant physics.

## 2.4. Intrinsic Simultaneity as Equality of Action

own merits.

A crucial and interesting point to emphasize is that two spacelike separate events which belong to the same apparent instant in the above sense will be simultaneous in the conventional sense in only one inertial frame. To put it another way, if they are linked telepathically as Heinlein imagines—that is, such that the link is instantaneous in some inertial frame when the two telepaths are relatively at rest in that frame—the link will not actually be instantaneous in all frames. Some frames will judge the reception to precede the transmission, others the other way around. (This is a point that Heinlein does not make very clear in his story. He speaks of the mindlink as instantaneous without being careful to state with respect to which inertial frame. I suspect that Heinlein understood the problem, but did not wish to overcomplicate his story.) Although this violates the presumed invariance of causal order, I do not think it is by itself a reason for rejecting the possibility of such a link. If there is any sort of spacelike causation then we would just have to accept that causal order is frame dependent. In fact, probably the most useful approach to this problem would be to distinguish between the *extrinsic* causal order of various events in terms of time coordinates as defined in various coordinate systems and *intrinsic* causal order in terms of proper time along the worldlines linking those events. The latter is, of course, invariant.

There is another interesting point. It is reasonable to assume that a human's specious present is not infinitesimal in duration, but occupies a certain definite amount of proper time—some small fraction of a second—along that human's worldline. This means that the specious present of the spacefaring twin will be much longer than that of the Earthbound twin; a tick of Tom's clock might take a week in Pat's frame of reference, if their relative velocity is high enough. If this is so, then the hypersurfaces of intrinsic simultaneity as defined here in terms of psychologically apparent 'instants' would not really be surfaces *per se* but open regions bounded by two spacelike hypersurfaces which could, in general, be curved in interesting ways. This is a point which would have to be clarified in a more detailed theory.

### 2.4 Intrinsic Simultaneity as Equality of Action

The spacelike separate event points that we have hypothesized would belong to the same apparent instant for the twins has a further interesting and elegant property—given certain initial conditions, they have the same *action*.

Return to the twin scenario, and again let Pat be the Earthbound twin and Tom the space voyager. Assume that just before the voyage began, both twins possessed the same initial energy $E_0$. Let $\tau$ be a given value of Pat's proper time after the voyage has begun. At this proper time $\tau$ Pat will possess an action $E_0\tau$. (Note the interesting fact that although action is an invariant, it is not conserved—i.e., assuming no net energy interchange with the environment, it increases as the time.[5]) At Tom's corresponding proper time

$$\tau' = \sqrt{1-\beta^2}\tau$$

(i.e., the reading of Tom's clock that I suggest is intrinsically simultaneous with Pat's clock reading $\tau$), relativity tells us that Tom will have an energy

$$E = \frac{E_0}{\sqrt{1-\beta^2}}. \tag{2.2}$$

Hence Tom will have an action

$$E\tau' = \frac{E_0}{\sqrt{1-\beta^2}} \times \sqrt{1-\beta^2}\tau = E_0\tau \tag{2.3}$$

also, just the same as Pat's.

In other words, it may be that points in spacetime which (at least if we were telepathic) we would identify as belonging to the same apparent instant are just those which have equal *action*. If there is an invariant notion of global simultaneity (which I suggest should be called *intrinsic* or *dynamic* simultaneity), perhaps it attaches to hypersurfaces of equal action, not coordinate-dependent hyperplanes of equal time (which would define sets of *extrinsically* or *kinematically* simultaneous events).[6]

There are some obvious complications to this picture. Real twins, in real spacecraft, will not always have precisely the same masses, and they will often exchange mass-energy with other parts of the universe in the course of their journeys. Therefore, intrinsically simultaneous events on different worldlines will not usually have precisely the same action; they will have a difference in action which depends only upon differences in initial conditions. This does not seem to be an essential complication, but it muddies the nice simplicity of the theory. We can salvage our original scheme, however, by noting that each macroscopic twin is really an assemblage of elementary particles. We do not know how many 'elementary' particles there are (hundreds, perhaps an infinity) but we do know that the spectrum of particles is discrete. Each particle of each type (each electron, say) has precisely the same proper mass. Now, each particle of which each twin is made up will be affected by the overall time dilation that the twin experiences. Hence all the particles of which the twins are composed will have the same actions at intrinsically simultaneous events.

We can easily generalize this picture to one in which any number of spacefarers, or particles, radiate from a common origin. And we can go further, too: most contemporary cosmologists favour a model of the universe (the

---

[5] Thanks to Mike Kernaghan for pointing this out to me.
[6] Alex Korolev suggested to me that this could be generalized in terms of the Langrangian of the system.

so-called Big Bang model) in which all matter and energy, and in fact all space itself, radiated outward from a highly compressed initial state. If this is correct, then we could identify sets of points on the worldlines of all particles which are globally or intrinsically simultaneous in the sense described here; we could then think of spacetime as being built up of 'layers' of constant action which could be interpreted as invariant hypersurfaces of intrinsic or dynamic simultaneity. Let's call such layers the *action surfaces*.

Nothing said here is an addition or correction to presently accepted spacetime physics. No one would dispute that given suitable initial conditions one can define something like action surfaces in the spacetime of general relativity. The question is whether these surfaces so defined have any special physical significance or interest; that is, whether they could (to borrow Dieks' phrase) play 'a direct role as a determinant in physical processes' [64, p. 456].

I do not claim that they do here (although I think that an argument can be made in favour of this claim); however, I do claim that they have a special psychological interest as the sets of hypersurfaces that would correspond to the most psychologically natural choice of sets of events belonging to one 'apparent instant', if there could be such sets of events.

I think it is a very interesting fact that the spacelike separate points which on a natural psychological interpretation can be thought of as intrinsically simultaneous have this elegant property of having the same action. I do not profess to understand the significance of this odd fact, but I think that it should be better known.[7]

## 2.5 Conclusions

I hope my readers have enjoyed this fictional excursion, even if they do not find the argument compelling. Indeed, much of the plausibility of Heinlein's view comes simply from his skill as a storyteller, which I can hardly convey here.

My conclusion is conditional: if there is a Now, it is associated not with equal time slices but with corrected proper time hypersurfaces, which, interestingly, given certain initial conditions are hypersurfaces of constant action. These hypersurfaces are invariant; so there is no contradiction between the psychological intuition (illusion, if you insist) of the universality of this sense of Nowness and the relativity or observer-dependence of simultaneity in the Einsteinian sense. It may, therefore, be just a mistake to insist that the common specious present of several observers must be tied to hyperplanes of constant time. If I am correct then it may, after all, be possible to define hypersurfaces in spacetime which invariantly represent what Stein calls a 'cosmic present' [215, p. 162], in spite of the relativity of optical simultaneity. This would, of course, radically change our interpretation of the philosophical significance of

---

[7]C.W. Rietdijk [185] has also introduced a notion of simultaneity in terms of equality of action, although from interestingly different considerations, having to do with quantum nonlocality.

relativity, although it would not make any difference to the mathematical form of the theory and might not make any difference to the way the theory is used and applied in physics. (I say only 'might not' because the territory of overlap between relativity and quantum physics is still a conceptual demilitarized zone, and it is quite possible that a reconsideration of the meaning of 'simultaneity' may help to resolve some of the enormous difficulties in constructing a truly satisfactory relativistic quantum theory.) However, nothing I have said in this paper directly resolves the question of probabilism that concerns Maxwell and Stein; it is thinkable that the corrected time hypersurfaces could represent a cosmic present which divides spacetime into two disjoint sets of actual and potential events, but it is also thinkable (and in fact I am sure that many would insist that this is the only thinkable alternative) that these hypersurfaces have no special physical significance beyond their psychological interest for human beings. Indeed, some authors (see, for instance, Rucker [228]) have suggested that the fact that we humans experience a only certain small interval of our worldline as 'present' is only a peculiarity of the four-dimensional structure of the human brain/mind. My own guess is that the 'corrected proper time' cosmic present indicated here does separate an actual unsettled future from a definite past; however, I could only defend this intuition by appealing to questions of quantum physics which are beyond the scope of this paper. This paper will have accomplished quite a lot if it has convinced anyone that there may be a new way of thinking about simultaneity (even though it is a way of thinking that is, after all, not all that new).[8]

---

[8]I am very grateful to J. W. Crichton and C. Normore for encouragement in the early stages of development of these ideas, and G. Solomon for useful discussions. Thanks also to Virginia Heinlein for her gracious response when I sent her a copy of this paper. This work was supported by doctoral and postdoctoral fellowships from the Social Sciences and Humanities Research Council of Canada.

Chapter 3

# On the Edge of a Paradigm Shift: Quantum Nonlocality and the Breakdown of Peaceful Coexistence[1]

**Abstract** I present a thought experiment in quantum mechanics and tease out some of its implications for the doctrine of 'peaceful coexistence', which, following Shimony, I take to be the proposition that quantum mechanics does not force us to revise or abandon the relativistic picture of causality. I criticize the standard arguments in favour of peaceful coexistence on the grounds that they are question-begging, and suggest that the breakdown of Lorentz-invariant relativity as a principle theory would be a natural development, given the general trend of physics in this century.

...we have considered worthwhile to illustrate explicitly the general proof of the impossibility of superluminal transmission, even though it is quite elementary, to stop useless debates on this subject.
—G.C. Ghirardi et al., 1980, [93, p. 208]

It is one of the chief merits of proofs that they instil a certain scepticism as to the result proved.
—Bertrand Russell [194], quoted in Lakatos 1976 [126, p. 48]

---

[1]This was first published in *International Studies in the Philosophy of Science* 12(2), 1998, 129-150. My thanks to the Taylor and Francis Group for permission to reproduce this paper in *Quantum Heresies*.

## 3.1 Introduction: A Call For a Fresh Approach

In this paper I undertake a critical review of the doctrine of 'peaceful coexistence', which, following Abner Shimony [201, 203], I take to be the proposition that quantum mechanics (QM) does not force us to revise or abandon the usual picture of relativistic causality:

> Quantum mechanics is undoubtedly a non-local theory when it treats correlated spatially separated systems. When one examines closely the character of this non-locality, however, one does not find reasons for modifying the causal structure of space-time as described by special or general relativity theory, but rather reasons for refining the concept of an event. [203, p. 182][2]

The notion of peaceful coexistence has been what one might call the 'received view' in foundations of physics for some time, but it has recently been coming under increasingly sceptical scrutiny from a number of quarters [159, 160, 136, 137, 48, 121]. Here I will review and extend these critiques, with the aid of a thought experiment. My main aim, however, is not so much to establish any particular result, but to argue for the reasonableness and plausibility of a major redirection of research on quantum nonlocality.

Broadly speaking, a great deal of the foundational work that has been done on nonlocality has been directed at showing that we can defend QM from the charge that it conflicts with relativity; this has often involved placing technical restrictions on the full generality of the quantum mechanical formalism. While this approach served a pragmatic purpose in the early stages of the development of quantum field and particle theory (since it enabled physicists to derive a host of useful predictions with a minimum of conceptual fuss), it is beginning to bear a remarkable resemblance to what Lakatos [126] called a degenerating research programme. As evidence for this I take Fine's recommendation (couched in strangely postmodernist jargon[3]) that we abandon attempts to understand the puzzle of nonlocality, and a similar quietism advocated by van Fraassen [225].

---

[2]Shimony has later (e.g. 1990) [204] conceded the possibility that our picture of causality may require some repair; however, his statement of 1986 is, I think, a very clear expression of what many believe, and so I will take it as a point of reference without, I hope, any prejudice towards Shimony's more recent views.

[3]Fine recommends that we abandon our outmoded 'essentialist cravings' [86, p. 183], and adopt a 'nonessentialist attitude toward explanation' that will lead us 'to accept that what requires explanation is a function of the context of inquiry' [p. 193]. Fine does make a very interesting suggestion: that we simply accept quantum events as inherently random, but that we recognize 'patterns between sequences as part of the same natural order as patterns internal to the sequences themselves' [p. 193]. The problem is that we entirely lack any theory of probability that can provide the kind of account of patterns between sequences that probability theory can now provide for patterns within sequences; indeed, to the extent that mathematics can say anything about such correlations, it seems to say that they are a natural indication of measurement bias [174]; i.e., in this 'context of inquiry', nonlocal influences of some unclear sort.

It is now high time to turn the whole problem around. I entirely agree with Chang and Cartwright, who remark,

> It is unreasonable to require or even expect that whenever relativity and quantum mechanics clash it is quantum mechanics alone that has to yield. [48, p. 186]

What we should do, I suggest, is thoroughly purge QM of any lingering quasi-classical locality assumptions, and directly challenge relativity. If relativity can stand on its own in the face of the quantum challenge, well and good. If it falls, that does not mean (as I suspect many fear) that physical science collapses into postmodernist rubble; it simply means that we need to seek a deeper invariance principle that directly takes into account the quantum of action. (If we get it right, we will still be able to recover classical relativity as a useful approximation in appropriate limits.) Seen in the light of this sort of research programme, most or all of the standard arguments in favour of peaceful coexistence can be seen to be more or less question-begging.

I want to make it especially clear that the problem of nonlocality is not purely or merely a question of seeking some suitably subtle (or sophistical) reinterpretation that will let the fly out of the flybottle; nor is it merely a question of elucidating the formal structure of quantum theory (although such investigations can be extremely valuable). On the contrary, there is almost certainly new physics to be revealed. Furthermore, I think that philosophers could well contribute to uncovering this new physics because the problem is not purely technical (although technical innovation is certainly required), but at least partially a matter of conceptual reorientation. Here is a sterling opportunity for practitioners of philosophy of physics (or *philosophysics*, as F.A. Muller has jocularly dubbed it [148]) to defend their discipline against recent charges of its utter irrelevance to actual scientific progress.[4]

## 3.2 Some Basics

Let us quickly review a few facts about quantum nonlocality that are especially relevant to our concerns here.[5] A typical example of an Einstein-Podolsky-Rosen (EPR) system is an apparatus in which a certain decay process emits pairs of photons whose spin angular momentum must sum to that of the parent particle. The photons travel in opposite directions and strike polarizers. The photons either do or do not transmit through the polarizer. The probability

---

[4] I refer, of course, to Weinberg's insistence [230] that the main value to science of philosophy of science is to defend scientists from the errors perpetrated by other philosophers of science!

[5] See Redhead [181] for a very thorough overview of this subject. The seminal paper is Einstein et al. [78]; the reply by Bohr [36] is also essential, although frustrating, reading. On the history of Einstein's concerns about nonseparability, see Howard (1990) [114]. Pitowsky (1994) [174] is one of the most lucid and penetrating analyses of Bell's theorem; see also Shimony (1990) [204] for a very concise and clear derivation of Bell's theorem and the properties of correlated photons used in this paper.

that a given photon will pass through its polarizer is just $\frac{1}{2}$ and an observer stationed near one of the polarizers will merely see a random sequence of pass/no pass events, like the results of a series of coin tosses. Nevertheless, if measurement results at each polarizer are tabulated and then later compared, it will be found that there are remarkable correlations between them.

Suppose the left and right polarizers were oriented at angles $\theta_l$ and $\theta_r$ respectively with respect to a common horizontal axis. Then it will be found that there is a correlation $\cos 2(\theta_l - \theta_r)$ between the results for each particle pair; or equivalently, the results for each pair will be found to agree (either both pass or both not pass) a fraction $\cos^2(\theta_l - \theta_r)$ of the time. Information about the relative angle of the two polarizers is somehow encoded in the pairs of observed results, even though it is not available locally to observers at either detector.

These correlations simply express the fact that the total spin of the two particles must be conserved, but they have two striking features. First, they are established instantaneously; that is, there exists an inertial frame (the lab frame, if source and detectors are relatively at rest) in which the distant measurements on members of a pair of particles can be simultaneous. Second, as the various versions of Bell's theorem show, one gets into a severe contradiction with the predictions of QM if one presumes that the particles were in definite states of polarization (with respect to a given direction) before they impinged upon the polarizer. It is precisely as if the measurement of the left photon actually causes, instantaneously, the right particle to go into a certain definite state. A great deal of the literature on nonlocality from Bohr (1935) [36] onward can be said to be focussed on finding a way of denying that this is literally what is going on while simultaneously accepting the undeniable nonlocality implicit in the entangled state.

The question naturally arises as to whether the left observer can communicate with the observer at the right by varying the angle of her detector in step with some code. In fact, she can, but not superluminally. Varying the relative detector angle will indeed modulate the correlations between left and right outcomes, but the right observer can only detect these variations if both sets of data are available to him; he would have to receive the left observer's data by normal means in order to compare them with his own, and thereby read the message. No matter what the left observer does, in any kind of EPR apparatus we presently know how to build the right observer's local data will always look like a random string of passes and fails. (I will shortly return to the question of whether this must always be the case.) The most we can conclude (and this with a large pinch of salt) is that if the left observer changes the relative detector angle, the right observer receives a different random string of results than he would have received had the left detector not been manipulated.[6]

---

[6]The pinch of salt is required because this presumption, obviously, is not directly testable, since we can hardly know what random sequence the right observer would have received under

This, incidentally, is the basis of various quantum encryption schemes which have been proposed [29]. Nonlocality seems to offer the perfect encryption method; a message can be built into the correlations, but the correlations can only be read if one has both sets of data; each data set serves as the unique key for the other.

## 3.3 Is there a Bell Telephone?

But why, one might insist, is it not possible for one of the observers to send a superluminal message to the other? Is it not conceivable that one observer could somehow twiddle his detector in just such a way as to allow him to vary the statistics collected by the distant observer? A host of authors have published papers attempting to show that this is in principle impossible; that is, these authors argue that according to QM, one observer will always see the long-run frequency of photon transmission to be just $\frac{1}{2}$, regardless of what manipulations the other observer performs. This claim is generally known as the no-signalling theorem (more technically, it is the statement that QM obeys *parameter independence*, the statistical independence of the left series of results on the right detector parameter or knob setting); and many authors, following Jarrett,[7] take it to be the foundation of the doctrine of peaceful coexistence.

Many technical approaches have been employed to demonstrate the no-signalling theorem (or, as I shall call it here, the no-controllable-signalling theorem, or NCS); most fall into three broad categories—all of which, I argue, are question-begging in one way or another.

In the first category of NCS proof, one assumes that the Hilbert space of the composite multi-particle system is localizable; that is, operators that act on one branch of the system act only trivially on the other branch [120, 93, 19, 192]. There are several ways to express this assumption algebraically, but unsurprisingly they all give the desired result. Kennedy [121] has argued in detail (and, I think, very convincingly) that this sort of NCS proof is question-begging, since one can insist that the very thing one needs to show is that all conceivable operations performed on one particle have no effect on the other. Indeed, Kennedy shows that the key algebraic restriction appears to have been written into the general formalism of quantum theory by von Neumann precisely because of a prior belief in NCS.

Another way to approach the problem is to appeal to the standard form of local quantum field theory, which contains a special rule (usually called either microcausality or local commutativity) that says that all measurements performed on particles at a space-like separation must commute. This rule again secures a NCS result rather directly [70, 57, 71]; but one can again argue [159, 160, 121, 147] that it assumes the very thing one needs to show.[8] This

---

the counterfactual circumstance.

[7]See his [119]. Essentially the same distinctions are drawn by Eberhard [70].

[8]P. Eberhard has insisted (private communication) that all he meant to show was that within

follows partially from a historical reprise of quantum field theory—which was deliberately set up by its founders such as Pauli [157] in order to ensure its agreement with relativity—and partially from the uncomfortable fact that relativistic QM does indicate the reality of operators that violate microcausality [87], in spite of attempts to postulate them out of existence.

A third approach—and one that especially bears on considerations I shall raise in this paper—works from the assumption that particle dynamics is local (see, especially, Shimony [202]). Technically, this is embodied in the assumption that the Hamiltonian of the multiparticle system is fully local; that is, that there are no terms in the Hamiltonian that represent direct interactions between the distant particles. Again, with this assumption in hand, one can derive a NCS result; and again, the whole procedure is arguably question-begging. I shall return to this point shortly; for the question of the locality or otherwise of the particle dynamics may be the key to the whole matter.

## 3.4 A Fiendish Device

We can think of an EPR apparatus as being like a telegraph in which the key transmits dots and dashes to a remote location with some appreciable accuracy, but which is nearly unusable for communication because the key sends dots or dashes randomly and uncontrollably. How near is nearly? A version of Schrödinger's infamous *Höllenmaschine* [199] underscores the fact that with suitable prior arrangements and highly efficient detectors, even uncontrollable signalling poses some very interesting challenges to relativistic causality. In the following I do not claim to demonstrate any new result; I wish simply to issue a reminder that the nonlocal correlations can be remarkably informative of distant events even if we set aside any worries about the NCS proofs and grant the uncontrollability of local outcomes.

Let us set up a source that produces correlated pairs of photons and sends them in opposite directions toward polaroids, which are at some considerable distance $D$ from each other. Source and detector are all relatively at rest in some inertial frame, which we shall call the lab frame. The source is exactly halfway between the two detectors, so that the transit times will be equal and the arrival of the photons at the left and right detectors will be simultaneous in the lab frame. Recall that the fraction of photons that will either both transmit through the polaroids or both not pass is $\cos^2(\theta_l - \theta_r)$, where $(\theta_l - \theta_r)$ is the relative angle between the polaroids; while regardless of relative detector angle, the probability of getting a given result at either detector is always

---

local quantum field theory, microcausality is a necessary and sufficient condition for no-signalling. Indeed it is, but if one reads the references cited one finds much ambiguity regarding the logical status of the NCS claim; in setting forth these proofs, are we merely elucidating a no-signalling assumption, or trying to show that NCS follows as a theorem from the general formalism of quantum theory? Unfortunately, the cited proofs have been widely interpreted as having established the latter claim, whatever the precise intentions of their authors may have been.

## 3.4. A Fiendish Device

just $\frac{1}{2}$. Suppose the source emits many pairs of photons in succession, and the observers occasionally change the relative detector angle. Granting NCS, neither observer will be able to tell whether the other has made a change, even though the information about $(\theta_l - \theta_r)$ will be encoded nonlocally in the pairs of results.

Now, let us suppose that we do a run of the apparatus in which the left observer knows in advance that $(\theta_l - \theta_r) = \pi/2$. There is no way she could know this without prior arrangements having been made; on the other hand, there is no reason in principle why such arrangements could not have been made. In such a case, even though there is only a 50% probability that a given photon will pass her detector, the left observer knows with certainty (or more precisely, with an uncertainty dependent only upon left and right detector efficiencies) that if a photon passes at a certain time in the lab frame, then the corresponding photon incident upon the right detector will not pass. On the other hand, she knows (again, with a certainty dependent only upon detector efficiencies) that if the photon is absorbed by her detector, then it must pass the other. The left observer knows these facts because the outcomes are perfectly anticorrelated at $(\theta_l - \theta_r) = \pi/2$. In other words, with this arrangement, she can obtain near-certain knowledge of a distant event that she could otherwise never predict with more than 50% confidence. Hence, an EPR apparatus certainly enables someone in the right location in spacetime, and with the right (and in principle realizable) knowledge of background conditions, to know instantaneously something about an event at a space-like separation.

In order to dramatize this, we can place a cage near the right detector with an unfortunate cat imprisoned within it. A photomultiplier behind the polaroid is linked to a device such that an instantly lethal gas will be released in the cage if and only if a photon fails to pass the polaroid at a certain time (say 12:00 noon). (That is, if a photon passes it will disarm the device.) As before, we have $(\theta_l - \theta_r) = \pi/2$, and the left observer knows, by prearrangement, that a pair of photons will be released from the source just in time to arrive at the detectors at noon.

The left observer waits patiently. Up until noon, the left observer has absolutely no way of knowing what pertains at the distant measurement site, at noon or any other time up to $D/c$ in the past. However, at noon, she immediately knows what is happening at the other site. If she detects a photon, she knows that the cat is presently dying for science; if she does not detect a photon, she knows that the cat lives. Furthermore, she can use this knowledge to make testable predictions. Suppose it has also been prearranged that another observer near the right detector will immediately call the left observer by cellular telephone to inform her whether or not the cat was killed. If the left observer does not detect a photon, she can predict with confidence that at the time $D/c$ past noon she will receive a telephone call telling her that the cat has survived. On the other hand, if she does detect a photon at noon, then she can predict that she will receive a message saying that the cat has perished. Even one bit of information about a local event—whether or not a photon passes a certain filter—can in a realizable context serve as information about events at a space-like separation. Whether or not it is controllable is a separate question. I take it that there clearly is, in this precise and perhaps limited sense, usable information being shared or transmitted instantaneously between the two distant particles. The only way out of this conclusion might be to deny that it is possible to make sufficiently reliable detectors, which has a flavour of the *ad hoc* but is a possibility that had to be explored.[9]

Note a remarkable feature of this story: even a complete and exhaustive knowledge of all events in the past cone (the causal past) of the cat at its location at noon would be insufficient to predict whether it would be alive at 12:01; but just one bit of information about an event at a space-like separation (whether or not the left photon passed), combined with knowledge of all the prearranged relevant factors in the cat's past cone (such as whether or not the device is armed, etc.) is sufficient to allow an observer located space-like separate from the cat to predict this much of its future. Examples such as this show that in a universe obeying QM, the future of a localized macroscopic system (such as a cat) can be determined, in part at least, by events outside its own past cone. This is hardly a novel observation; but still, it is striking—and insufficiently remarked upon, I believe—that so little extra information from outside the light cone is enough to predict so much. This surely casts a shadow on Shimony's statement [203] that QM gives us no reason to revise our understanding of the causal structure of spacetime.

Please note that I am not attempting to make the usual suggestion that the cat's state is indefinite until observed because it is coupled to a quantum system that was for a while in a superposition of states. The cat can be in a glass pen, under continuous observation by humans or any recording device we wish throughout the whole course of the experiment. Indeed, what interests us here is precisely the striking fact that at noon the cat will undergo a definite change of macrostate partially as a result of a distant micro-event. The emphasis on controllable communication as a violation of relativity has, I suspect, led most people to neglect the fact that even uncontrollable space-like availability of information poses a very serious challenge to the usual view of relativistic causality.[10]

---

[9]Fine [85] and others have suggested this. Maudlin [137] places an upper bound on detector efficiencies that would permit local instruction sets to mimic quantum statistics.

[10]A. Elitzur is one of the few who have not made this mistake [79, p. 534]: '...the fact that no communication can be transferred by the correlations between [left and right particles] cannot negate the passage of information about [the left particle] to [the right particle].' And Chang and Cartwright state, '...quantum measurements are situations in which spacelike-separated events behave, despite relativistic claims, exactly as if information were being passed on at a speed faster than that of light' [48, p. 182].

## 3.5 But Why Can There Not Be a Common Cause?

People sometimes say that the violation of the Bell inequalities (BI) shows that there is no 'common cause' explanation of the quantum correlations. This depends upon what one means by 'common cause'. Certainly the preparation of the state at the source is a sufficient explanation of the long-run correlations between left and right measurements in the sense that (given the rules of QM) it is sufficient to predict those correlations.[11] However, the way the source was prepared cannot possibly account for the particular way a particular run of the experiment turns out—the particular sequences of spins up and down we got at each measuring station. If we were to assume that the measurements merely reveal properties of the particles that were established at the source, but also demand that observed correlations must satisfy the predictions of QM, we find that some combinations of properties must be assigned to the particles with *negative* frequencies[12]—a result that is surely at least as troubling as superluminal influences, and possibly even harder to interpret. It is in this sense that we can quite accurately say that there is no common cause explanation for sets of correlated results that violate the BI; and it is this that, at least *prima facie*, warrants us to suppose that these correlations are established by some sort of direct causal influence or commonality between the distant measurements.

In spite of this, there is, perhaps, a loophole in my argument for information transmission. It is perfectly true that the long-run statistics of such two-particle systems violate the BI. However, it may seem as if each individual run of the experiment could be explained by a locally-causal story. (As emphasized by Mermin (1990), this would not be the case for the three-particle GHZ [Greenberger-Horne-Zeilinger] state. However, the properties of the GHZ state have not yet been directly verified by experiment.[13]) After all, both experimenters have agreed to measure the same observable, and each obtains definite results that obey the relevant conservation law. Considered out of context, it seems just like a case in which the two particles were mailed from their common source with the values to be obtained by the measurements already gift-wrapped.

In the usual EPR scenario the experimenters are allowed to switch their

---

[11]Chang and Cartwright [48] have a very useful discussion of the notion of common cause. They conclude that the event of the creation of the EPR particle pair can serve as a *'partial* [my emphasis] common cause, which acts in conjunction with each of the apparatus settings to produce the outcomes...' [p. 181]. This is a perfectly reasonable way of speaking; however, in asking whether there is any communication across the space-like gap between the detectors, the issue is whether conditions and events at the source of the particles can serve as a complete common cause of the experimental outcomes. To this question the answer would seem to be an emphatic no.

[12]See Maudlin [137, Chapter 1] for an especially elegant and accessible demonstration of this fact.

[13] Note added in 2018: the predicted non-classical properties of the GHZ state are now well-established experimentally; see, e.g., [37].

detector parameters between runs, and this bare possibility will not save local realism. We would need a different causal story for each run of the apparatus, and this would mean that there had to have been differences in the state preparation for each run that were not reflected in the state description. One might think that there is an EPR-type argument for the incompleteness of QM lurking here somewhere. However, this option would not be open in the GHZ case. Furthermore, we could scuttle any such local cause alibis by allowing for delayed choices; that is, we let the observers make their parameter choices after the particles have left the source.

Unfortunately, though, we cannot get off the hook in the case of my thought experiment by appealing to the possibility of delayed choice, because that would obviously make the prearrangements impossible. It is essential to the experiment that the observers know beforehand that the detectors will be set parallel or anti-parallel, and that they agree not to manipulate the detectors during the crucial run of the experiment at 12:00 noon. It might seem as if we cannot rule out the bare possibility of a common cause explanation for the particular kinds of results we get just in this case.

Why, then, am I not very worried about this? Because such prearrangements and choices of detector settings do not seem to have any possible causal bearing on how we prepare the particles emitted at the source. If they could, we would have to accept that precisely in the cases in which we (verbally, standing outside the laboratory door) make certain prearrangements, some odd, subtle (but not superluminal) influence from the event of our conversation jiggles the source in such a way that just for that run of the experiment there is a common cause built into the particles; even though the source has been prepared in exactly the same way as it would have been in a sequence of runs that would directly demonstrate the violation of the BI. This would be to allow that a mere conversation can have a physical influence on particle preparation, a notion more in keeping with the writings of Richard Rorty than anything else.

I find this extremely implausible, but I acknowledge that I cannot absolutely rule it out. But just to highlight the implausibility, suppose we did a run in which the prearrangements are made but then one of the experimenters arbitrarily decides to subvert the experiment (after having repaired to his remote site), and switches his detector angle at random. If the prearrangements that had been made earlier had that influence on the particles could not be altered by our experimenter's sudden change of plan, and thus statistics taken on many runs of this nature might well satisfy the BI. And yet, is there anyone who could believe that the accumulated correlation statistics would in fact not show the usual violation of the BI? Such prearrangements as we require to carry out our thought experiment could not build sufficient common causes into the particles by any mechanism that I can conceive.[14]

---

[14]There are two more remote but logically possible explanations for the correlations that do not necessarily involve nonlocal causation. One would be to imagine that a sort of Leibnizian

## 3.6 Information and the Locality of Particle Dynamics

I will take it, then, that in suitable quantum mechanical contexts localized outcomes can be informative of space-like separate events, and that this fact cannot be explained by any common cause model. If this is right, the implications for particle dynamics are crucially important, and bear in the most direct way possible on the question of peaceful coexistence.

To see why, let us first consider some remarks by Tim Maudlin. Few have done as much as he to insist that there is indeed superluminal information transmission in QM, and that it poses a fundamental challenge to relativity. (Indeed, all I have really done in my thought experiment above is to add a little colour to Maudlin's cogent and detailed arguments to this effect.) However, in spite of this, Maudlin himself accepts the NCS demonstrations; and in particular cites the local dynamics class of arguments in favour of that claim:

> In fact, quantum theory requires that there be no matter or energy transfer between the correlated particles, at least in the following sense. *After the paired photons or electrons have separated, the so-called interaction Hamiltonian between the particles decays to zero.* [Emphasis added.] The Hamiltonian governs the time evolution of the system, and is intimately connected to its energy. If the interaction part of the Hamiltonian goes to zero, the evolution of the two wings decouples in certain ways. It follows that (1) no manipulation on one wing... can affect the expectation value of the energy on the other. As a consequence (2) if the particles have definite energies after they separate... then nothing done on one side can change the energy on the other. In this sense, no energy or matter can be transmitted between the wings. Quantum correlations do not require any superluminal matter or energy transfer. To the extent that Relativity forbids such transfer, all is still well. [137, p. 71]

Maudlin accordingly argues (as does Elitzur [79]) that the information transmission endemic to quantum phenomena is a special and unique sort of information transmission that, unlike any other, somehow occurs without exchange of energy or momentum. But this entire line of thought depends upon the assumption about the locality of the Hamiltonian that I highlighted above. Surely the entire issue is to determine precisely whether or not the interaction

---

pre-established harmony prevails, in which (for reasons that please the Deity, perhaps) distant micro-events just happen to be correlated in the ways predicted by QM. Another would be superdeterminism; if experimenters do not really have free choice then one can suppose, perhaps, that both the experimenter's choice of parameter and the experimental outcome, even in a delayed-choice experiment, were determined by common local causes. (I thank the late Niall Shanks for pointing this out to me, in conversation.) Like solipsism, these positions are probably irrefutable but are intellectual dead ends. I prefer to assume that there is some point to further inquiry, although I freely admit that this is largely an emotional commitment!

Hamiltonian does indeed decay to zero after the particles have separated. I emphasize that *no proof has ever been offered of this assertion*; it has simply been assumed.[15]

Abner Shimony is one of the few who have even acknowledged that the locality of the particle dynamics could be an issue:

> The quantum mechanical predictions concerning ensembles of pairs of particles do not violate Parameter Independence, provided that nonlocality is not explicitly built into the interaction Hamiltonian of the particle pair. [203, p. 191]

But why are we entitled not to worry that nonlocality might not be 'built into' the interaction Hamiltonian? In fact, both Shimony and Maudlin are simply adopting the standard view of virtually all physicists who have studied this question. These physicists, if pressed, would probably argue that what is really in question here is burden of proof. The irreverent critic such as myself will say that we cannot just assume that there is no unmediated interaction between the distant particles; that gives the whole game away. Others will reply, with some justice, that the critic must demonstrate the existence of some positive physical motivation for supposing that there might be nonlocal terms in the Hamiltonian; otherwise, they will say, the suggestion that there are nonlocal terms is purest ad hoccery. Richard Feynman once jokingly observed that one might well imagine that angels push the planets around in their orbits. Many people seem to feel that any suggestion of nonlocal dynamics in QM is like postulating superluminal angels—an importation of a purely fanciful, ad hoc and possibly untestable hypothesis that has insufficient independent justification.

In fact, one can point to some positive physical reasons for taking the idea of nonlocal interaction seriously. Let us go back again to the question of information transmission. I entirely agree with Maudlin that we should accept that the information somehow got across the gap between the two measurement sites. But if we are willing to accept this, however, then we need to pay careful attention to what is known of the physical conditions under which information can be transmitted. In fact, there is a well worked-out body of theory, known as information theory, that is concerned precisely with this question (see, e.g., [172]). And a general result of information theory is that information cannot be encoded in any physical structure or system without expenditure of energy. The reason is very fundamental: to encode information

---

[15]Ghirardi and Weber [94, p. 13] state, 'It is absolutely incorrect to use the tested behaviour of quantum systems to assert that quantum theory implies the possibility of an instantaneous transfer of energy and/or information between spacelike separated observers'. But in support of this claim they cite [93], which *assumes* the dynamic localizability of the subsystems of the EPR system and then merely shows (as do the other NCS proofs) that QM does not allow one to violate this condition. Whether or not the subsystems really are dynamically local is the very thing one needs to establish in the first place.

## 3.6. Information and the Locality of Particle Dynamics

in a structure, one lowers entropy in that structure (in fact, these are equivalent ways of saying the same thing); and to lower entropy one must do work. Any device that could transmit interprtable information without doing work on the structure in which that information becomes encoded would be a perpetual motion machine of the second class (i.e. one that violates the second law of thermodynamics).[16] Either QM violates the second law of thermodynamics, or there is a nonlocal aspect of energy which should be reflected in nonlocal terms in the interaction Hamiltonian of multiparticle systems. If this is right, then the defenders of peaceful coexistence are faced with a rather stark choice: give up relativity in its present strict interpretation, or allow that QM somehow miraculously violates the laws of thermodynamics. And it was Einstein himself who said that if there is any one branch of physics that will stand when others fall, it is thermodynamics.[17]

Much of the literature in this field is characterized by lack of attention to the fundamental requirements of information theory. A striking and instructive example of this is the explanation offered by Bohm and Hiley for their concept of 'active information'.[18] They note that particles seem to be guided by information encoded in the form of the wave function, in such a way as to allow a distance-independent effect:

> Such behaviour would seem strange from the point of view of classical physics. Yet it is fairly common at the level of ordinary experience. For example we may consider a ship on automatic pilot being guided by radio waves. Here, too, the effect of the radio waves is independent of their intensity and depends only on their form. The essential point is that the ship is moving with its own energy, and that the form of the radio waves is taken up [sic] to direct the much greater energy of the ship. We may therefore propose that an electron too moves under its own energy, and that the form of the quantum wave directs the energy of the electron. [32, p. 32]

---

[16]There are cases in which the nonoccurrence of an event may be informative of distant events. For instance, if I plan to meet a friend for lunch at 1:00 unless she is called in to work, and if she does not appear at 1:00, then I can conclude that she was called in to work. Such cases do not imply any transmission of energy or signal from my friend to me at 1:00. (Some work had to be done, of course, in order to arrange the circumstances under which my friend's absence at 1:00 could be interpreted. But that energy did not have to be transmitted from her location at 1:00 to me.) But there must be work done in cases in which the definite occurrence of an event (such as a particle passing through a polarizer) is informative of some distant state of affairs (such as the death of a cat), whether that energy is transmitted via a common cause, or directly from event to event.

[17]Quoted in [123, p. 6]: '...classical thermodynamics...is the only physical theory of universal content which I am convinced will never be overthrown, within the framework of applicability of its basic concepts'.

[18]In the following I am indebted to M. Guarini for useful discussions, and to the thought-provoking review of Bohm and Hiley's *Undivided Universe* by Dickson [62].

Bohm and Hiley suggest that both in the case of a ship being directed by a radio signal, and a particle being directed by a quantum wave form, we see the effect of what they call active information. They suggest that the wave function can carry 'enfolded' or 'implicate' information that can guide particle motions without necessarily having to impart energy directly to the particles.

> The basic idea of active information is that a form having very little energy enters into and directs a much greater energy. The activity of the latter is in this way given a form similar to that of the smaller energy. [32, p. 35]

But Bohm and Hiley do not offer a very clear picture of how the information encoded in the wave form can have this remarkable effect:

> The puzzle in this approach is that of how information that is merely passive... is able to determine actual objective processes... [p. 37]

What Bohm and Hiley are apparently trying to describe is the familiar phenomenon of *amplification*. Consider a 100,000 ton ship receiving a radio message warning of icebergs ahead. The captain prudently alters course. The change in the massive ship's momentum constitutes, in effect, an amplification of the energetically feeble but significantly informative signal received. As Bohm and Hiley rightly insist, the tiny (but non-zero) energy-momentum transferred to the ship's radio antenna certainly does not push the ship into its new course. Instead, the signal modulates a much larger flow of energy within the ship itself.

Bohm and Hiley perform a valuable service by bringing this sort of process to the fore. But what is missing from their account is a clear recognition that even this sort of indirect influence requires a transfer of momentum-energy from the carrier of the information. There are numerous ways that modulation can occur, but the important point is that since any sort of modulation is a causal process the original signal must have been carrying some small amount of momentum-energy. For amplification to occur, there has to be a signal to amplify, however weak. Amplification does indeed offer a promising model of what happens in quantum measurement; but the notion that measurements amplify a signal present in the wave function offers no support whatsoever for the idea that measurement can occur without the exchange of momentum-energy between the wave particle system and the measuring apparatus.

In fact, Bohm and Hiley do, in passing, acknowledge that the quantum 'information field' may also have some 'negligible' energy [32, p. 38]. However, I think that we have to go much farther than merely conceding this as a possibility. It is the heart of the matter; the quantum field must impart some energy to the (particle + detector) system in order for the amplification to be possible. And the theoretical importance of this fact is anything but negligible. For instance, it would make a huge difference to the structure of the Bohm

## 3.6. Information and the Locality of Particle Dynamics

theory itself, which (like the usual NCS proofs cited above) starts from an explicit assumption of dynamical locality [32]. And it is hard to see how it can fail to have large implications for our theoretical understanding of relativity.

This discussion brings to mind Bohr's insistence (frequently cited by John A. Wheeler (see, e.g., [234]) that any completed measurement involves a thermodynamically irreversible act of amplification. What we seem to have to add to this is that the amplification is of a signal delivered nonlocally—a notion with which Bohr himself would have obviously been most uncomfortable![19] The details remain unclear, but perhaps we can say that under certain conditions that remain to be elucidated, systems may be potentiated to amplify the very weak nonlocal signal generated by a distant measurement event, with the 'collapse' of the wave function being essentially a dramatic increase in entropy which entails a macroscopically significant reweighting of possible measurement outcomes.

Unfortunately, I cannot pursue the measurement problem itself here. The crucial point is that if we accept superluminal information transmission (controllable or otherwise), then information theory tells us (at least *prima facie*) that we have to accept nonlocal dynamics; and this undermines all the standard arguments for NCS and challenges the usual picture of relativistic causality in a very direct way.

One can also briefly indicate other reasons to think that the possibility of nonlocal dynamics should be taken seriously.

First, Bohm showed us that a nonlocal potential is implicit in the basic mathematics of standard nonrelativistic wave mechanics. This quantum potential contributes directly to the total energy of the system and (formally at least) seems to be capable of transferring momentum to particles—since as a potential it can be differentiated with respect to distance to give a force. If my worries about the local Hamiltonian are correct then the Bohm theory cannot be exact; but it seems rather unlikely that a more accurate development of the theory would be any less nonlocal than Bohm's original version.[20]

Another crucial point to note is that the concept of localization is not relativistically invariant. A concentration of energy that was localized within a small region $\Delta x$ in one frame of reference could appear to be spread over a very large volume of space in other frames of reference. (In fact, it is not unreasonable to conjecture that the existence of the nonlocal quantum potential is directly related to the nonlocality of the position operator.) This is something that is not likely to go away even if Lorentz invariance should be found to be

---

[19] Recall Bohr's remark: 'Of course there is in a case like [the EPR thought experiment] no question of a mechanical disturbance of the system under investigation during the last critical stage of the measuring procedure' [36, p. 699]. The point of this discussion is that Bohr very likely was simply mistaken when he said this.

[20] A peculiarity of the Bohm theory is that particles do not reciprocate; they do not transfer momentum-energy back to the quantum field. This may be yet another indication of the provisional nature of the Bohm theory.

inexact.

There is another point that is more difficult to express precisely. QM shows that nonlocality is pervasive; it seems to suggest (although not clearly) that in some sense much of physics is fundamentally nonlocal. As Leslie Ballentine remarks, 'Perhaps what is needed is not an explanation of nonlocality, but an explanation of locality' [18, p. 786]. Now, it may turn out in the end that all particle dynamics are local after all. But in view of the presumption in favour of nonlocality apparently set by QM in so many cases, are we really entitled to assume with only scanty discussion that dynamics are local? Should this not have to be *argued* for, and should not alternative conceptions of dynamics be explored?

There is another sort of objection that is often raised to the suggestion that there is superluminal causation of some sort in EPR experiments. It will be said that one has confused the 'space of reasons with the space of causes'. The correlations yielded by the formalism of QM are sufficient reason to allow the left observer to make the inferences about the distant site that she can indeed make; why need we speak of causes at all? The point is that information certainly is available to the left observer that relativity seems to say she cannot have, and this must entail, at the very least, a careful reinterpretation of the usual relativistic picture of causality. I do not find it to be at all sufficient merely to issue a reminder that the formalism gives an unambiguous procedure for calculating the correlations, and wash one's hands of the whole affair.

## 3.7 Could Relativity Really Be a Principle Theory?

The opinion of most physicists and philosophers of science is that relativity is a 'principle theory', which Paul Teller defines as 'a set of general constraints which any more detailed theory must satisfy' [219, p. 212].[21] In many ways this seems very reasonable. Relativity[22] is extremely well confirmed by experiment; it has provided a framework within which highly successful particle and quantum field theories could be constructed; it is supported by a profound and searching analysis by Einstein of the origins of our notions of space and time; and moreover, it is a theory of great conceptual and mathematical elegance. Is it even reasonable to entertain the possibility that it is not, after all, exactly right?

The issue of confirmation is easy to deal with. Newtonian mechanics is also very well confirmed within certain realms of applicability, but that hardly prevented it from being superseded. Certainly, what we can say in relativity's favour is that if some broader theory $T$ replaces it, relativity must

---

[21] The distinction between 'principle' and 'constructive' theories was first mooted by Einstein [77]. See [42] for an instructive and sympathetic discussion of principle versus constructive theories. Einstein's notion of a principle theory may be somewhat irreverently characterized as a sort of de facto *synthetic a priori*.

[22] What I mean by relativity here is the theory of spacetime structure founded by Einstein, according to which spacetime is a Riemannian manifold characterized by a locally Lorentz metric.

## 3.7. Could Relativity Really Be a Principle Theory?

be embeddable in $T$, and $T$ must closely approximate to relativity in contexts in which relativity is already known to work well. However, there seems to be no intrinsic reason why relativity could not be superseded as have so many other theories in the past.

Einstein's analysis of kinematical concepts clearly captured a vital element of the truth. However, Einstein himself was well aware of the limitations of his approach. In particular, he made it clear from the outset that he chose to gloss over the whole problem of defining the very term 'local', which would have entangled him in difficulties that would have been hopeless at the time he wrote:

> We shall not here discuss the inexactitude which lurks in the concept of simultaneity of two events at approximately the same place, which can only be removed by an abstraction. [74, p. 39]

There is no reason to suppose that Einstein's reworking of the concepts of space and time, no matter how much of an improvement it was over earlier views, is the last word.

A very fundamental problem is that if there really are dynamic interactions between space-like separate events then there is an invariant concept of simultaneity; and if such interactions (*pace* the NCS theorems) could ever be controlled there would be a way of directly synchronizing clocks at a distance. But this fact would not necessarily be a *reductio ad absurdum* of the notion of nonlocal influences. As a number of authors have suggested [48, 159, 161, 151], there may be a variety of concepts of simultaneity above and beyond what Brent Mundy [151] has dubbed the 'optical simultaneity' defined by Einstein.

Should the mathematical elegance and coherence of relativity be taken as evidence of its completeness and adequacy as a physical theory? Not necessarily; Dirac rightly emphasized mathematical beauty as a heuristic guide to theory construction, but theoretical elegance and simplicity can sometimes be deceptive. One need not be a fan of chaos theory to acknowledge the possibility that nature might at some deep level be inherently complex or asymmetric. Furthermore, aesthetic standards, while certainly not entirely arbitrary or relative, are notoriously dependent upon culture and personal taste. For centuries astronomers were hobbled by the assumption that planets must move in circular orbits because the circle is highly symmetric. Perhaps some day Lorentz-invariant theories will seem as awkward and arbitrary as Ptolemaic astronomy does to us now.

Relativity has a special kind of appeal that makes it especially difficult for the theoretician to abandon. The academic mind loves an orderly scheme, with everything assigned its proper place, and no items that are unaccountable or out of control. And relativity provides just such a scheme, with its neat division of spacetime by the lightcones into distinct causal regions, and its definite and exception-free classification of the sorts of causal relations that are possible. QM upsets all of this. According to QM, it is not strictly impossible, but merely extremely *improbable*, that the next time I open my office door I shall be precipitated into a Jurassic swamp. Perhaps (although I cannot substantiate this guess by textual reference) the fact that such apparent absurdities cannot be somehow ruled out by their very nature is another reason why theoreticians still find the indeterminism and nonlocality of QM to be so difficult to accept. If there are indeed 'essentialist cravings' [86] to be rooted out, this could be where they lie.

Some calculations by H. Ardavan [12, 11] indicate possible limitations for Lorentz invariance, and need to be taken far more seriously than they appear to have been. Ardavan showed rigorously that there are apparently realizable configurations of rotating electromagnetic and gravitational fields in which certain field potentials diverge, posing a difficult interpretational problem.[23] He pointed out that either there would have to be some as yet unknown, sweeping physical principle prohibiting the establishment of such rotating field patterns, or else one would have to assume that the divergence indicates the breakdown of the assumption that the relativistic vacuum is nondispersive.[24] It is interesting to note that in aerodynamics one encounters a formally similar problem: there is a simplified linear theory of aerodynamics (due to Ackeret) in which one takes air to be nondispersive with respect to the propagation of sound waves. This theory predicts that transonic motion is impossible, since according to it the coefficient of pressure diverges at Mach 1! (See von Karman [229, pp. 110–118].)

The problem is that if a theory (such as standard Lorentz-invariant relativity) predicts a divergence for some value $v_0$ of some parameter $v$, there are two possible interpretations. One is that it is in fact physically impossible for the parameter to assume that value. The other is that the theory breaks down at that critical value. Physics is, of course, rife with theories that are applicable for some range of some controlling parameter, only to break down elsewhere. An example is the linear theory of the simple harmonic oscillator, which predicts

---

[23] Ardavan offers a specific example. Suppose that a tenuous but electrically conductive plasma extends throughout a solar system. Suppose also that there is a distant pulsar, and the rotating beam of radiation from this pulsar sweeps through this solar system. Consider a plane through the plasma perpendicular to the bisector of the pulsar beam. If the solar system is far enough away from the pulsar, the beam will rotate with superluminal tangential velocity where it intersects this plane. (This is essentially the familiar searchlight-beam effect.) This rotating field will induce a pattern of charge separation in the layer of plasma. The locus of this pattern will rotate superluminally, and it will itself radiate a rotating field pattern. Ardavan shows that the field potentials in any such superluminally rotating field pattern will diverge, according to standard Maxwell-Lorentz electromagnetic theory. And yet it is difficult to see what could guarantee that this sort of scenario could not occur. Ardavan is cautious in his conclusions, and yet it seems likely that this is simply a case where the standard theory does not work.

[24] The latter possibility was also mooted by K. Fujiwara [90]; see also Pavlopoulos [158]. A dispersive medium is one in which the velocity of propagation of disturbances is a function of frequency. This spreads out the pressure gradients near the critical velocity that would be infinitely sharp in a nondispersive medium.

## 3.7. Could Relativity Really Be a Principle Theory?

infinite amplitude at the resonant frequency $\omega = \omega_0$. This does not pose an interpretational problem, because no one expects the theory to apply rigorously at the resonant frequency. The challenging thing about Ardavan's results is that they tend to rule out the first possibility for electrodynamics, since there seems to be no fundamental reason at all why the types of rotating field patterns he considers could not actually occur. It is conceivable, therefore, that the divergences predicted at $v = c$ in Lorentz-invariant theories may be just as unphysical as the divergence at resonance in the linear theory of the harmonic oscillator. The puzzle set forth by Ardavan may be related to one of the most fundamental difficulties with relativity, which is that it is a continuum theory. It assumes that position, time, energy, momentum, and action are continuously variable quantities, and takes spacetime positions and trajectories to be definable to arbitrary precision. But we know that at least some of these quantities can only assume a discrete spectrum. Action, in particular, is always quantized, and action is crucial, the king-pin that links kinematics with dynamics.[25] Furthermore, Lorentz-invariant relativity takes no direct account of the existence of conjugate quantities such as position and momentum, between which stand uncertainty relations. It is hard to see how Lorentz-invariant relativity could be precisely correct.[26] The uncertainty relations imply that spacetime trajectory is only an approximate concept; furthermore, a wide range of experience with particle phenomena indicates that we are not necessarily entitled to assume that particles have continuous trajectories between the locations at which they are detected. As Misner, Thorne, and Wheeler state, 'That object which is central to all of classical general relativity, the four-dimensional spacetime geometry, simply does not exist, except in a classical approximation' [146, pp. 1182–1183].

If Misner *et al.* are right, there exists a yet to be discovered quantum theory of spacetime, which would bear roughly the same relationship to classical relativistic spacetime theories as the quantum theory of fluids bears to classical fluid dynamics; that is, the classical theory would be a frequently useful (and yet sometimes dead wrong) limiting approximation to the more fundamental quantum theory. It is foolish to predict the development of science with any degree of dogmatism, and yet given the general trend of physics in the past century, a development of this nature seems highly likely, if not more or less inevitable.[27]

---

[25] Bohm's guidance condition takes momentum $\mathbf{p} = \nabla S$, where $S$ is action. This equation has no meaning unless $S$ is continuous and differentiable to at least first order in position. Since action is always discrete this fact alone is sufficient to indicate that the Bohm theory, as illuminating as it is, cannot be exact.

[26] Schrödinger many years ago argued that we 'have to "quantize" the Lorentz transformation', but he was not able to suggest what that might mean mathematically [198] (quoted in [17, p. 79]).

[27] Proponents of the Bohm theory will object, pointing out that Bohm showed us that it is possible to construct a version of quantum theory which is observationally equivalent to the usual theory, but in which particles can apparently have definite, continuous trajectories. See Cushing's lucid study [52] for details. However, the mathematical structures which Bohm identified (the quantum potential, the guidance conditions) need not have the specific interpretation which he

A further worry is that relativity as we understand it today takes metric relationships as law-like and dynamical structures as contingent. However, we know through quantum theory that there is an intimate relationship between metric and dynamic structures. Quantum phenomena teach us that metrical and dynamic quantities are linked through the quantum of action, a fact that is not expressed in the present formalism of relativity even though the interdependency between the metrical and the dynamic is prefigured in general relativity through Einstein's field equations. We need an invariance principle that expresses this directly, rather than requiring us to write in dynamical facts.

Finally, we should take note of the fundamental difficulty posed by quantum phenomena for the principle of relativity (PR) itself. The PR essentially expresses a realist intuition, that what things and events are in themselves is fundamentally unaffected by the way they are observed. We want to believe that whether I look at a rock from the west or from the east, it is still the same rock. The PR may be expressed mathematically by a variety of invariance principles or symmetries. Relativity theory as we presently understand it utilizes Lorentz invariance, the symmetry that makes Maxwell's equations of electrodynamics law-like. It is quite thinkable that we could express the PR by means of other symmetries that reduce to Lorentz invariance in suitable limits. (Such a symmetry might be based upon the invariance of action.) But QM presents a deep challenge to the whole realistic programme of basing physical theories on invariance principles of presumed universal applicability, for it tells us that the reality we observe can be in itself changed or determined in some unclear way by the means with which we chose to observe it.

I certainly do not want to advocate that we abandon realism in the deepest sense, which is essentially an acknowledgement that we humans live in and arose from a vastly larger nonhuman order to which we must remain responsive in order to survive. However, it may well be that QM will force us to acknowledge limits on the describability of that reality, and thus limitations on that ultimate predictive and explanatory completeness of fundamental physical theory that Einstein [76] identified as the deepest goal of the physical scientist.

## 3.8  Nonlocal Hidden Variables?

One naturally tends to suppose that anyone who countenances nonlocal influences is advocating a nonlocal hidden variables theory such as some versions of the Bohm theory. This is not necessarily the case. It depends upon what we mean by 'hidden variable'. In the Bohm theory, the hidden variables are simply the positions of the particles, and they are assumed to be what Dirac called $c$-numbers; continuous, real-valued quantities. They are hidden, according

---

and his followers prefer; and as I indicate in this paper there are reasons to doubt that the Bohm theory could be exactly right. Rather, the really significant thing which Bohm accomplished was to bring to the fore the fundamental nonlocality of dynamics in quantum theory. I hope to defend this possibly controversial position in a future study.

to the Bohm theory, only because of the uncertainty relations, which Bohm took to be purely statistical. Some authors apparently find the Bohm theory to be philosophically comforting, because it seems to allow us to think that 'particles are particles' [98] with definite spacetime trajectories and properly deterministic behaviour.

I fear that any such attempt to revert to the classical picture—even if it courageously accepts a rather radical nonlocality as did Bohm himself—is probably doomed from the start (although one can no doubt construct quasi-classical theories, such as the Bohm theory itself, which are useful and illuminating in limited contexts). I propose that we seek not a hidden variables theory, but something that might jokingly be called a hidden operators theory.

Everything that we presently know about multi-particle systems is consistent with the presence of nonlocal terms in the Hamiltonian, so long as these terms have the following characteristics: (i) they must be dependent on phase differences, which are distance-independent but which in phase-incoherent systems will wash out; (ii) they must be usually quite small in magnitude compared with local potentials and kinetic energies; and (iii) they may fluctuate randomly in sign from measurement to measurement on identically prepared systems, so that they do not necessarily appear in an ensemble Hamiltonian defined over a mixture of measurement trials. (It is not inconceivable that there could be phase-coherent systems in which the nonlocal component of the Hamiltonian could be quite large; this could have interesting technological implications.)

In one sense, therefore, my proposal is more radical than Bohm's, in that it seeks an explicitly nonlocal Hamiltonian and thus undermines the whole notion of particle localizability that Bohm thought his theory would defend. It is less radical in that it involves no change in the ontology of quantum theory. Or more precisely, it advances the deontologizing of physics that has been under way for quite some time now—if by an 'ontology' we mean a presumptive underpinning of a theory in terms of persistent 'objects'. This, sadly for some, will be an even more radical departure from the classical world view; but it may simply be the logical completion of the revolution sparked by Max Planck in 1900.

## 3.9 Two Alternate Approaches

I should say something about two other approaches to the puzzle of nonlocality that many people find attractive.[28]

A number of authors (e.g., Elitzur [79]) have noted that in any EPR scenario the distant particles are in fact topologically connected by a very large number of world lines. In particular, their back light cones will overlap, and subluminal world lines within those back cones may intersect as well.

---

[28] In this section I am indebted to Bryson Brown for illuminating comments in his review [40] of James Robert Brown's *Smoke and Mirrors* [43].

Thus, if we are willing to contemplate some sort of backwards causation, we already have a route for causal connection between the particles; why postulate superluminal world lines, nonlocal potentials, or the like? If we could thus find a way to make just one amendment to standard spacetime theory workable (the introduction of backwards causation), we would apparently have a very conservative solution to the problem of nonlocality. Furthermore, the importance of advanced potentials in electromagnetic theory does suggest that some sort of backwards causation could be taken seriously [115].

Backwards causation theories certainly merit further investigation. However, there are two objections to them.

First, from the viewpoint advocated in this paper, which takes as a hypothesis that abstract quantum theory is fundamental, the idea of explaining nonlocality in terms of spacetime trajectories of any sort is simply to get the whole explanatory problem backwards. Trajectories, on this view, are approximate, secondary constructs, not fundamental structures.

Second, any attempt to account for the BI violating correlations by any structures delimited in spacetime is almost certainly, in general, doomed from the start. (It may succeed in special cases.) I conjecture that a QM-violating BI will follow from any attempt to confine possible interactions between entangled particles to any region of spacetime less than the whole spacetime. This would apply even to attempts to explain interactions between correlated particles purely by means of tachyons. There may well be tachyons, but they would not suffice to explain the correlations; indeed, there would be nonlocal correlations between the tachyons! However, I reiterate that these remarks are conjectural; further work is required.

Another ingenious approach—in some ways more philosophically radical than anything considered in this paper—has been advanced by James Robert Brown [42, 43]. Brown avows a very literal Platonism, arguing that our intellects can have unmediated (although potentially fallible) access to universal entities and laws. He suggests that QM manifests the existence of information that is purely abstract not encoded in anything physical at all. Brown argues (private communication) that the approach I advocate here may be 'overly physicalistic and even question-begging, by insisting that information must be physically represented/encoded'.

Brown's view is cogent and challenging. However, I am going to stand by my physicalism for the time being. The sort of information available to our left hand observer in the thought experiment above is exactly the sort of information she could get from a telephone call. (Again, the fact that the caller on the right could not control whether he sends 0 or 1 is irrelevant to whether a bit of information was received; and because the right apparatus can be causally connected to other physical systems—it could trigger a bomb, for instance—that one bit of information can carry a lot of interpretative weight.) Hence, it is not unreasonable at all to insist that EPR information is subject

## 3.10 On the Edge of a Paradigm Shift

to the same general thermodynamic constraints as the information that one receives over a telephone wire—namely that it must be paid for in the currency of free energy because its presence amounts to a local reduction in entropy in the state of the receiver (the left apparatus).

### 3.10 On the Edge of a Paradigm Shift

I think that Thomas Kuhn [125] was essentially right in his depiction of science as going on comfortably for periods of time, solving expected problems by means of accepted methods, until it gets increasingly 'stuck'. At that point, a new Gestalt or 'paradigm' is needed. (Whether it truly makes sense to say that the new way of doing science is 'incommensurable' with the old is another question entirely. As Kuhn noted, scientists themselves tend to downplay this aspect of the story, probably because they do not like to admit that they were stuck!)

However else one may characterize Kuhn's paradigm shifts (and Kuhn himself unfortunately tended to mystify the whole process), they do resemble perfectly ordinary problem-solving in one crucial respect: when you are stuck, simply stuck, on a tough intellectual problem, you often do not make a breakthrough until you accept that you have to give something up. If there is just no way of reconciling all of your cherished assumptions with each other, then at least one of them must be abandoned or turned on its head. In physics we are presently in an acutely 'stuck' phase now, because of the problem of reconciling quantum nonlocality with relativistic locality. And relativistic causality as we presently understand it is very likely the thing we have to give up next.[29]

---

[29] Earlier versions of this paper were presented at the Interuniversity Centre for Postgraduate Studies in Dubrovnik, April 1993, at the meeting of the Eastern Division of the American Philosophical Association in Atlanta, Georgia, in December 1993, and at the Western Canadian Philosophical Association Conference, University of Lethbridge, November 1996. I am grateful to R.I.G. Hughes and Phil Hoffmann, respectively, for challenging commentary on those occasions. I have also benefited greatly from discussions with J.R. Brown, R. Clifton, K. de Laplante, R. DiSalle, P. Eberhard, M. Guarini, W. Harper, J.B. Kennedy Jr., M. Kernaghan, T. Maudlin, S. McCall, R. Mosher, I. Pitowsky, N. Shanks, A. Shimony, A.J. Stacey and S.R. Valluri. (Of course, none of these people are responsible for any errors on my part.) This work was generously supported by the Social Sciences and Humanities Research Council of Canada.

# Chapter 4

# An Adventure Outside the Light Cone[1]

**Abstract** This paper reviews and extends an approach to superluminal kinematics set forth by R. Sutherland and J. Shepanski [216]. This theory is characterized by a spacetime with positive *definite* metric, a Lorentz factor of the form $1/\sqrt{\beta^2 - 1}$, and real-valued proper times and proper lengths for superluminal reference frames.

## 4.1 Motivation for this Study

The central assumption underlying the standard approach to tachyon theory is that the usual Lorentz transformations apply to the superluminal case. One therefore simply takes the Lorentz factor $\gamma = \sqrt{1 - \beta^2}$ (where $\beta \equiv v/c$) and substitutes $\beta > 1$ into it. This leads directly to imaginary rest masses and proper times for tachyons, with many attendant difficulties of interpretation. (See, e.g., [83, 30].)

Instead of proceeding by substitution (often a risky business) it may be useful to attempt to derive transformations for the superluminal case from first principles; that is, assume the invariance of the speed of light and the usual Minkowski spacetime geometry following from that postulate, but make the *explicit assumption* that it is possible to transform to a superluminal reference frame. We shall see that this results in an interestingly different spacetime theory, characterized by a Lorentz factor of the form $\gamma = \sqrt{\beta^2 - 1}$ and a *definite* metric.

---

[1]This was first published as 'Superluminal Transformations in Spacetimes of Definite Metric' in G. Hunter, S. Jeffers, and J.-P. Viger (eds.), *Causality and Locality in Modern Physics*. Dordrecht: Kluwer, 1998, pp. 227–234. I thank Springer Publishing for permission to reproduce this paper in *Quantum Heresies*. I have corrected a sign error that appeared in the original version in Eqs. (12) and (13).

## 4.2. Derivation of Superluminal Transformations

The results derived here were first set forth by Sutherland and Shepanski [216], who establish a quite general theory of superluminal reference frames. L. Parker [156] also explored a theory with definite metric. The purpose of this note is to draw attention to this approach, and to present an alternative derivation of Sutherland and Shepanski's results that indicates in an especially clear way the physical differences between them and the usual theory. The definite-metric theory by no means solves all problems asssociated with the notion of superluminal motion; in particular, it does nothing to dispel the closed-loop causal paradoxes. However, in certain ways it does seem to satisfy the requirements of the Principle of Relativity in a more natural way than the usual approach. Furthermore, the theory has some very interesting (and indeed pleasing) mathematical properties regardless of the question of its physical relevance.

## 4.2 Derivation of Superluminal Transformations

### 4.2.1 Using Auxiliary Subluminal Frame

The method used by Sutherland and Shepanski [216] involves the use of an auxiliary subluminal frame. We will not repeat the whole calculation here. The essential geometric idea is very natural in the context of Minkowski geometry. Any boost involves the rotation of the time axis and the spatial axis in the direction of motion toward the light cone. This rotation is symmetric about the light cone—that is, given a choice of time and distance scales such that the light cone is at $\pi/4$ with respect to the time and space axes in the 'lab' frame $S$, both axes rotate toward the light cone through the same angle. Now, a superluminal boost will involve the rotation of the time and spatial axis (in the direction of motion) *through* the light cone; and again, of course, this will be symmetrical about the light cone line. Therefore, for every (hypothetical) superluminal frame $\bar{S}$, there exists a subluminal frame $S'$ with its axes at the *same* angle $\phi$ with respect to the axes of the lab frame, but with time and space axes (in the direction of motion) interchanged.

Let $\bar{v}$ be the superluminal velocity of $\bar{S}$ with respect to the lab frame $S$, and let $v$ be the subluminal velocity of the auxiliary frame $S'$ with respect to $S$. One readily shows that $\tan\phi = v/c = c/\bar{v}$, giving $v = c^2/\bar{v}$.

Let $(x,y,z,t)$ be coordinates in $S$, $(x',y',z',t')$ be the coordinates in $S'$, and $(\bar{x},\bar{y},\bar{z},\bar{t})$ be the coordinates in $\bar{S}$. Between $S$ and $S'$ there stand the usual subluminal Lorentz transformations

$$x' = \gamma_-(x - vt), \quad t' = \gamma_-(t - vx/c^2), \quad y' = y, \quad z' = z, \tag{4.1}$$

where we define $\gamma_- \equiv 1/\sqrt{1-\beta^2}$. Sutherland and Shepanski show that by making appropriate substitutions in these formulae, one arrives at the superluminal transformations

$$\bar{x} = \gamma_+(\bar{v}t - x), \quad \bar{t} = \gamma_+(\bar{v}x/c^2 - t) \quad \bar{y} = y, \quad \bar{z} = z. \tag{4.2}$$

where we define $\gamma_+ \equiv 1/\sqrt{\beta^2 - 1}$. Sutherland and Shepanski simply write the usual $\gamma$ factor with absolute value bars, but our notation emphasizes the physical distinction between the subluminal and superluminal cases.

### 4.2.2 Using the Galilean Limit

We now outline an alternative derivation of the superluminal transformations which makes their physical basis especially clear.

One familiar way of deriving the subluminal Lorentz transformations is to write down the transformation rule that would hold for position in the Galilean limit, and then construct the relativistic picture by assuming that there is a velocity-dependent correction factor to be determined. (See, e.g., [137, 46–47].) We will here apply this method under the explicit assumption that the frame to which we transform is moving superluminally.

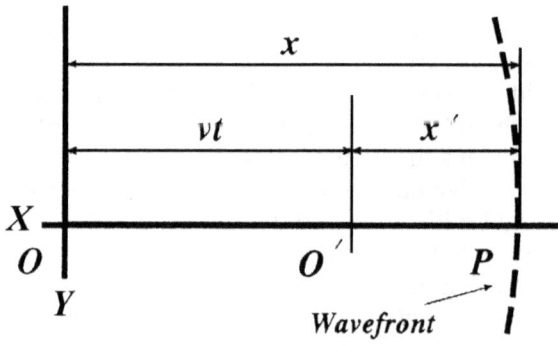

Figure 4.1: Subluminal Case

**Subluminal Case**

For clarity of comparison, we begin with a review of the familiar subluminal derivation.

Our first task is to establish what would hold in the Galilean limit. Accordingly, we will assume that light moves with some finite velocity $c$, but we assume Galilean rules for addition of velocities and the existence of an absolute time. Now suppose that there are two frames with origins $O$ and $O'$, with $O$ at rest in the laboratory frame and $O'$ moving along the common

## 4.2. Derivation of Superluminal Transformations

x-axis with constant subluminal velocity $v$. Assume also that a wave-front was emitted from $O$ at time $t = t' = 0$ and let $P$ be the point where the wave-front cuts the x-axis. Let $x$ be the distance $OP$ in $O$'s coordinates, and $x'$ be the same distance in $O''$s coordinates. As Figure 5.1 shows, we readily get

$$x' = OP - OO' = x - vt. \tag{4.3}$$

To get the inverse relationship we note, either from the figure or from inverting the last equation, that

$$x = x' + vt. \tag{4.4}$$

However, since this is the Galilean picture, the two observers agree on their time coordinates, and so

$$x = x' + vt'. \tag{4.5}$$

To derive the relativistic transformations we take

$$x = ct \text{ and } x' = ct'. \tag{4.6}$$

These relations express our assumption that $c$ is invariant for both observers; this is what forces the difference between the Galilean and relativistic cases. We also assume that there is some velocity-dependent correction factor $\gamma_-$ such that

$$x' = \gamma_-(x - vt), \tag{4.7}$$

with the inverse relationship

$$x = \gamma_-(x' + vt'). \tag{4.8}$$

Substituting (4.6), we get

$$ct' = \gamma_- t(c - v) \text{ and } ct = \gamma_- t'(c + v). \tag{4.9}$$

Multiplying the two expressions, we get

$$c^2 tt' = \gamma_-^2 tt'(c^2 - v^2); \tag{4.10}$$

i.e.,

$$\gamma_- = 1/\sqrt{1 - \beta^2}. \tag{4.11}$$

Straightforward substitutions yield (4.1).

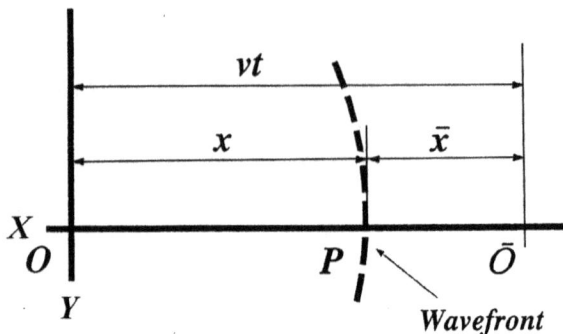

Figure 4.2: Superluminal Case

**Superluminal Case**

We now make the explicit assumption that the moving system $\bar{O}$ can outrun the wavefront, and carry out a parallel calculation. Consider Figure 5.2, which shows that $\bar{O}$ has *outrun* P. We let $x$ be the coordinate of P in $O$'s frame and $\bar{x}$ be its coordinate for $\bar{O}$.

Again, we begin with the Galilean limit. Because $\bar{x}$ must be negative, we have

$$\bar{x} = \bar{O}O - OP = x - vt. \tag{4.12}$$

Inverting, and again noting that the two observers agree that $t = \bar{t}$, we get the corresponding relationship for $x$:

$$x = \bar{x} + vt = \bar{x} + v\bar{t}. \tag{4.13}$$

Now we put these transformations for distance to work in order to arrive at a set of Lorentz-like transformations for the superluminal case of Figure 2. As before, we assume that there is some velocity-dependent correction factor $\gamma_+$ such that

$$\bar{x} = \gamma_+(x - vt), \tag{4.14}$$

with the inverse relationship

$$x = \gamma_+(\bar{x} + v\bar{t}). \tag{4.15}$$

We again take $x = ct$ and $\bar{x} = c\bar{t}$. Substituting this condition in (4.14) and (4.15), and multiplying as before, we get

$$c^2 t\bar{t} = \gamma_+^2 t\bar{t}(v^2 - c^2); \tag{4.16}$$

## 4.2. Derivation of Superluminal Transformations

i.e.,

$$\gamma_+ = 1/\sqrt{\beta^2 - 1}. \tag{4.17}$$

Appropriate substitutions, in this case, yield (4.2). It is therefore crucial to be clear from the outset whether or not $\tilde{O}$ is inside or outside the light cone.

### 4.2.3 Form of the Metric

Some authors (e.g., Bilaniuk and Sudarshan [30]) have defended the appearance of imaginary quantities in standard tachyon theory by arguing that it merely shows that there is no such thing as being at rest with respect to a superluminal frame. However, The Principle of Relativity (PR) implicitly assumes the possibility of local measurements of positions, times, and masses (which are taken to be invariants) for all frames of reference. Therefore, in order to properly test the PR, we ought to set up the theory in such a way that these quantities can be real numbers, and the only way to do this is to set $ds^2 \geq 0$ everywhere. This assumption is implicit in our construction above, since we take $\tilde{x}$, a proper distance in $\tilde{S}$, to be real-valued. If we could not do this then we would have no transition to the Galilean limit in the superluminal case, even though there is no clear reason why the Galilean limit (which would treat light like any other disturbance, albeit exceptionally fast) should not exist.

As one moves from inside to outside the light cone, therefore, the signature of the metric must change, whether expressed in sub- or superluminal coordinates. Specifically, time and the distance coordinate in the direction of motion must interchange so as to maintain the real-valuedness of interval. For instance, written in subluminal coordinates, the line element outside the light cone must have the form

$$ds^2 = c^2 dt^2 + dy^2 + dz^2 - dx^2. \tag{4.18}$$

This expresses the fact (evident from inspection of the Minkowski diagram) that the spatial metric outside the light cone is hyperbolic, not Euclidean.

A delicate question of interpretation arises. Sutherland and Shepanski [216] argue that the presence of the geometrically distinguished spatial direction indicates that the Principle of Relativity *cannot* be applied to superluminal frames. They believe that the PR implies that space must be locally isotropic, and therefore locally Euclidean. However, the PR simply requires that there exist a covariant 4-dimensional description of physical phenomena, consistent with the assumption that the speed of light is an invariant. Nothing suggests that the structure of events cannot look radically different in different frames. Also, there seems to be nothing in the *General* Principle of Relativity that would prohibit locally non-Euclidean frames. Furthermore, it would be very odd if some feature of Minkowski geometry were inconsistent with the PR, since

Minkowski geometry is constructed on the basis of precisely that principle. Hence, it may be that far from ruling out the possibility of tachyons, Sutherland and Shepanski's beautiful construction simply gives us (perhaps for the first time) an accurate picture of their kinematics.

It may seem paradoxical to suppose that we can conjoin the assumption of the invariance of $c$ with the supposition that $\bar{O}$, the origin of the moving frame, can be moving faster than light. The key is that in the superluminal frame $\bar{S}$ the wavefront must *recede with constant velocity c* from any point at rest in $\bar{S}$ regardless of how fast $\bar{S}$ moves with respect to any subluminal frame. This means that (as suggested by (4.18)) the wavefront in $\bar{S}$ along constant time slices is not a sphere (as it must be in subluminal frames) but an hyperboloid of revolution with axis along the direction of superluminal motion [216].

## 4.3 A Problem for Space Travellers

The familiar Twin Paradox takes on an interesting twist in the definite theory. Suppose there are identical twins Peter and Paul. Peter remains home on Earth, while Paul embarks on a subluminal space voyage. It is well known that Paul's elapsed proper time will be less than Peter's; if Paul travels at relativistic speeds he may even return home still physiologically young to find his brother an elderly man.

Now suppose, *per impossibile* perhaps, that Paul has the technological means to set out on a *superluminal* voyage. Let $\beta$ be Paul's velocity (with $\beta \geq 1$), $t(\beta)$ his elapsed proper time when he returns home, and $t_0$ Peter's corresponding elapsed proper time. Then we will have

$$t(\beta) = t_0 \sqrt{\beta^2 - 1}. \tag{4.19}$$

Paul's elapsed proper time is nearly zero when $\beta$ only slightly exceeds 1, but then begins to increase as $\beta$ increases, matching Peter's at $\beta = \sqrt{2}$, and then increasing roughly as $\beta$ thereafter! If Paul could travel at (say) $10c$, he would age almost 10 times as fast as his brother back on Earth. Superluminal travel would thus offer few advantages to the space traveller.

Space travel enthusiasts (such as this author) may at first find this result to be discouraging. However, it might not apply to hypothetical 'space warp' methods of travel [6], since conceivably a locally Euclidean spatial metric could be maintained on board the starship. Of course, this is highly speculative, but it does merit further investigation.

## 4.4 Causal Paradoxes

An adequate discussion of causal paradoxes is beyond the scope of this paper. However, it is easily seen that, *prima facie*, one still gets closed-loop paradoxes in the definite theory. These paradoxes depend upon the topology of the world-lines, and whether one parametrizes world-lines with real or imaginary

## 4.4. Causal Paradoxes

numbers makes no difference. Indeed, as Arntzenius [14] points out, there will be closed-loop paradoxes in any theory (even a Galilean theory) that allows for infinite signal velocities. The lack of an obvious resolution of the causal paradoxes in this model should not preclude the discussion of superluminal frames, however, because it is essential to explore, in an open-minded fashion, every avenue that may be mathematically feasible.[2]

---

[2] The author thanks James Robert Brown and participants in the Vigier Symposium for useful discussions, and the University of Lethbridge and the Social Sciences and Humanities Research Council of Canada for financial support.

# Chapter 5

# To Understand Anything We Have to Understand Everything[1]


It has become very fashionable these days to proclaim the end of physics or even the end of science itself. Several kinds of reasons are typically given for this: budget cuts (of course!), loss of societal interest in science, the end of the Cold War, the rise of illiteracy and religious fundamentalism [195], inescapable limitations of human intelligence itself (maybe we can no more understand the true laws of physics than rats can understand prime numbers),[2] worries (somewhat premature, I suspect) about the entropic decay of the universe [129]; and even, among a few, a belief that we really are just a few more calculations away from having wrapped up all the genuine problems.

In *From Physics to Metaphysics*, the distinguished Cambridge philosopher of science Michael Redhead demurs.

> I would submit myself that the further development of physics, about whose future course we can, admittedly, only speculate, will provide the most stimulating intellectual challenge of the new millennium. (86)

In the following I shall explain why I think there are good grounds for Redhead's apparently incautious claim. Indeed, to the extent that I disagree with him, I will argue that he has been, in regard to one crucial issue (peaceful coexistence between relativity and quantum mechanics), too cautious himself.

---

[1]This was first published as, 'Critical Notice of *From Physics to Metaphysics* by Michael Redhead,' *Canadian Journal of Philosophy* 28(2), June 1998, 287–309. I am grateful to the *Canadian Journal of Philosophy* for permission to reproduce this review in *Quantum Heresies*.

[2]See the interview with Colin McGinn, in John Horgan, *Limits of Knowledge in the Twilight of the Scientific Age* [113, pp. 56–59]. McGinn argues that the deep problems of philosophy (and presumably science as well) could be forever beyond human capability. I will leave unspoken the obvious retort.

However, the important issue here is not to play the futurist's game of guessing what the next big scientific advances might be, but to see the philosophical interest of the problems that might give rise to those advances.

Redhead states that a main purpose of his book

> is to consider the relevance of developments in modern theoretical physics to metaphysical questions about the ultimate nature of reality. (xi)

And in the end he concludes:

> physics and metaphysics blend into a seamless whole, each enriching the other, and that in very truth neither can progress without the other. (87)

In historical fact, the discipline we now call physics grew out of philosophy, and well into this century major advances in physics have been driven partially by philosophical motivations.[3] Redhead's claim for the philosophical significance of physics and vice versa is therefore, in part, simply a timely reminder of a tradition going as far back as the Presocratics. However, in recent years philosophy of physics (or 'philosophysics' as this field has been jocularly dubbed by F.A. Muller [148]) has received fresh impetus from the dramatic experimental confirmation of Bell's Theorem, which forces physicists to face issues of interpretation that some of them would rather brush under the carpet, and forces philosophers to realize that certain cherished 'metaphysical packages' [181] are almost certainly obsolete. Redhead believes that Bell's Theorem shows that we almost certainly must abandon local realism (which I will define below) in favor of something—and here I grope for a term as well as an adequate description of what is indicated—that might be called nonlocal or perhaps holistic realism. (I must grope for a term because Redhead, oddly, does not name it himself, even though his commitment to realism in general and his rejection of local realism together leave him, as we shall see, with only this option.) And this in turn has large implications for the possibility of completing scientific knowledge.

There is a lot in Redhead's book. Its terse, unadorned style should not deceive the reader. Others have said far less with far more words. There are many interesting things I cannot comment on here (for instance, Redhead's masterful critique of what he calls the 'disreputable procedure' of coarse-graining in statistical mechanics, 28–33) . Let's just say that if you want a short, tough book that will give you a spirited defense of scientific realism together with an accurate but opinionated sense of why some very smart *philosophers*

---

[3]See Pierre Kerszberg, *The Invented Universe: The Einstein-de Sitter Controversy (1916- 17) and the Rise of Relativistic Cosmology* [122] for extensive documentation of this fact in the case of the development of general relativity.

60  Chapter 5. To Understand Anything We Have to Understand Everything

are terribly interested in Bell's Theorem, nonlocality, and the measurement problem, this would be an excellent place to look.

In the following I will examine four main themes of Redhead's book: realism, holism, nonlocality, and the completeness of scientific theories. All bear on each other. I will treat these questions in roughly the order in which they are brought up by Redhead, using his chapter headings.

## 5.1  Isms and Schisms

The first chapter of the book is the least technical (apart from bits of expository material that can be skimmed if need be) and makes the most contact with issues that might be immediately familiar to the non-specialist. Redhead begins by offering what he calls 'caricatures' (2) of the mutual misunderstandings of philosophers and physicists. (In fact, his picture is not entirely a parody.) All too often, he says, physicists dismiss the ruminations of philosophers, who, say the physicists, simply don't understand the subtle technicalities of their field and just get themselves all confused about nothing.

> Philosophy, like religion, abounds in isms and schisms, which it is a waste of time to try and sort out [say these Philistine physicists]. Much better to keep one's nose to the grindstone, and produce good physics, than to indulge in idle fancy and speculation. (1–2)

On the other side, the philosophers 'regard physicists as naïve' (2)—naive in the sense that they are too willing to spin their theories without critically examining the pedigree and grounds for those theories. It is high time for a *rapprochement*; and a reminder, in particular, of the nature of philosophy itself.

> Philosophy in the sense in which I shall employ the term looks at the credentials of the cognitive enterprise, and in its specialization to the philosophy of physics asks the question: What exactly is it that the physicist claims to know about the natural world, and how should we evaluate those claims? (2–3)

Redhead then sketches what he calls a 'potted history' (6) of modern particle physics leading up to quantum chromodynamics (QCD), the closest thing we now have to a syncretic view; the point being primarily to give the reader a sense of the type of claim that the physicist makes. What emerges is that our best current theories, terribly sophisticated and predictively powerful as they are, are provisional not only because of their employment of the trick of renormalization[4] and their somewhat promiscuous reliance upon a large number of empirical constants (or 'fudge factors' as they are sometimes irreverently

---

[4]In standard quantum field theory a number of quantities (such as particle rest masses) are calculated to be infinite, in spite of the fact that they have perfectly definite experimental values. One of the major technical innovations during the 1940s was the invention by Feynman, Tomonaga, and Schwinger and others of a technique called renormalization, which is a consistent way of

## 5.1. Isms and Schisms

dubbed in first-year physics labs), but because they brush under the carpet the fundamental puzzles of quantum mechanics (QM). And, says Redhead, 'dirt under the carpet is still dirt, I would submit' (7).

An interesting question arises: do physicists actually believe in QCD?

> The answer is 'yes,' for certain limited purposes of theoretical modelling of phenomena, but not in the sense that it is a serious candidate for being dead right. (8)

In spite of this, many physicists do hold to a faith that before too long we may be in sight of a Theory of Everything (TOE)—a grand unification of particle physics, electrodynamics, and gravitation. But perhaps even that would be provisional in some sense. Will we ever be able treat any physical theory as essentially anything other than what Plato referred to as 'a likely story'? [175]—a phrase that suggests a number of things, but in particular a certain ironic withdrawal from full ontic commitment. In fact, however, as Redhead says, physicists do tend to be 'realists about the entities they deal with' in their own inimitable 'unreflective and intuitive attitude to their work' (9). Why? Because they know that whatever these mysterious subatomic entities may be, they are manipulable in a variety of rather definite ways.

> To physicists the deep inelastic scattering experiments manifest the quarks just as surely as holding them, one at a time, in the hollow of one's hand, so to speak. (9)

What we have here is therefore something like the distinction Hacking usefully draws between theory and entity realism [101, 102]. Both Redhead and Hacking suggest that scientists tend to be realists about the entities they can manipulate,[5] even though they are also (or should be, if they have the slightest shred of philosophic sophistication) ironists about the theories that describe those entities.

Doesn't this ironic stance place us at the top of the well-travelled slippery slope leading down into the swamp of relativism? Redhead himself even seems to slide a little further down, when he goes on to declare that he rejects foundationalism because he thinks that Cartesian rationalism, Kantian a priorism, and Machian positivism 'have been satisfactorily discredited in the philosophical literature' (10). But then he firmly applies the brakes. There is, he says, one core 'presupposition' (10) of foundationalism that we just can't

---

getting around this problem. Opinion tends to be sharply divided as to whether renormalization genuinely solves the problem of the infinities or is merely a clever dodge. See [218] for a lucid introduction to the problem.

[5] As Hacking famously puts it, 'physicists believe that electrons are real because they can spray them' [101, p. 23]; that is, electrons can be used as tools with which to manipulate or influence something else. I am not sure that this can be honestly claimed, as yet, for quarks; hence Hacking's criterion for the reality of entities may be a little more stringent than Redhead's although they both are in the same spirit.

let go of because without it coherent discourse is impossible—a 'minimalist' (11) correspondence theory of truth. This presupposition insists that surely 'it makes sense to talk of truth simpliciter, of how things actually are in themselves or how they are represented to us in phenomenal experience' (10). The usual alternative is the coherence theory of truth, according to which 'beliefs are true if they cohere with other beliefs' (11). But one can hardly even express this notion of coherence unless one can somehow say, and indeed mean, that it is simply true that a certain belief does or does not cohere with another. So, concludes Redhead,

> if there are facts about how beliefs relate to one another, perhaps it is not so large a step to accept that there are facts about how beliefs relate to the world. (11)

Well, some philosophers would argue that it is a pretty big step, since the whole problem is that while we do have a rather direct access to our beliefs, we do not have the same sort of access to facts or events which are not directly experienced. There might be very important differences between the ways in which beliefs relate to beliefs, and the ways in which beliefs relate to nonintentional realities.

Setting this worry aside, though, there are other and more effective ways that one can argue against relativism. The most important point is just that 'the world kicks back; we cannot just make it up any way that pleases us' (15). Arch-relativist Richard Rorty says that the only 'constraints on inquiry' are 'conversational' [187], but to most physicists (and certainly to Redhead) this is merely irresponsible posturing; working scientists must spend most of their time endlessly trying to adjust to the nonconversational constraints imposed on inquiry as nature repeatedly kicks back.

The right approach, says Redhead, could be along the lines set forth by his 'old mentor Popper' (15) (even though Redhead concedes that Popper may have placed too much weight on the work done by refutation as opposed to confirmation). That is, grant that our theories may be at least partially true but at the same time never forget that they are largely conjectural; so that the more remote they may be from the possibility of immediate experiential confirmation or disconfirmation, the larger the grain of salt we should take with them. This will engender a suitable degree of skepticism and caution but at the same time allow us to mean what we are literally saying when we talk about the theory.

Redhead insists that what keeps us off the slippery slope is to not 'allow the first, subtly alluring move, of going soft on truth' (15).

> For quarks it may not matter so much, but in everyday life I believe it really does make a difference whether we believe in medical science as against witchcraft and spells, and I know for sure which jetliner I want to travel in—the realist's, not the relativist's! (15)

I suspect that worrying about this elusive quality 'truth,' while certainly not

## 5.1. Isms and Schisms

unimportant or uninteresting, is somewhat beside the point in comparing the merits of realism and relativism. Consider the problem, alluded to by Redhead, of designing and building a successful jetliner or other engineering work. An engineer may ponder whether a certain alloy should be used for the wing spars. But what determines whether or not he makes a sound choice is largely what factors he chooses to pay attention to. If he pays sensitive and primary attention to the 'kick back' of nature, he stands some chance of designing a good wing. If he pays primary attention to the political (which, according to Rorty, is the only thing we can pay attention to), he will produce either a mediocrity or an outright disaster.[6] Realism in the deepest sense is not a doctrine about truth or the kinds of entities that can exist, but an attitude and a practice.

With this in mind, is there any use or sense in saying that quantum chromodynamics is 'true'? Redhead is confident that there is no reason we cannot 'slide'

> from a robust realism about tables and chairs to a definitely more conjectural realism, but realism all the same, about quarks and QCD. (16)

I would agree unhesitatingly if we mean a realism in the deep sense I indicate above. But I think that we need to do a lot more work before we can say confidently what we mean by the 'truth' of a theory like QCD or any other theory informed by quantum mechanics. Consider a statement like 'The electron has position $x$ at time $t$.' As Bohr very rightly emphasized, this statement has meaning only in an experimental context, which is implicit whenever we choose to speak of positions or times; there is no such thing as the fact of the electron's position without the measurement of its position. Furthermore, the very language in which the statement is posed is misleadingly tendentious, for it speaks of the electron as if we could be sure that there was one definite entity sitting somewhere waiting for its position to be determined. In fact, QM strongly suggests that the whole notion of a continuously and independently existent object is a construct, something that Leibniz might have termed a 'well-founded phenomenon.' Redhead expresses much sympathy with the 'presupposition' of foundationalism that surely it makes perfect sense to talk 'of how things actually are in themselves' (10). But he knows as well as anyone that in a certain precise sense QM does not even have a way of talking about how things are 'in themselves'; reference always has to be made

---

[6] One of the most instructive examples of the contrast between the relativist's and the realist's approach is the story of the R101 disaster in Nevil Shute's memoir *Slide Rule: The Autobiography of an Engineer* [206]. In 1925 the British Government commissioned a private firm (Vickers) to design and built a prototype passenger-carrying airship, in direct competition with the British Air Ministry's own design team. Vickers produced the R100, a brilliant technical success; the government team, which allowed engineering to be dominated by political considerations, produced the R101, a botched lash-up that crashed on its maiden voyage, killing over 40 persons.

to the type of experimental or observational question to be asked. Under these maddening constraints, the whole notion of 'truth' as some sort of external relation between a representation and an independent reality seems hopelessly simplistic. I certainly do not think that the words 'truth' or 'reality' are obsolete; but I think that we have to do a lot more thinking to say what they can mean, given what we now know—and what we now know that we don't know.

Redhead concludes the first chapter with a crisp treatment of several other problems for scientific realism, such as underdetermination (some say the facts do not uniquely determine a theory), the problem of defining truth-likeness of theories, and the claimed lack of convergence (some say that the history of science actually denies that there is convergence to a best theory). Redhead acknowledges that these problems challenge realists to articulate their position with greater precision—'philosophy of physics is no more a finished enterprise than physics itself' (20)—but insists that they do not fundamentally threaten realism.

In the second chapter we face challenges to realism of a different kind, namely those that many people believe come from within physics itself.

## 5.2 Science and Subjectivity

Does physics force us to acknowledge an irreducible element of subjectivity in our descriptions of nature? The burden of the second chapter is to defend realism by showing that

> there are no compelling arguments that we can discover from developments in modern theoretical physics that human consciousness and subjective awareness are more intimately involved in the physical world than we previously supposed. (40)

To this end Redhead considers grounds for subjectivism or idealism that have been alleged to arise in relativity theory, statistical mechanics, quantum mechanics, and in connection with the anthropic principle. He believes that what has to be defended is the possibility of what Nagel [152] has called the 'view from nowhere'—the essentially personal-perspective-free account of the world sought by science.

I fear that this may be an irrelevant diversion from Redhead's central concern, which was to defend realism. Does it really follow that realism demands that everything can be given an objective description? Perhaps we will be able to salvage and articulate the vital core of realism only when we decouple it from the possibly gratuitous insistence on *describability*—which, as I have already indicated, is rendered highly dubious by quantum mechanics.

Most (but not all!) of the problems treated by Redhead in this chapter are fairly elementary confusions that can be cleared up by some careful attention to how the theories considered actually work. I will pass over Redhead's treatment of the anthropic principle (which can hardly be improved upon), his

## 5.2. Science and Subjectivity

patient (and certainly unobjectionable) explications of why there is no element of subjectivity in relativity and statistical mechanics, and turn directly to the huge problems posed by the quantum.

There is much to be said about the impact of QM on realism, but in this chapter Redhead's main concern is to scotch fears that QM requires the intrusion of human whim or consciousness into physical law.

One potential confusion is easily dealt with. First, the frequent reference to 'observables' in QM does not ascribe a special role in the theory to conscious observers. 'Observable' is only a technical term (reflecting a 'positivist influence in the historical development of the theory' [33], as Redhead notes) for quantities that are measurable by certain classes of definite procedures. These procedures could be carried out by an automaton just as easily as by a human.

The second and somewhat more subtle problem comes from the fact that many of the properties that can be ascribed to quantum mechanical systems come in complementary pairs (the terms conjugate or incompatible are also used), meaning that a precise measurement of one precludes the precise measurement of the other. Position and momentum are the paradigmatic examples of conjugate variables. Between any two mutually conjugate variables stands an uncertainty relation of the type first set forth by Heisenberg; the product of the uncertainties must always exceed a multiple of Planck's constant of action. This is quite far-reaching, and is one of the (some might say the) distinctive features of QM.

Now, the immediate point is that in an experimental arrangement that manifests position it is not possible to manifest momentum; and if we switch from measuring position to momentum, and then go back to measuring position again, we will find (in general) that the position has changed in an unpredictable way. What properties we can ascribe to a quantum system seem to be essentially conditioned by the method with which we chose to observe the system. As in relativity, though, 'this brings in no subjective element,' for

> The experimental arrangements in quantum mechanics play an analogous role to the reference frames of rods and clocks in relativity theory, in establishing what one might want to call a perspectival aspect to reality. (34)

This is certainly correct up to a point, for there is absolutely nothing in the specification of (say) a position measurement that requires the participation of a conscious observer. However, there is an important disanalogy between frames of reference in relativity and measurement procedures in QM. Relativity is based on the assumption that the spacetime perspective from which we observe a system can make no intrinsic difference to the reality of that system; the mathematics of relativity (the language of tensors and invariants) expresses this assumption. In QM, though, the choice of measurement procedure partially, and in ways that remain importantly unclear, determines the intrinsic reality

66  Chapter 5. To Understand Anything We Have to Understand Everything

of what is to be measured. There is no way, in general, to make the context of observation transparent, as there is in relativity.

There is a third way in which some believe that conscious subjectivity enters physics, through the measurement problem of quantum mechanics. We can describe the measurement problem roughly as follows. (Redhead's account of it is just about as accurate as can be without the use of mathematics; I shall wave my hands a bit here.) Any quantum system to be observed will in general be not in some definite state, but in a so-called superposition or linear combination of states.[7] However, when we make an observation (of, say, position or spin) we get one and only one definite outcome, with a probability that can be calculated by a simple rule. The problem is that the formalism of the theory says that this cannot happen! What must happen instead when we allow a system to interact with a measuring apparatus, if the system plus apparatus is assumed to evolve according to the Schrödinger Equation, is that the apparatus will itself disperse into a superposition of states, each corresponding to a different possible pointer reading. Measurements, according to the theory, will only rarely have definite outcomes at all, contrary to all our experience.

The contradiction is highlighted by Schrödinger's fable about an unfortunate cat imprisoned in a cage. A two-state quantum system with a definite probability of flipping from one state to the other is to a device that releases a fast-acting poison. According to the formalism of the theory, the cat is in a superposition of states, neither truly alive nor truly dead. And yet we know perfectly well that if we look into the cage at any given time, we shall see a cat that is either definitely alive or definitely dead. The formalism, so accurate in predicting the probability of the cat's demise within a given period of time, yields apparently absurd results if employed to describe the observable condition of the cat itself at any particular time.

Many ingenious solutions have been proposed for the measurement problem. The usual textbook approach, which many (including Redhead) view as a stop-gap, was codified by John von Neumann. It says that there are really two ways that quantum systems can evolve. When the system is not being observed it evolves in the deterministic, unitary, reversible, continuous manner described by the Schrödinger Equation; but when an observation is made it undergoes an indeterministic, nonunitary, irreversible, discontinuous 'jump' or 'collapse' to one definite state. This cuts the Gordian knot and gives a pragmatically useful picture for many practical purposes, but it is conceptually very unsatisfying.

Redhead's special target in this chapter is a solution to the measurement problem proposed by Eugene Wigner [235], who surmised that superpositions are resolved into definite macro-outcomes only in the minds of conscious

---

[7] And what is a 'state'? Mathematically, it is represented by a vector in a complex linear vector space. These vectors are combined in a straightforward way to give an amplitude for a process to occur; amplitudes (which are complex numbers) may be thought of as a square root of a probability.

## 5.2. Science and Subjectivity

observers. Some variant of this claim is quite appealing to many people, in spite of the obvious paradoxes to which it gives rise. (Could a mouse wandering into a laboratory glance at an apparatus and collapse a superposition? Is there not an infinite regress of collapses, since even if I seem to myself to observe a definite result, won't some other observer judge me to still be in a superposition?) However, Redhead dismisses this line of thought with a sniff:

> It is really amazing that such a solution has been proposed by physicists of the calibre of Eugene Wigner and John Wheeler... I think it would only be reasonable to take such a solution of the measurement problem seriously if there were absolutely no other viable way of proceeding... quantum mechanics may be queer, but it is certainly not clear that it is *that* queer. (38)

In fact, I entirely agree with Redhead that the rather rather simplistic model sketched by Wigner couldn't be exactly right; nevertheless, I am a bit disappointed in the way Redhead brushes this approach aside with so little principled argument. David Albert and Barry Loewer [5] have advanced a more sophisticated version of Wigner's approach, called the 'Many-Minds' interpretation of QM,[8] which, though decidedly weird, is by no means foolish. It is also possible to turn the problem around and, instead of supposing that consciousness is necessary in order to understand QM, explore whether quantum nonlocality may be necessary in order to understand some of the peculiar features of consciousness.[9]

To conclude: I am in sympathy with, but do not precisely agree with Redhead's conclusion that

> the realist view of a physical world which exists quite independently of our musings and imaginings survives. (40)

This has to be qualified by the observation that we still do not really understand the relationship between consciousness and matter, and that it is not out of the question that quantum mechanical processes could be essential to understanding the operations of the mind. Our 'musings and imaginings' must themselves be accounted physical processes and therefore essentially quantum mechanical in nature. This does not necessarily mean that our musings have an unmediated influence upon or participation in physical processes outside the skulls they customarily inhabit, but it does mean that the clear separation between the subjective and the objective is a little more difficult to define and maintain than Redhead would like to believe.

I do, however, wholeheartedly agree with Redhead that whatever the physical world may be, it is probably

---

[8]See also the discussion in [137].
[9]See, e.g., [213].

68  Chapter 5. To Understand Anything We Have to Understand Everything

very different in fundamental aspects from anything supposed in classical physics. (40)

Just *how* different, we may begin to appreciate when we consider nonlocality, the theme of the next chapter.

## 5.3 Experimental Metaphysics

Another apparently conceivable approach to the measurement problem is to assume that QM just has it wrong—that particles really do possess all of their properties all of the time, so there is no sense in which measurement 'creates' those properties. This approach was carried to its logical conclusion by Einstein, Podolsky, and Rosen (EPR) in a classic paper of 1935 [78], in which they showed, by means of an ingenious argument, that either QM allows for unmediated influences over arbitrary distances or QM is 'incomplete' in the sense that it does not describe all the properties that particles actually have.

The argument goes roughly like this: suppose two particles are created by a common source in a so-called 'entangled' state, as QM allows that they may be, and that they then fly away in opposite directions to arbitrary distance. It can be shown that both the total momentum and the difference in position of the particle pair are conserved quantities. Consider the left particle. From its position, the position of the right can be inferred by appeal to the global conservation rule, and similarly for momentum. But recall that position and momentum are incompatible observables. They cannot be measured for the left particle at the same time. Nevertheless, an experimenter near the left particle could have freely chosen to measure either position or momentum at some definite time—say, 12:00 noon. And this would allow that experimenter to attribute to the right particle either a definite position or a definite momentum at 12:00 noon. But (according to EPR) it is absurd to suppose that procedures carried out locally on one particle could affect the other at the same time. Therefore the right particle must have had both a definite position and a definite momentum at 12:00 noon, in spite of the Uncertainty Relations. Thus QM, by its own admission, cannot describe all the properties that particles can simultaneously possess.

The EPR argument by itself, however, seemed to leave the choice between nonlocality and the incompleteness of QM to philosophical taste, and most physicists dismissed the problem as unresolvable. EPR could not suggest any way of resolving the issue experimentally, let alone of finding a more complete theory, a so-called 'hidden variables' theory, that would reveal the hidden machinery responsible for QM.

In 1964, J.S. Bell [25] (taking advantage of a clearer formulation of the EPR argument due to David Bohm [34])[10] found a way to put the issue to

---

[10]It is a matter of acute embarrassment for the international scientific community that neither Bell nor Bohm was awarded the Nobel Prize, even though the groundbreaking significance of their

## 5.3. Experimental Metaphysics

experimental test: if we accept 'local realism' (to be defined below) then we must accept that the correlations between observations on particles in EPR experiments obey a certain set of mathematical inequalities, now known as the 'Bell Inequalities.'[11] On the other hand, Bell also pointed out that the predictions of QM violate these inequalities, and since the late 1970s, numerous experiments have richly confirmed the predictions of QM. It seems, therefore, that experiment has settled a critical metaphysical question; local realism is false. Does that mean that we must accept action at a distance?

Not necessarily, Redhead tells us. Local realism is the conjunction of two claims:

> Realism: 'entities ... possess definite sharp values for all their attributes at all times' (41);
>
> Locality: 'these attributes cannot be affected instantaneously by operations such as measurements performed on other microentities at different spatial locations' (41–42).

Now local realism (made suitably precise) can be shown to imply the Bell Inequalities (BI). The BI are false. Hence, by *modus tollens*,[12] local realism is false. But logic by itself compels us to reject only one of its two clauses, though it could turn out that both are false.

Redhead then announces (and this is the move to which I shall object) that rejection of Locality 'is closed off by appeal to relativity theory,' 'the other great pillar of modern theoretical physics' (42). Hence we must reject the 'realism of possessed values' itself, and the burden of this chapter is to show just what that actually entails.

Redhead thus offers us a version of the familiar thesis that relativity and QM stand in a relation of 'peaceful coexistence.'[13] This doctrine concedes that QM is indeed nonlocal, but in a way that does not allow for controllable superluminal effects and thus overt violations of the relativistic prohibitions on faster-than-light causation.

Redhead expresses the notion of peaceful coexistence in a way that draws special attention to its ontological implications. He distinguishes two locality principles: Ontological Locality (OLOC) and Environmental Locality (ELOC). Loosely, they are defined as follows:

> OLOC: all local observables[14] can be specified independently of

---

work was quite clear by the times of their deaths in 1990 and 1992 respectively.

[11]Itamar Pitowsky has shown that the Bell Inequalities turn out to be special cases of the 'conditions of possible experience' set forth by George Boole [174].

[12]This has inspired a spate of puns in the literature, suggested by the phrase 'for whom the bell tolls,'

[13]The phrase, deliberately ironic, is due to Abner Shimony [201].

[14]By 'local observable' we mean an observable that is fully specifiable in terms of measurements made at a point or very small region of space.

## Chapter 5. To Understand Anything We Have to Understand Everything

global properties (the 'measurement context') of the combined system.

ELOC: values that can be observed for any local observable 'cannot be changed by altering the arrangement of a remote piece of apparatus which forms part of the measurement context for the joint system' (48–9).

These principles are more precise formulations of Realism and Locality as defined above. ELOC and OLOC, in conjunction with two other technical principles which are not in doubt, lead to a contradiction;[15] hence at least one of the two is false. However, if ELOC were violated we would be able to instantaneously, and at will, affect the measurement statistics at a distant location in an EPR experiment. Redhead therefore indicates with no further ado that the violation of ELOC is to be ruled out because of this 'prima facie' conflict with relativity (50). In conclusion, we accept the violation of OLOC.[16] (Redhead's wording in this passage (50) is ambiguous, since it seems to suggest that we have an option as to whether we reject OLOC—which we certainly do not, since its violation is implicit in virtually all quantum phenomena.)

Redhead's argument at this point suffers from the same blind spot that mars the reasoning of all the proponents of peaceful coexistence, which is an odd unwillingness to seriously consider the possibility that relativity itself might be wrong. Given the pervasive nature of nonlocality, it seems perfectly reasonable to explore the possibility that the relativistic picture of causation must ultimately break down. And yet, almost all investigations of the relationship between relativity and quantum theory have not attempted to probe loopholes in relativity, but instead set out to protect quantum mechanics from the charge that it conflicts with relativity. Some of the arguments to this end have almost assumed the flavor of special pleading; indeed, for example, the entire edifice of quantum field theory is constructed under the explicit requirement that its predictions should not conflict with relativity, and to ensure this result a special restriction on the generality of quantum theory ('microcausality') was written into the formalism of the theory [157].

The defenders of peaceful coexistence will point out that it is apparently possible, using the formalism of quantum theory, to prove ELOC; this is often called the 'No-Signalling Theorem' (NST).[17] In recent years these proofs have come under long-overdue skeptical scrutiny [160, 121] The essence of the critique is that the various NST proofs are question-begging because they all depend on special technical locality assumptions which are in fact extraneous

---

[15]The way in which Redhead arrives at this conclusion makes appeal to the Kochen-Specker paradox. There is a detailed exposition in Redhead's *Incompleteness, Nonlocality, and Realism* [181].

[16]The violation of OLOC is sometimes referred to in the literature as 'contextuality,' a sort of tamed nonlocality.

[17]Redhead himself has given such a proof; [181, pp. 115–16].

## 5.3. Experimental Metaphysics

to the general formalism of QM, and which, arguably, are the very things that one needs to establish in the first place in order to defend peaceful coexistence. These assumptions generally amount to the claim that left and right particles in the EPR set-up are dynamically independent; technically, this may be expressed in a number of ways. It is frequently done either by assuming that the so-called Hamiltonian (an expression for the total energy of the multi-particle system) is local, or by assuming that the time evolution operator for the system factorizes into independent left and right components.

To my knowledge, no argument has *ever* been given in the literature for this assumption, except the observation that if one did not make it then there would be a possibility of signalling, and the fact that the macrodynamics with which we are presently familiar tends to a local form (possibly merely as a limit). Even the Bohm theory, the most explicitly nonlocal version of QM available, starts (without discussion) from a local Hamiltonian and, not surprisingly, upholds a no-signalling result [32].[18] As Redhead explains, QM shows that part-whole reductionism is in general false. But the no-signalling proofs depend essentially upon the applicability of a part-whole reductionism as applied to particle dynamics. Perhaps in the end it will turn out that we can get away with this, but I cannot see why we are entitled to assume it from the outset.

Both the strengths and the weaknesses of Redhead's position are apparent in his invocation of David Lewis's 'bilocal hand':

> We emphasize that giving up OLOC does not involve causal action at a distance. The following simple analogy proposed by David Lewis may be helpful here. Lewis invites us to contemplate a bilocal hand, i.e., a hand which occupies two spatial configurations at the same time ... suppose that we are introduced to a person with a bilocal hand, and endeavour to shake her right hand ... her left hand would also move up and down in mysterious harmony, not because there is causal interaction between the two hands, but because the left hand just is a (bilocal) manifestation of the right hand, or, perhaps, more correctly, of the unique hand, bilocally manifested. (51)

A 'bilocal' entity is therefore something that just happens to be in two places at the same time; and indeed that is roughly what the mathematics says of the particles in an EPR experiment. Quantum systems are multilocal, or more precisely *a*local—their fundamental reality (if we could express that at all) does not require reference to position.

Lewis's metaphor is therefore rather apt, and I shall make further use of it. However, as employed in the defense of peaceful coexistence, it is just

---

[18] David Peat observes that Bohm's 'hidden variable approach is essentially a local theory that gives what appear to be nonlocal results!' [169, p. 222].

another typical example of an attempt to make the physical into the definitional. Whether we should call what is going on action at a distance is a nice verbal point, since putative cause and effect would be simultaneous in one frame of reference, but it is not clear why we should be entitled to assumed that the dynamics of the particles are not part and parcel of their multi- or a-locality

The other major problem discussed by Redhead in Chapter III is the breakdown of part-whole reductionism. Implicit in the failure of OLOC is the startling fact that collective properties of groups of particles cannot fully supervene on the properties of constituent particles because constituent particles in general cannot possess enough properties for this to be possible! In QM wholes do not in general have parts independently of the way those parts are examined experimentally. It is not too much of an exaggeration to say, therefore, that atomism, because it leads to quantum mechanics, refutes itself.

It is fascinating that in spite of the failure of part-whole reductionism the notion of multi-locality still apparently allows us to retain entity realism ('entities ... possess definite sharp values for all their attributes at all times' [41]) so long as we are willing to generalize our notion of 'entity.' The trick is to grasp that, like Lewis's bilocal hand, the entities themselves must be multilocal. In the EPR experiment, for instance, the particle pair is to be thought of as the entity under study, while the single particles belonging to the pair (which we carelessly imagine as separable entities) cannot in fact qualify as distinct entities. Nevertheless, considered as a whole, the pair will be found to possess definite sharp values of certain globally conserved quantities such as linear and angular momentum, and it seems perfectly natural to accept these as the 'attributes' of the extended entity. So we may be able to keep to a kind of realism after all—call it nonlocal or holistic realism—so long as we are willing to drop the localizability of entities. This is the point that Redhead does not make (except indirectly, 61); a possible reason for his reluctance to take a step that is easily open to him will emerge in the next section.

In spite of my worries about peaceful coexistence, I like Redhead's approach. He shows that it may be possible for scientists to admit and philosophers to discuss holism without lapsing into New Age mysticism or postmodernist obscurantism. The death of part-whole reductionism does not signal the death of reason, much less the end of science. As we shall see, it probably does, though, signal a change in what we can expect of science in the way of explanatory completeness.

## 5.4 Theories of Everything

Redhead, in conclusion, turns to two related questions: can there be a Theory of Everything (TOE)? And is the end in sight for theoretical physics?

Physicists in the past have not been especially modest about the scale of their explanatory ambitions. For instance, Einstein once remarked,

> The supreme task of the physicist is to arrive at those universal

## 5.4. Theories of Everything

> elementary laws from which the cosmos can be built up by pure deduction. [76, p. 226]

For reasons we shall discuss here this aim now seems hopelessly naïve. Nevertheless, some physicists still maintain similar hopes. In a famous lecture of 1980 ('Is the End in Sight for Theoretical Physics?'), Stephen Hawking surmised that a scheme known as '$N = 8$ extended supergravity' might well, by the end of the century, allow us to solve (at least in principle, since the calculations required might be intractable) all the fundamental puzzles of physics [104]. Since then, as Redhead reports (65), this theory has fallen by the wayside and superstrings are now touted at the best contender for Theory of Everything.

In fact, predictions like Hawking's have not fared well in the past. Consider, for example, the following statement by A.A. Michelson, published in 1903, which has the flavor of 'famous last words':

> The more important fundamental laws and facts of physical science have all been discovered, and these are now so firmly established that the possibility of their ever being supplanted in consequence of new discoveries is exceedingly remote ... our future discoveries must be looked for in the sixth place of decimals. [145, pp. 23–24]

Redhead presents an urbane and sensible perusal of the possibilities for a TOE, but concludes:

> even if from a God's eye point of view we hit on a totally correct TOE, we would certainly never know it. The infinity of its empirical content could never be surveyed by human scientists. (69)

He then turns to a perhaps more tractable problem: is there genuine scientific progress? He thinks there clearly is; for not only can we point to a record of increasing technological capabilities, but it is obvious that QM solves some problems (such as the spectrum of the hydrogen atom) that classical methods cannot.

Still, some argue that succeeding scientific theories are incommensurable, so that successive theoretical realms cannot be compared and that the notion of progress is not meaningful. Redhead sets out to disabuse this worry by graphing scientific advances in terms of the behavior of physical properties as functions of parameters such as the speed of light or the quantum of action. The object is to see if incommensurability can be demystified by describing it mathematically. I shall not attempt to explain Redhead's model here. The important point is that one sees that the behavior is sometimes discontinuous; that is, new theories will often predict qualitatively different phenomena. Thus

> the mathematical reflection of incommensurability is just that some aspects of the classical world are not even approximately true in the new theories, but are simply and misleadingly false. (74)

Thus we can see 'how radically different structure emerges in physics' (78); but we can also see that it can be clearly related to earlier structure. Thus, the imputation of incommensurability, Redhead feels, is quite unjustified. The discontinuities between theories in significant part simply represent the fact that newer theories often treat phenomena which were not treated by the older theories; the theories themselves, however, are certainly comparable.

But how long can progress continue? If science is progressive, must we not eventually come up against some sort of wall where all the interesting problems have just run out? Redhead admits readily that a law of diminishing returns will often apply in probing the limits of any particular parameter (such as particle energies in accelerators). However, we can give no secure a priori grounds for thinking that there could be an end to the appearance of discontinuities! Thus, we can meaningfully speak of progress without being committed to a definite limit or end to progress. There could well be 'boojums all the way down' (70)—or there could not, but it is unlikely that we will ever be able to tell.

This immediately should suggest that some sort of incompleteness must apply to scientific theories, analogous to or perhaps even identical to the incompleteness of formal mathematical theories famously identified by Gödel. Indeed, Redhead points out (as have many others) that this would seem to be inevitable, if we (like Einstein) conceive of a scientific theory as a formal deductive structure. It is not clear, however, that scientific theories, even in physics, really should be conceived of in this way; certainly, in practice, most theories that are actually used to solve problems outside the realm of the textbook have a much looser structure. In any case, I agree with Redhead that it could certainly be interesting to clarify the implications of Gödel incompleteness for what we can expect scientific theories to be able to accomplish.

There is yet another, and perhaps even deeper reason to be skeptical about TOEs, stemming from fundamental facts about quantum nonlocality. Earlier I suggested that the metaphor of multilocality offers a way of salvaging Redhead's notion of entity realism; we can think of multilocal systems (such as the EPR pair) as a single spatially extended entity with definite global properties. But a little consideration shows that this, too, is only an improved approximation, a somewhat better 'likely story'; for if anything like the Big Bang cosmology is true, all particles in the universe were dynamically entailed at some early stage in cosmological history, and therefore all particles in the universe belong to one vast 'entangled' state. Any attempt to isolate parts of the universe and describe them as if they were 'all there' is bound to be slightly wrong at least, and perhaps very, very wrong. This seems to entirely rule out the possibility of descriptive or predictive completeness.

> But overarching all these considerations is the conclusion of the last chapter, that knowing the properties of a single elementary particle is never enough, that the classic method of analysis for dealing with

## 5.4. Theories of Everything

> complex wholes must in principle fail... To understand anything requires us to understand everything. (86)

I would still insist, though, that realism as an *attitude* survives—indeed, must survive if we as a species hope to survive. But, as Redhead says, realism as a set of beliefs about entities must always remain a little conjectural. Holistic realism gives us a richer conception of the sorts of entities that may exist, but it hardly removes the necessity for a mild but chronic skepticism.

In the end, the questions as to whether we are close to an ultimate theory, or whether there could be such a theory, are (for the time being, at least) more or less moot. It is much more useful to ask if we are near another revolution or breakthrough, as Redhead believes we may be. Could there be any grounds for anticipating the imminence of discovery, beyond a sort of *ad ignorantiam* plea that for all we know there is no reason there could not be such? Here it may be useful to let history be a guide.

Consider some of the factors that led up to Einstein's enunciation of special relativity in 1905. There was little if any anomalous experimental evidence that could have forced this move. True, there was the infamous Michelson-Morley ether-drag experiment of 1887, with its puzzling negative result. However, Michelson himself was totally unworried that this posed a fundamental challenge; and the whole thing might just as well have been dismissed as an inconsequential *Dreckeffekt*.[19] Einstein made it very clear that what primarily motivated him to realign mechanics with electrodynamics was the *conceptual inelegance* of the existing scheme. He begins his momentous paper of 1905 with the following observation:

> It is known that Maxwell's electrodynamics—as usually understood at the present time—when applied to moving bodies, leads to asymmetries which do not appear to be inherent in the phenomena. [74, p. 34]

It was not even that there was an outright *contradiction* between prediction and observation; there was simply a redundancy, an awkwardness in the description. And there are other examples like this as well. History suggests, therefore, that a good predictor of coming scientific growth is precisely the existence of this sort of theoretical awkwardness; something in the way we describe things is simply *clumsy* in the sense that it is done without clear justification, paper it over as we will, or as practically inconsequential as it may immediately seem to be.

Now, the interesting question is whether we are faced with a similar situation today. As in 1903, there are certainly those who will insist that all

---

[19]Michelson noted the negative result of his own efforts to determine the motion of the Earth through the ether, and conceded that ether theory was in 'an unsatisfactory condition' [145, p. 163]. However, he seemed to think that this was merely a technical difficulty that would soon be cleared up by some clever calculation or model within the existing framework.

is well in the house of physics, so long as we learn to talk about things the right way (and in a hushed, respectful voice). But in fact, in spite of the impressive explanatory and predictive power of modern physics, there are indeed a number of things that have a decidedly jury-rigged look to them. Notable among these is our obstinately holding onto part-whole reductionism with respect to particle dynamics in spite of the general failure of part-whole reductionism in QM, as awkward an example of theoretical awkwardness if ever there was one. There are other sorts of awkwardness connected with QM as well—the measurement problem, the difficulty of describing state reduction relativistically, various defects in particle physics (such as our complete inability to calculate the spectrum of particle masses, and the dependence on arguably dodgy renormalization techniques), and the sheer mystery of where QM comes from in the first place. (As Redhead says, 'one couldn't accept that the end of physics has arrived until the interpretational problems of quantum mechanics have been sorted out' [66].) Awkwardnesses abound if one looks for them, and I cannot believe that even a partial resolution of any of them would not mark a large if not discontinuous change in our world picture.

In summary: I entirely agree with Redhead that physics may yet surprise even the physicists and issue forth intellectual challenges to compare with any it has produced in the past. However, whatever rough conceptual beast slouches our way may be even more revolutionary than Redhead envisions.

## Chapter 6

# Bub and the Barriers to Quantum Ontology[1]

Quantum mechanics is certainly the most successful physical theory known, if one defines success of a physical theory as predictive power over a large range of phenomena. Most of us (naïvely, perhaps?) value scientific theories not only for their pragmatic efficacy, however, but also for their ability to explain phenomena in terms of general principles. In this respect, quantum mechanics, at least in its orthodox Copenhagen formulation, may well be an utter failure—for while it is enormously effective in predicting what we can expect to observe, it offers us almost no clue at all (apart from the features of the mathematical formalism itself) as to why things turn out the way they do, and may even imply that this question makes no ultimate sense at all. After all, Schrödinger's cat shows us that quantum mechanics cannot be talking about ordinary objects, even though it can make very reliable predictions about what will happen to a huge variety of ordinary objects (and some very extraordinary objects). Surely, we feel, a theory that is so predictively successful must be about something, if only we could figure out what that could be.

In this book, the respected philosopher of physics Jeffrey Bub conducts us through a detailed and masterly review of some of the best work that has been done in the attempt to say what quantum mechanics could be about. I'll summarize (very sketchily) the contents of this rich book and then offer a few comments.

Bub begins with some personal notes recounting high points of his career. After studying mathematics and physics as an undergraduate, he was 'hooked' on foundations of quantum mechanics when he encountered the Einstein-Podolsky-Rosen paradox. A scholarship took him to Birkbeck College and work with David Bohm, to whom Bub acknowledges his 'most important

---

[1]This was first published in *International Studies in the Philosophy of Science* 16(3), 2002, 285–289. My thanks to the Taylor and Francis Group for permission to reproduce this paper here.

intellectual debt' (xiii). Bohm and Bub published in 1966 a no-collapse proposal for the solution of the measurement problem. (Their theory, unlike Bohm's better-known theory of 1952 based on the quantum potential and guidance condition, does predict small differences from orthodox quantum mechanics.) Not long after, at the Minnesota Center for the Philosophy of Science, Bub was introduced to quantum logic and von Neumann's tantalizing suggestion that quantum systems obey a logic different from the Boolean logic of classical systems. Bub states that ever since then Bohm and von Neumann have remained his 'two main influences' (xiii) in the study of quantum mechanics, though much of the work described in this book arose out of recent collaboration with Rob Clifton.

Chapter 1 begins with an insightful review of the interpretational challenges posed by the irreducibly probabilistic nature of quantum theory and the problem of the role of the observer. It has offended the philosophical common sense of many (including, famously, Einstein) that the observer is apparently needed in order to make Schrödinger's cat be definitely alive or dead; and yet, it seems inescapable that in quantum mechanics 'what there is depends in some essential way on how we look' (8). How can we reconcile the intuition that there has to be something there regardless of how we look at it, with the fact that observed results often are inconsistent with the presumption that the system has all its properties before we examine it? Again, is it possible, in other words, for quantum mechanics to have a subject matter other than the phenomena that it is so adept at predicting?

The real problem, Bub states (12), is that 'the properties of a quantum system "fit together" in an essentially non-Boolean way'. However, while the 'rejection of the "ideal of the detached observer" is the Copenhagen response to non-Booleanity' (12), there are other possible responses to this starkly non-classical feature; and the overall message of Bub's book is that suitably formulated modal interpretations of quantum mechanics are (with certain qualifications) the best way we have found so far to acknowledge the irreducible non-Booleanity of quantum mechanics in a way that does at least some justice to Einstein's realist intuitions.

Bub then reviews quantum lattice theory, which flowed out of Birkhoff and von Neumann's pioneering attempts to set up a quantum logic. Lattice theory highlights the conundrum for the property realist:

> we can take the propositions corresponding to the properties in the property state as true, but we can't take the propositions that correspond to all the properties that are not in the property state as false, for this will involve a contradiction. (p. 31)

It is mathematically impossible for quantum systems, in general, to have at one time all of the properties that our various possible measurement choices could reveal them to possess. The most natural way out of this, Bub argues, is to follow van Fraassen [224] in thinking of the theory as describing not definite property states, but possibilities, with the Schrödinger equation describing the evolution of these possibilities through time.

In some respects this makes a great deal of intuitive sense. It is hard to see what it could mean to say that Schrödinger's cat is actually both alive and dead, but it is perfectly natural to say that before the box is opened the possibilities coexist that the cat is either alive or dead. The possibilities for incompatible outcomes certainly can be compatible. But this still does not really solve the measurement problem, which Bub defines as the 'inability of the orthodox interpretation to provide an internal account of measurement (in terms of the dynamics of interacting systems)' (p. 32). We still don't know what actually happens when we open the box; what causes (if that is even the right term) the statistical weighting of the various possibilities to change suddenly and globally when we make a measurement? Bub reviews the orthodox von Neumann answer to this question, which is that, upon measurement, superpositions discontinuously and suddenly collapse or project on to pure states, but, as do many authors, he rejects this as little more than a convenient stop-gap. What we want, he insists, is a 'no-collapse' theory that will show us how quantum systems evolve to yield observable results according to some definite dynamics stated in terms of determinate observables.

Chapters 2 and 3 offer very detailed treatments of the Einstein-Podolsky-Rosen thought experiment and the key 'no-go' theorems of quantum mechanics, the most spectacular of which are Bell's Theorem and the Kochen-Specker Theorem. (Bell's Theorem is, in fact, a special case of the Kochen-Specker result.) A 'no-go' theorem rules out underpinning the statistics of quantum theory with any sort of mechanism in terms of local hidden variables. Bub's discussion of the Kochen-Specker theorem and related matters is extraordinarily thorough, and covers much recent work that has not yet been brought together in one volume.

Chapter 4 introduces and proves the Bub-Clifton uniqueness theorem for no-collapse interpretations of quantum mechanics. The overall aim is to find out 'how large we can take the set of determinate observables without generating a Kochen-Specker paradox' (p. 119). This would be the closest we could come to specifying pictures that could satisfy Einstein's realist instinct, and is an essential prerequisite for setting up the type of quasi-realistic no-collapse picture that Bub seeks. It turns out that it is always possible to choose an observable (such as position) as determinate (at the price of indeterminacy in its conjugate), and every such choice of determinate observable uniquely characterizes a possible no-collapse theory. Not just any observable will do, however; for (as Bub explains in Chapter 5), the choice of a preferred observable is 'constrained by the nature of the interaction between open systems and their environments in our universe' (p. 163). Still, there are as many no-collapse theories as there are practicable choices of observables for the class of systems under consideration. The realist thus secures a Pyrrhic victory.

Chapters 5 and 6 cover 'Quantum theory without observers', and detail some possible interpretations of quantum theory, especially the so-called 'modal' interpretations. I have sought diligently throughout this book for a succinct but general explanation of what a modal interpretation of quantum mechanics is supposed in recent parlance to be. It is not just that we follow van Fraassens suggestion that quantum mechanics speaks of possibilities and 'only indirectly about what actually does happen' [224, p. 229]. The many recent authors who have constructed a bewildering variety of modal interpretations try to attach to van Fraassen's suggestion some way of making precise some intuition about what could still be treated as definite despite the modality of quantum language. The key technical move is that one drops the orthodox eigenstate eigenvalue link in favour of taking an 'appropriate preferred observable as having a determinate value independently of the quantum state' (p. 232). Bub is much in sympathy with such approaches, but also shows that it is possible to be very precise about how well they can expect to succeed.

Chapter 7 ('Orthodoxy') is an insightful and original review of Bohr's Copenhagen interpretation. Bub distinguishes it from the Dirac-von Neumann view in terms of the sort of sublattices selected as determinate. I found especially valuable Bub's analysis of Bohr's reply to Einstein, Podolsky, and Rosen.

Chapter 8 ('The new orthodoxy') is a review and critique of some other recently popular interpretations of quantum mechanics, namely the decoherence, many-worlds, and consistent-histories theories. Bub argues that these are merely much more sophisticated versions of the Copenhagen 'gentle pillow for the true believer' (Einstein's sarcastic phrase); they still give no principled way of determining which outcomes will actually be found.

> The only way to get definiteness or determinateness into the story is to put it in somewhere. One way to do this ... would be to reject the orthodox interpretation principle and take the quasiclassical domain as generating a suitable preferred observable $R$. In such a quantum world, specific events correlated with the determinate values of $R$ actually happen to [observers] like Schrödinger's Cat ... as those values evolve stochastically in time ... So probabilities cash out in the usual way as measures over a set of alternative histories, only one of which is actual, and we preserve the core features of Einstein's realism. (p. 236)

A 'Coda' sums up the line of argument, and the book concludes with an appendix summarizing, succinctly and clearly, many of the key technicalities of quantum theory. This appendix will serve as an extremely valuable reference for anyone contemplating the serious study of the philosophy of quantum mechanics.

The punch line of the book is that it can now be shown quite clearly the sense in which a no-collapse picture of measurement is possible, and that modal interpretations are the best candidates for such pictures. Bub concedes, however, that the problem of understanding quantum mechanics is still unsolved because no clear way has been found of making any no-collapse theory Lorentz covariant. He warns us that the task of constructing a genuinely relativistic 'no collapse' rewriting of quantum mechanics 'cannot be avoided without giving up on quantum mechanics' (p. 245).

Like almost everyone in the field, Bub seems still unwilling to consider seriously the alternative possibility, which is that Lorentz covariance itself may turn out to be only an approximate symmetry. It is perfectly true that progress in physics is achieved through what John A. Wheeler has called 'daring conservatism', but it is beginning to look as if hanging on to Lorentz covariance at the expense of a more complete picture of the measurement process in quantum mechanics may be the less conservative direction. Surely what we should be seeking—and I hardly mean to suggest that this would be an easy thing to find—is a fully quantized theory of space and time, which presumably would reduce to the ordinary relativistic picture in suitable limits.

Bub's discussion of signalling in the Bohm theory (pp. 242–243) is very sketchy. He argues that we cannot signal superluminally in a Bohmian quantum world because we could never, in practice, have a sufficiently precise knowledge of the trajectories of correlated particles. But this is not exactly what is relevant to the question of signalling. What matters is the dynamics of the multiparticle system. If the Hamiltonian is local (and here I discuss only non-relativistic systems) then there is no controllable signalling; this has been demonstrated by several authors. However, it is very reasonable to question the locality of the system dynamics, especially in a picture such as Bohm's theory which explicitly contemplates action at a distance. (For a critique of the attempted no-signalling proof offered by Bohm and Hiley [32], see Peacock and Hepburn [168].[2] )

I have another worry about Bub's treatment of the Bohm theory, which is one of a class of modal theories that Bub champions. He says, and I think quite correctly, 'The really essential thing about a quantum world is the irreducible indeterminism associated with non-commutativity or non-Booleanity...' (p. 240). However, the whole point of Bohm's original theory was to attempt to show that it is possible (by introducing the quantum potential) to underpin quantum physics with a theory that is, in principle at least, dispersion-free, and therefore Boolean at base (although Bohm himself did not use that term). Now, the Bub-Clifton theorem apparently guarantees that it will always be possible to assign some observable as determinate, but always at the price of indeterminacy in other observables of the system. We can move the indeterminacy around

---

[2] An up-dated version of this paper appears in the present volume, as "The Truth is (Still) Out There," Ch. 11.

but we can't make it go away. But does this not mean that Bohm's aspiration to create an in-principle dispersion-free theory must be abandoned? Is it not the case that after 50 years of intensive investigation, we must now concede that the ontological interpretation has failed? This momentous conclusion seems to be a very nearly immediate implication of the investigations that Bub reports, but he does not seem willing to say it in so many words. And if this implication is correct, then someone should tell the supporters of the Dürr-Goldstein-Zanghì version of 'Bohmian Mechanics', who still believe that "particles can be particles". (See, e.g. [69].)

I have expressed some reservations about Bub's reading of a few contentious points, but the fact remains that this book is a masterwork. It is simply essential reading for serious students of the foundations of quantum mechanics, especially for anyone interested in a clear, detailed, and authoritative review of very recent work on the modal interpretations. Note that Cambridge University Press has issued a revised paperback edition (1999).

# Chapter 7

# Quantum Logic and the Unity of Science[1]

John Woods[2] & Kent A. Peacock

**Abstract** This paper is an exploratory prolegomenon to the construction of a quantum logic that could shed some light on the thesis of the unity of science. We attempt to take account of the following factors, among others: the difficulty of saying just what a logic *is*, the startlingly *simple* queerness of quantum mechanics from the classical point of view, the consequences of the breakdown of bivalence and individuation in quantum mechanics, and the implications of recent work in quantum computation for quantum logic. We tentatively endorse modal interpretations of quantum mechanics, and suggest that quantum computation points to ways in which quantum logic could be extended beyond the traditional Birkhoff-von Neumann lattice theoretic approach.

## 7.1 Motivating Quantum Logic

The unity of science is the idea that all of the sciences are partially ordered by a set of reduction relations. This notion has been found attractive to thinkers at least as far back as Descartes, who posited the familiar metaphor of the tree of knowledge, with metaphysics as its roots and physics as its trunk.[3]

---

[1] This was first published as John Woods and Kent A. Peacock, 'Quantum Logic and the Unity of Science', in S.Rahman, J. Symons, D.M. Gabbay, and J.-P. Van Bendegem (eds.), *Logic, Epistemology, and the Unity of Science*. Dordrecht: Kluwer, 2004, pp. 257–287. My thanks to Springer Publishing for permission to reproduce this paper in *Quantum Heresies*.

[2] Department of Philosophy, University of British Columbia, Vancouver, British Columbia, Canada.

[3] To be more precise, Descartes himself believed that the roots of the tree of knowledge would be metaphysics, or first philosophy; (see, e.g., *Principles of Philosophy*, especially the Letter to Abbé Picot, in [236].). But Descartes' own attempts to construct a rationalistic theology were never convincing, and such projects have been largely abandoned. Instead, we tend, perhaps too uncritically, to think of logic itself as having a kind of metaphysical import, at least insofar as it governs the forms of *possible* worlds; and to this extent the modern version of the Cartesian view is that it is mathematical logic itself that should be at the root of the tree.

# Chapter 7. Quantum Logic and the Unity of Science

Since its heyday under the sway of logical positivism, the thesis of the unity of science has growingly been judged plausible in highly localized junctures of the universe of science—which is just to say that the thesis itself has not been found very convincing.

Nor has every local candidate for reduction (logicism in mathematics is a case in point) returned the promise of its youth. Notwithstanding the general discouragements that have fallen on it, the idea of unity in the sciences retains some minimal credibility in two main respects. One is that all of science is driven by essentially the same methodology. The other is that there is one science, namely logic, to which all of science must answer, a suggestion which we examine here. It would be natural to suppose that it is classical logic (or some near thing) that lays rightful claim on the status of this *ur-science*. Not everyone takes this view, however. Ambitious claims have been made by Putnam [179, 178] and Deutsch [58, 59] (in different ways) to the effect that classical (Boolean) logic is a *special case* of quantum logic. If such a claim is correct, then the roots of Descartes' tree must be the logic of quantum mechanics.

This is an exploratory paper that will be limited to three related questions which bear on the challenge posed by Deutsch and Putnam. One is whether quantum physics in any way discredits classical logic. For example, does the failure of distributivity in the quantum domain (when statements about noncommuting observables are involved) show that the classical principle of distributivity is invalid? The second issue is whether quantum physics requires or allows for a logic of its own. And, third, would this be one that gave the unity of science thesis any encouragement?

We want to lay some emphasis on the preliminaries of our intentions in this chapter. We do not have a smoothly coherent view to propose. This will come in later work, now in progress. Our task here is to assemble the bits and pieces that a smoothly coherent positive account will have to take into account.

Possible answers to our questions cannot help being heavily conditionalized by a rather substantial *pluralism* in present-day logical theory. Our answers must include the rider: 'It depends on what you mean by "logic".' We intend to expose enough of this pluralism to help determine whether there is a *respectable* notion of logic which meets the following conditions: that there are features of quantum mechanics (QM) which require that there is a logic in this respectable sense; that this logic is nonclassical; and that it is indispensable or especially conducive to the logical business of QM itself.

With appropriate tentativeness we call this logic or possible logic QL, appropriating the acronym from Birkhoff and von Neumann [31] and giving it a more comprehensive use than it had originally. We are asking therefore whether there is reason to suppose that QL exists and that it meets the conditions we have just set out; and whether it instantiates a respectable notion of logic.

Fully identifying the logical concerns of QM (or any other empirical

## 7.1. Motivating Quantum Logic

science, for that matter) is a bigger task than we have time for here. Even so, certain undertakings stand out as fairly obvious. For example, it is certainly part of the logic of an empirical science to articulate a principled distinction between its valid and its invalid deductions and its correct and incorrect entailments.

Logicians have long held that the laws of logic are prior to those of the other disciplines. In one way of representing this priority, logic is seen — as Wittgenstein saw it in the *Tractatus*—as an account or model of the logical structure of the world. There are two ways of reading this notion, one silly and the other interesting. On the silly view every truth about the world instantiates a law of logic. On the interesting view, no truth about the world contradicts a law of logic (minimal unity of science, again).

If, for example, a logic must accommodate strong logicism, then nothing counts as a logic unless it accommodates everything that counts as mathematics, including the mathematics peculiar to QM.

Here are some further questions that will guide our enquiry. If logic is, or is in part, a theory of certain properties of linguistic structures, and if the type of language that is appropriate to such an investigation is an ideal or artificial language, how can it be the case that the logical laws of such structures have any bearing on natural language structures, such as deductions in QM? (We return to this important question in 7.5.2 below.) Another question is that if logic is, or is in part, the theory of certain properties of reasoning, is it necessary to restrict the notion of reasoning to what human beings do? Or is there room for a logic of reasoning for any type of system for which a concept of higher order computation is definable?

Answers to these questions assist the would-be quantum logician in a non-trivial ways. If strong logicism is true and if its accommodation is a requirement of anything aspiring to be a logic, then QL must exist and must be very different from classical logic. Strong logicism is the view that all of mathematics can be reproduced without relevant loss in logic. QM contains some mathematics that classical logic cannot accommodate. Hence, on the present assumption, QL would be a needed alternative to classical logic in the quantum domain. If, on the other hand, logic is a theory of reasoning, or of aspects of reasoning, for any system for which the concept of higher order computation is definable, then there is reason to suppose that accounts of *quantum computation* may embed a nonclassical logic.

Examples could be multiplied, but we shall forbear for the present. We have exposed enough of the structure of logic's pluralism to be getting on with here.

Here is a point on which we wish to lay some emphasis. It is one thing to show that a purpose-built QL is needed or deserved by QM. It is another thing entirely as to what such a logic would look like, apart from its not looking classical. In this chapter we concentrate on the first issue. Concerning the second we leave a promissory note.[4]

## 7.2 Feynman's Problem

We can now say something more definite about what our starting position is. If it is necessary or justified to posit a QL, the following conditions must be met:

1. The positing of QL is driven by particular traits of the *physics* of QM.

2. Whether or not these physical traits constitute a refutation of classical logic, QL itself must be nonclassical.

3. The objective of QL is to discharge the *logical* requirements of QM; e.g., it must provide an account of validity which honours the distinction between valid and invalid QM-deductions.

What, then, is it about the *physics* of QM that calls out for a purpose-built nonclassical logic? A loose and informal (and very common) answer is the utter queerness of QM.

What is so special about quantum mechanics? What makes it 'utterly queer'? And is it *these* considerations that call for a special logic? Of course, one automatically thinks of startling phenomena such as nonlocality or Bose-Einstein condensation; but Richard Feynman has argued that the deepest puzzle is that we can't see why anything so terribly *simple* is true.

QM *simple*? How can this be? Aren't the elaborations of quantum theory often of great mathematical complexity? But, as Feynman points out, the basic rules are terribly indeed simple and can be grasped by anyone with a slight familiarity with *probabilities, complex numbers*, and the most elementary parts of *linear algebra*. Here we review just enough of the structure of quantum theory to make Feynman's point clear. It should also be enough to satisfy condition (1) of three paragraphs ago.

The basic notion is that we think of a physical system as being capable of passing from some initial prepared state, via some definite procedure acting on the system, to a final output state. Input (or preparation) states are represented by so-called *kets* of the form $|\psi\rangle$; these are column vectors in a Hilbert space, which is a linear space of complex-valued vectors. There are many possible Hilbert spaces with different dimensionalities, depending on the number of states that the system can assume. By saying that a Hilbert space is linear, we mean that the superposition principle holds: any linear combination of allowable state vectors is an allowable state vector. (There are some special restrictions on superposition, called superselection rules, but we need not be concerned with them here.)

---

[4]To be redeemed in a future work of ours. We hardly mean to suggest that we would be the first to develop a quantum logic. Apart from the pioneering work of Birkhoff and von Neumann themselves [31], one can point to, among other notable attempts, [23, 173, 95].

## 7.2. Feynman's Problem

Output (or outcome) states are represented by *bras* of the form $\langle\phi|$, which are row vectors; the components of a bra are the complex conjugates of the corresponding ket. The scalar product of a bra and a ket is represented by a *probability* or *transition amplitude*, written as a 'bra-ket' of the form $\langle\phi|\psi\rangle$. Although Dirac notation can be manipulated with great ease and read in any direction, if the transition amplitude is read from right to left (like Hebrew) it has a natural interpretation as tracing the evolution of the experimental set-up from preparation to outcome. Such transition amplitudes are complex numbers of the form $e^{i\theta}$, where $\theta$ is a phase angle. All the predictions of QM come directly or indirectly from phase relationships between transition amplitudes.

State vectors (bras and kets) can be transformed into other state vectors by linear operators, represented by square matrices. If a linear operator $\hat{O}$ is such that

$$\hat{O}|\alpha\rangle = \alpha|\alpha\rangle, \tag{7.1}$$

where $\alpha$ is a real number, we say that the operator is Hermitian, and the state $|\alpha\rangle$ is said to be in an eigenstate of $\hat{O}$ with eigenvalue $\alpha$. In the conventional reading of QM, Hermitian operators represent possible observations on the system, and are called *observables*; the spectrum of eigenvalues are the possible results that one could obtain. (In some versions of the modal interpretation, discussed below, this eigenvalue-eigenstate rule is modified.) Some eigenvalue spectra are discrete (such as spin states, or the energy states of bound systems); others are presumed to be continuous, such as the energy of open systems. (It may eventually turn out that the appearance of continuity for some observables is an artifact of coarse-graining.)

Observables can also be thought of as definite procedures applied to prepared systems. The probability amplitude to move from input $|\psi\rangle$ to output $\langle\phi|$ by means of procedure $\hat{O}$ is

$$\langle\phi|\hat{O}|\psi\rangle. \tag{7.2}$$

The *probability* that the system will undergo this transition is given by

$$|\langle\phi|\hat{O}|\psi\rangle|^2. \tag{7.3}$$

This is a real number, and the description can be normalized such that it comes out in the interval $[0,1]$.[5] In other words, to get from probability amplitudes to probabilities, we square up (i.e., take the modulus) of the complex amplitude to get a real number. Or to put it another way, in QM probabilities have complex-valued square roots, a fact that has no counterpart in classical probability theory. This notion (which remains to be defined more precisely) of 'square root of a classical concept' may have quite wide applicability, and points toward a way in which the quantum view is a natural generalization of the classical view.

---

[5] Note added in 2018: this way of calculating probabilities is known as the Born Rule.

Suppose now that the system can be taken from an initial state $|\psi\rangle$ to a final state $\langle\phi|$ via two possible operations $\hat{O}_1$ and $\hat{O}_2$. Let us suppose that these two routes are mutually exclusive, and—most important—that when the system arrives in its final state we cannot tell, without further experimentation, which route the system took. Then the probability that the system will get from the initial to the final state will be of the form

$$|\langle\phi|\hat{O}_1|\psi\rangle + \langle\phi|\hat{O}_2|\psi\rangle|^2. \tag{7.4}$$

We add the amplitudes *first* and then square up to get the probability. Now, had the systems been classical (meaning in important part that it would be possible in principle to distinguish which paths the system took *by independent means*, without disrupting the system), we would find the probability that a system followed either of two mutually exclusive paths by directly adding the probabilities for each path. In other words, in the computation of probabilities in quantum systems there is an *extra* step (i.e., summing up the amplitudes). This step makes all the difference in the world, for transition amplitudes are complex exponentials, and if they are not perfectly in phase there will be interference terms that have no counterpart in the classical realm.

As Feynman *et al.* say, that's it; all of quantum theory is merely an elaboration upon these simple rules.[6] But these rules are as deep as anyone has been able to go: 'We have no ideas about a more basic mechanism from which these results can be deduced' [84, I-10]. And this strikes us (and has struck others) as the deepest mystery about QM, nonlocality notwithstanding: why can we not see the reason for a mathematical structure that is so utterly simple, and yet so widely applicable? It should be *obvious* why something as basic as this is the way to go—but it is not. In the following we shall call this the Feynman Problem.

Feynman *et al.* state correctly that we get interference so long as we do not have a way of distinguishing the paths in the experiment; but how would you distinguish the paths that the system can take? The answer is that, one way or another, you would have to end up measuring observables that fail to commute with the first observables you thought you were measuring. That's what it takes to destroy interference. For instance, if you try to pin down the trajectories of the particles as they zip through a double-slit apparatus, an apparatus which measures the positions of the particles as they hit a detector plate, you have to measure their momentum vectors; this destroys the interference because position and momentum fail to commute.

---

[6]Feynman really should have added one more rule, which would be a statement of the value of Planck's fundamental constant of action. If action were not quantized, there would be no uniquely quantum phenomena, and the existence of interference and Bohm's quantum potential (another *sine qua non* of QM) must be somehow deeply connected with the basis of Planck's constant. But at present we have absolutely no idea why action must be quantized, much less how to calculate the value of the constant of action.

So to explain the mathematical structure we must take account of the *physical* fact of non-commutativity. However, we still don't have a complete story of why non-commutativity forces upon us the Hilbert space structure. And, then of course, there is the wholly central question as to whether the contradictions implied by commutativity assumptions (such as the Kochen-Specker paradox; see [44]) are *fruitfully* construable as logical.

Very well, then. We have this mathematical structure to take note of. It is in a number of ways odd, even though it is not as mathematically complex as it appears to be conceptually. Is there any feature of it that tells us that we must have a purpose-built QL? If there is, it is far from obvious that there is. So we shall keep looking.

## 7.3 Lattice Theory: A mined-out vein?

Historically, quantum logic originated in the 1936 paper of Birkhoff and von Neumann. It arose as one of several rival interpretations of QM. Birkhoff and von Neumann's essential idea was that we try to read a logic off from the mathematics of quantum theory. They did not presume to offer a deeper analysis in terms of which QM could be explained; rather, they seem to have realized from the outset that they were simply *redescribing* the formalism of QM in a way that would, they hoped, be more perspicuous. And they showed us that while a classical, or more precisely a Boolean logic has the structure of an orthocomplemented distributive lattice, quantum lattices are nondistributive—a mathematical condition that reflects or encodes the physical fact of noncommutativity, the fact that observable quantities come in conjugate pairs.

So conceived, the distinction between quantum and Boolean lattices is essentially topological; they connect in different ways. That is why a quantum lattice cannot be mapped homomorphically onto $Z_2$, the simplest Boolean lattice. This is the same thing as saying that it is not possible to evaluate all possible observation-claims about a quantum system at once. It is not that they are not all known at once, but rather that it is contradictory to even suppose that they all have a truth value at once! (We are not aware whether anyone has done any studies of quantum lattice theory from an explicitly topological point of view, but it seems that this approach could be fruitful.)

This non-Booleanity was anticipated by Schrödinger in the same paper of 1935 in which he annunciated his cat paradox:

> At no moment does there exist an ensemble of classical states of the model [the quantum mechanical system in consideration] that squares with the totality of quantum mechanical statements of this moment. ...if I wish to ascribe to the model at each moment a definite (merely not exactly known to me) state, or (which is the same) to *all* determining parts definite ([not] merely not exactly known to me) numerical values, then there is no supposition as to these numerical values *to be imagined* that would not conflict with

some portion of quantum theoretical assertions. [199, p. 156]

It is this apparently irreducible non-Booleanity that is behind the several 'no-go' theorems of quantum mechanics, the most central of which is the Kochen-Specker Theorem. (See [44] for extensive review.) A no-go theorem places limitations on our attempts to reproduce the predictions of quantum theory with a Boolean model. It is often said that such a model would be expressed in terms of so-called 'hidden variables'— although this is a misnomer since the most promising hidden variable theory, the Bohm-de Broglie causal interpretation, is based simply on position as a determinate variable. What really counts for the 'ontological' aspirations that motivated Bohm (and other authors such as J.S. Bell who sought to interpret QM in terms of 'beables') is whether or not the statistics of QM can be underpinned by a Boolean structure [24, 32, 44].

It is undoubtedly too soon to say that Bohm's project must be accounted a failure, although we must go on record as conjecturing that it will be very unlikely that anyone can find a way to make the non-Booleanity of QM 'go away.' As Bub says, 'The really essential thing about a quantum world is the irreducible indeterminism associated with non-commutativity or non-Booleanity' [44, p. 240] Does this mean that Bohm's efforts were wasted? No; the really interesting thing that Bohm showed, almost in spite of himself, was the pervasive *nonlocality of dynamics* in QM. But it would take us too far afield to justify this claim here.[7]

In summary: it would be nice if the Birkhoff-von Neumann logic could give us insights into why the quantum world is the way it is. However, in the end, we simply read this logic off the physics. This gives us an interestingly different way of looking at the physics, but it could not be convincing as any sort of explanation of why quantum phenomena are the way they are unless quantum logic had some sort of *independent* motivation. And this is what we utterly lack; the facts of QM were forced by Nature upon more or less unwilling but open-minded physicists such as Planck. Nature said, if you want to get good predictions, these are the sorts of calculations you have to do. Compare this with classical statistical mechanics, which depends upon the classical laws of probability, themselves having an intuitive justification in terms of elementary set theory and Boolean reasoning. There is nothing like that for QM.

We now have a clear question to ask. Classical propositional logic is Boolean. QM is non-Boolean. Doesn't this mean that, at a minimum, QM

---

[7] There exists an offshoot of Bohm's pilot-wave theory called 'Bohmian Mechanics', which has been advocated with missionary zeal by Sheldon Goldstein and co-workers; [69, 52]. These authors downplay the nonlocality of quantum dynamics, and proclaim that 'particles can still be particles'; by which they apparently mean that the Uncertainty Relations are only statistical constraints because position and momentum really *do* commute, after all. It is beyond the scope of this paper to carry out an adequate critique of Goldstein's Bohmian mechanics. We can only point to the abundant (though arguably not completely conclusive) evidence that without fundamental non-commutativity there would be no interference phenomena and thus no quantum mechanics.

## 7.4. Discrediting or Underdetermining?

requires a non-Boolean propositional logic? It is true that the vertices of the lattices can be interpreted as propositions of a sort, and the meet and join operations have a formal resemblance to the meet and join of classical logic; but it is not clear that we do any discursive *reasoning* in the language of quantum mechanics—we just calculate with it. If you look through the pages of any paper or text using quantum mechanics, you will find quantum-mechanical calculations set within text written in perfectly ordinary classical language, with the reasoning done by means of classical natural deduction, and with the predictions of the theory being interpreted and described classically. No physicists, to our knowledge, actually use quantum logic in their day-to-day work. Furthermore, one can point out that quantum logic has no obvious *semantics* (unless we follow Dickson [63] and just say that the entire lattice structure itself is the semantics). There is a very clear syntax, but we are not at all sure how to interpret it. (Indeed, this is another way of expressing the Feynman problem.) Is a logic without a semantics a logic at all?

This discussion harks back to important conceptual questions about the relationships between mathematics and logic. Is all of mathematics a form of logic, as Russell and Frege hoped? Or is logic a form of applied mathematics? What would we say, for example, if it turned out that the *mathematics* of quantum theory permitted interestingly expanded methods of reasoning? So, again, if logic must accommodate strong logicism, a *QL must* be deployed. And if logic is a theory of reasoning or computational systems, a *QL might* also have to be. (We return to this point in **7.5.8** below.)

But we have left a question dangling. What if a theory—any theory—has a non-Boolean propositional structure? Doesn't that show decisively that its propositional logic must be (at least) non-Boolean? Let us see.

### 7.4 Does Quantum Physics Discredit or Undermine Classical Logic?

QM is formulable in any scientifically mature natural language. This is important. Logicians long since have wondered what the logic of a natural language is, and this has given rise to some peppery contentions. If we know how to settle this more general question, this might help us box our compass with respect to those parts of natural languages in which QM is formulated.

Classical logic is the extensional logic of truth functions extended to a theory of quantification. There is a wide (though hardly unanimous) consensus that in such a logic quantification is restricted to domains of individuals; hence classical logic is first order logic.

Classical logic is a theory of certain properties definable for linguistic structures. These latter are constructions of elements of a designated formal language, which is a language whose atomic sentences are uninterpreted and whose molecular sentences are constructions of atomic sentences attached to connectives and/or quantificational symbols, both of which bear weak interpretations by way of truth conditions. The net effect is that the sentences of classical logic are devoid of *propositional* content.

The target properties of classical logic are properties such as consequence, truth in a model, entailment, consistency, and so on. These properties are either properties of linguistic structures alone, or of linguistic structures in virtue of relations they bear to non-linguistic set theoretic structures.

### 7.4.1 Classical Logic

Consider a logical truth S of classical logic, e.g., "$q \supset (p \lor q)$". To say that S is a truth of logic is to say that S is true for all valuations. Valuations are functions taking truth values into truth values. In our example, if '$p$' and '$q$' are both true, then so is S itself. Consider now any pair of true sentences, $E$ and $E^*$, from an empirical theory. Suppose that we assign $E$ and $E^*$ to $p$ and $q$ in S. Are there *any* such substitutions in S that produce a false sentence? The answer is No. Any such interpretations of $p$ and $q$ in S will either have a classical truth value or not. If the former, the resulting interpretation of S will be a logical truth by the classical definition of logical truth. If the latter, the resulting interpretation of S is defective. If either $E$ or $E^*$ is not classically truth-valued, then it is not an admissible interpretation of $p$ (or of $q$, as the case may be), since it is a requirement of $p$ and $q$ that they be classically truth-valued. So there is no admissible empirical interpretation of a logical truth that itself is other than true.

Similar considerations apply to the quantificational component of classical logic.

### 7.4.2 Quantum Logic

Here is the nub of the problem at hand. There are quantum states that are complexes of simpler structures. Some of these states are describable by sentences in the form '$X \oplus (Y \otimes Z)$', in which '$\oplus$' denotes an operation which set theorists call *join* and '$\otimes$' denotes an operation which they call *meet*. Now join is a kind of disjunction and meet a kind of conjunction.[8] So, *informally speaking*, it would not be wrong to read our sentence as '$X$ or ($Y$ and $Z$)'.

Of course, classical logic sanctions the law of distributivity. Expressed in purely natural language terms, this law provides that if '$X$ and ($Y$ or $Z$)' is true, so necessarily is '($X$ and $Y$) or ($X$ and $Z$)' also true. But in quantum mechanics, if '$X$ and ($Y$ or $Z$)' is true it does *not* follow that '($X$ and $Y$) or ($X$ and $Z$)' is true. Indeed both '$X$ and $Y$' and '$X$ and $Z$' are contradictions in QM, if $X$ and $Y$ ($X$ and $Z$) assert the joint measurement of non-commuting observables. This leads some theorists to the view that the validity of the classical distributivity principle is overturned by certain established facts about the quantum domain.

---

[8]To be precise, in a quantum lattice the meet of two vectors is their intersection, while their join is the subspace they span. See Hughes [116, 117] for very clear expositions.

## 7.4. Discrediting or Underdetermining?

It is easy to see that this case against classical logic turns on an elementary mistake. It is an error that involves a fundamental misconception about formalization. The claim in question is that there are true quantum physical sentences of the form '$X \otimes (Y \oplus Z)$'. It is demonstrable that there are cases in which a sentence of the form '$X \otimes (Y \oplus Z)$' is true and yet '$(X \otimes Y) \oplus (X \otimes Z)$' is not true. It follows from this that for sentences '$X$', '$Y$' and '$Z$' and for operators '$\oplus$' and '$\otimes$', the distributivity rule fails in the micro-domain. The question is whether this shows that it also fails in classical logic. If so, there will be valuations which make

$$A \wedge (B \vee C)$$

true, and which make

$$(A \wedge B) \vee (A \wedge C)$$

false, where '$A$', '$B$' and '$C$' formalize classical sentences and '$\wedge$' and '$\vee$' are the connectives for truth functional conjunction and disjunction. It take no more than a simple review of the truth table definitions of '$\wedge$' and '$\vee$' to see that no such valuation exist. There *is* no valuation which makes '$A \wedge (B \vee C)$' true and '$(A \wedge B) \vee (A \wedge C)$' false. The distributivity law is valid in classical logic.

Of course, in *QM*, 'and' and 'or' are interpreted as $\otimes$ and $\oplus$, for which distributivity fails, whereas in classical logic 'and' and 'or' are interpreted as $\wedge$ and $\vee$, for which distributivity does not fail. But it is no part of the empirical adequacy of *QM* that $\otimes$ and $\oplus$ are correct or even plausible interpretations of the meaning of the English connectives 'and' and 'or'. Nor is it a condition of the completeness and soundness of classical logic that $\wedge$ and $\vee$ capture the ordinary meanings of 'and' and 'or'. It is true, of course, the $\{\otimes, \oplus\}$-pair and the $\{\wedge, \vee\}$-pair are incompatible interpretations of 'and' and 'or'. But since the $\{\otimes, \oplus\}$-pair have no occurrence in classical logic, there is no treatment of 'and' and 'or' in classical logic in which distributivity *could* fail.

We note in passing Hilary Putnam's bold claim that since distributivity fails for the English connectives 'and' and 'or', *QM* gets them right and classical logic gets them wrong [179]. This may be so, but it is of no mind. Neither *QM* nor classical logic is a linguistics for 'and' and 'or' in English.

We conclude, therefore, that there is nothing good to be said for 'the fundamental claim' of quantum logic:

> QL claims that quantum logic is the 'true' logic. It plays the role traditionally played by logic, the normative theory of right-reasoning. Hence the distributive law is wrong. It is not wrong 'for quantum systems' or 'in the context of physical theories' or anything of the sort. It is just wrong, in the same way that '($p$ or $q$) implies $p$' is wrong. It is a logical mistake, and any argument that relies on distributivity is not logically valid ... [63, p. S275]

We note that it is a consequence of the constraints that Putnam places on ¬ and ∨ that the classical rule, disjunctive syllogism, also fails. This suffices to suppress *ex falso quodlibet*, the classical theorem that establishes the equivalence of negation-and absolute inconsistency. This makes Putnam's system a paraconsistent logic. In some ways, this is an attractive outcome, in as much as it innoculates the purported logic of QM against any of the contradiction-making paradoxes. (Another way of saying this is that a paraconsistent logic is not intrinsically hostile to paradox. For an exploration of old quantum mechanics from a paraconsistent viewpoint, see [39].)

On the debit side is the complexity of systems that lack laws such as disjunctive syllogism. To take just one example, the propositional system *LR* is a system of relevant propositional logic of the Anderson and Belnap kind [9], except that the distributivity principle fails in *LR*. This makes the decision problem for *LR at best* ESPACE hard [221, p. 7].

### 7.4.3 The Quantum Question Again

We now turn to the question of the kind of fit that can be constructed between QM and the semantics of **Pred**, the predicate calculus. For example, if the basic entities of QM are *not* representable as arbitrary elements in an arbitrarily large domain $D$ of individuals, then the issue is settled. The sentences of QM could not have classical models. Hence they could do no violence to the sentences of **Pred**, which do have classical models. On the other hand, if the quanta of the quantum domain are legitimately construable as first-order individuals, then they are classical objects model-theoretically.

It is also necessary to determine whether the predicates of QM are representable as $n$-tuples of model-theoretically classical objects from $D$. If they are not, then the issue closes negatively. If, contrariwise, they are, then the properties of QM have classical representations.

But what of quantifiers? In a classical (Tarski-Henkin) semantics, a universally quantified sentence $\ulcorner \forall \alpha_k(\Psi) \urcorner$ is satisfied by a countably infinite sequence $\sigma$ of objects in $D$ if and only if every countably infinite sequence of such objects that differs from $\sigma$ at most in its $k_{th}$ element satisfies $\Psi$. We note a particularly important condition on sequences: Sequences of individuals must be enumerable; i.e., they must stand in a one-to-one correspondence with the the natural line. It must be possible to refer unambiguously and with definiteness to the $k_{th}$ element of every sequence. That is to say, the members of $D$ must satisfy strict conditions on *individuation*.

Some logicians are of the view that since the basic entities of the quantum world are intrinsically stochastic, they lack the determinancy required for individuation. To say that objects are not well-individuated is, among other things, to say that there is no function that takes them to the natural line. If this is right, then two consequences fall out. One is that the quantified sentences of QM can't be modelled classically. The other, relatedly, is that it is a mistake to suppose that the basic entities of *QM* are in the classical sense members of *D*. If so, *QM* lacks a classical semantics.

It is important, by the way, that we emphasize the distinction between a theory's ontology and a theory's model. Ontologies are structures that facilitate the distribution of truth values over a theory's interpreted sentences. Models are set theoretic structures which facilitate the distribution of target logical properties over (sets of) its uninterpreted sentences. From the point of view of model theory, a model is all the ontology that an uninterpreted theory can have. By these lights, then, the original *QL* of Birkhoff and von Neumann may qualify as an ontology for *QM* but not as a model for it.

## 7.5  The breakdown of bivalence; or *ex superpondendo quolibet*?

We shall have no more to say about whether *QM* contradicts any law of classical logic. Our position is that it does not. And that, as they say in a presently popular TV game-show is our 'final answer'. Much more interesting is whether, granting its consistency with *QM*, classical logic meets our condition (of **10.3**); i.e., takes care of the *logical* business of *QM* itself. Well, what *is* the logical business of *QM*?

One of the most logically dramatic features of *QM* is the apparent collapse of bivalence. Not every sentence about quantum states will be either true or false without exception. This again follows from the 'no-go' results such as the Kochen-Specker Theorem, noted above. As Bub has it, 'we can take propositions corresponding to the properties in the property state as true, but we can't take the propositions that correspond to all the properties that are not in the property state as false, for this will involve a contradiction' [44, p. 31].

It also appears that if we must say that Schrödinger's cat is both alive and dead at the same time, we are open to all the consequences of a classical contradiction—in particular, that any proposition whatsoever could be deduced. Let us call this phenomenon *quantum detonation*. But this sort of logical detonation takes a special form in quantum mechanics.

In classical logic we have the principle *ex falso quolibet*: from a classical contradiction we can deduce any proposition whatsoever. Quantum mechanics, however, does not exactly allow us to infer from the supposed contradiction of the cat being in a superposition of live and dead states to the conclusion that any state whatsoever is allowable; rather, it says that any superposition (linear combination) of allowable states is an allowable state. But there are often a lot of ways in which a number of given states can be linearly combined, including states that violate locality and other classical expectations. Hence we might say, with tongue in cheek, that in quantum mechanics we should replace the classical *ex falso* with *ex superponendo quolibet*.[9] If it is not strictly accurate to say that *anything* can happen in quantum mechanics, it is certainly true that

---

[9]We thank Chris Epplett for his dipomatic reminder that we should use the gerund in this expression.

some very strange things can happen. Strictly speaking, for instance, it is only highly improbable, but *not* impossible, that the next time Harry steps out of his office at his University that he should find himself in the court of King Henry VIII. We have something in QM that is analogous to what happens in statistical mechanics, according to which it is possible (though *highly* improbable) that a pot of water might freeze solid the next time it is put on a gas flame. One can hardly say that there are no constraints in nature, but the few truly global constraints (such as mass-energy conservation) that do seem to stand up tend to be of an extremely general nature; and within those broad constraints the laws of probability are free to work their magic. Sam Treiman's sardonic remark comes to mind: 'Impossible things usually don't happen' [28].

Thus in quantum mechanics we really do stand, as Pitowsky aptly puts it, 'on the edge of a contradiction' [174]. But, as noted above, it is still not enough to discredit Boolean reasoning *where Boolean reasoning applies* (technically, because meet and join are defined differently for quantum and Boolean lattices). There is a discontinuity between the Boolean and the quantum world (indicated, as we have noted, by the essential discontinuity between Boolean and quantum lattices) that acts as a kind of protective membrane sealing off the classical world from the contagion of logical paradox. Does this really mean that we live in two metaphysically distinct worlds? No thinker with an instinctive taste for the unity of science will find this a comfortable conclusion. As we shall note below, however, there is a way out of this colossal dilemma, which is to consider the possibility that the distinction between quantum and classical talk is *modal*. We return to this point in **7.5.4**.

### 7.5.1 Putnam's Analogy With Riemannian Geometry

Hilary Putnam [179, 178] has suggested that a very attractive analogy may stand between the relationship between quantum and Boolean logics, on the one hand, and Riemannian and Euclidean geometry on the other. Gauss and Riemann famously showed that ordinary flat Euclidean geometry (which Kant thought was *a priori*) can be seen simply as a special case of more general curvilinear geometries; namely, the special case in which the curvature is zero. Einstein then found that in order to describe gravitation in a way that accords with the general principle of relativity (no preferred frames, accelerated or otherwise), one must presume that the geometry of space-time is, in general, Riemannian. So Putnam has argued that just as Nature tells us that Riemannian geometry is the appropriate generalization of Euclidean geometry, Nature is also telling us that quantum logic is the appropriate generalization of Boolean logic.

There is one difficulty with this appealing analogy. There is a smooth transition between a curved and a flat space; the curvature can go continuously to zero. However, as noted above, the difference between quantum and Boolean lattices has to do with how they connect, and there is no *smooth* transi-

## 7.5. The breakdown of bivalence; or ex superpondendo quolibet?

tion between structures with different connectivity. (This difference between quantum and classical lattices is a consequence of noncommutativity and the existence of a finite quantum of action.) This is *not* to suggest that it is impossible to embed Boolean logic within a more general quantal scheme; as we shall see, the truth is quite the contrary. But Putnam's analogy must break down. The best we can do to salvage it is to note that there is frequently (but by no means inevitably) a *statistical* transition from quantum to classical behaviour; for instance, quantum interference phenomena will often be washed out in systems with large numbers of particles, so that the behavior of such systems will tend to *numerically approximate* the behavior of purely classical systems.

### 7.5.2 Trivializing Validity in Quantum Contexts

As we said at the beginning, an important question for any logic is whether it has interesting external *applications*. There are two main ways in which this question receives an affirmative answer.

1. A logic has an interesting application to natural language structures when, or to the extent that, for certain target properties, the natural language structure instantiates that property in virtue of *logical forms* recognized by the logic.

    EXAMPLE: Arguments in English that are *valid* in virtue of having a valid form in first order logic.

2. A logic has an interesting application to natural language structures when, or to the extent that, for certain target properties the natural language structure instantiates that property in virtue of its satisfying the logic's *definition* of that property.

    EXAMPLE: The argument

    a) The shirt is red
    b) Therefore, the shirt is coloured

    has no valid form in first order logic; but it satisfies that logic's definition of validity, namely, that any valuation making (i) true also makes (ii) true.[10]

How, then, do these matters bear on nonbivalence?

The short answer is that nonbivalent sentences have no formalization in classical logic. So deductions from nonbivalent premisses cannot, even if valid, be so in virtue of having valid classical forms.

Beyond that, let **I** be a class of nonbivalent English sentences. Let $D$ be any deduction of a sentence of English from a set $\Sigma$ of I-sentences and let $\mathbf{I}_{qm}$

---
[10] For a more detailed discussion see [237].

be a subset of **I** containing nonbivalent quantum sentences. It is easy to see that all such deductions are classically valid. Since there is no valuation that makes the sentences of $\Sigma$ true, $\Sigma$ is classically inconsistent. But any statement is classically deducible from an inconsistent set of premises.

We have it, then, that *all* Ds in *QM* satisfy the classical definition of validity, and therewith is lost the essential distinction between valid and invalid quantum deductions. It is obvious that if *QM* has any logical business to perform, it is to show a certain favoritism for valid, rather than invalid deductions. The classical account of validity cannot serve that end. So *QM* has a stake in someone's providing an account of validity that *can* serve that end; and this, we may suppose, is a fundamental task of *QL*. However, for this to be the case, it is not in slightest degree necessary that any law of classical logic fail.

It is well to be clear about what motivates the quest by quantum logic for quantum validity. If classical validity were the only validity, then every deduction from $I_{qm}$-sentences would be valid. This alone would dispossess validity of any reasonable standing as a deductive target for quantum physics. It follows, then, that either validity sets no applicable or defensible deductive standard for quantum physics or that the validity of quantum deductions is non-classical.

So long as we retain the assumption that quantum theory contains **I**-sentences indispensably, then the set of *QM* sentences will fail to have the Lindenbaum property. That is, there will be non-contradictory sentences that cannot be extended to a consistent and complete set of sentences *K* such that for any wff $\Phi$, either $\ulcorner\Phi\urcorner \epsilon K$ or $\ulcorner\neg\Phi\urcorner \epsilon K$. Informally, the *K* of a theory *T* is the set of all its (logically) true sentences. If *T*'s every sentence is such that either it or its negation is in *K*, the sentences of *K* must without exception have the classical truth values. Accordingly, were a theory to contain an **I**-sentence, it cannot be consistently extended to a *K* that is in the requisite sense complete.

So far, we have been considering the consequences of supposing that some sentences of *QM* are indispensably members of a set of **I**-sentences. The loss of classical bivalence is deeply enough consequential to motivate a quantum logic even at the level of sentential logic. Since the story of the classical truth values *T* and *F* is in turn laid out in the semantical theory of the quantifiers, we may expect some corresponding deviation from classical norms in the semantic theory of *QL*'s non-classical truth values. Another way of saying the same thing is this. The classical logic of quantification gives a model theoretic account of the logical truth values. It is easy to see that no such account can be a wholly accurate story of the *non-classical* truth values. We may expect in turn that the model theory that delivers the goods for the nonclassical truth values will also make nonclassical provision for the quantifiers themselves.[11]

---

[11] It may appear, then, that the lack of numberability does give rise to nonbivalence, contrary to what we say late in **7.5.3**. Again, it all depends. If by bivalence we mean that every sentence is either true or false, bivalence need not be a casualty of a nonstandard theory of truth just because it

## 7.5. The breakdown of bivalence; or ex superpondendo quolibet?

This expectation is met in the failure of the Existential Instantiation rule. For we may have it that it is provable that some individual (i.e., particle) satisfies an open sentence ⌜$\Phi v$⌝ but no individual $\alpha$ satisfies ⌜$\Phi v$⌝. For this to be a coherent outcome we need a model theory in which quantification is possible even when individuation is not. In classical model theory, quantification and individuation go hand in hand; 'no entity without identity', in Quine's nice quip.

Just as we had it that the physics of $QM$ gave a principled reason to deny classical bivalence to at least some of its sentences, so too would we expect that the failure of the classical quantifier law is occasioned wholly by the physical provisions of $QM$. For this to be so, it is essential that the ontology of physics not be that of classical individuals and the requisite set theoretical constructions on them.

A final conjecture regarding the breakdown of bivalence in $QM$: just as probabilities in $QM$ have complex-valued square roots (i.e., the corresponding probability amplitudes), perhaps it will be possible to define something like a square root of a truth value. But we shall have to leave this as a conjecture for now.

### Further Conditions on a QL

We now find ourselves in a position to say something more about what a $QL$ should be. Given classical nonbivalence, we have reason to postulate a $QL$ and to mandate it to produce a validity relation that will facilitate the logical work of $QM$. What else might we say of $QL$? We might propose that $QL$ is a bona fide logic for $QM$ only if

1. for some deductions in $QM$ it is essential to their correctness in $QM$ that they employ a nonclassical consequence relation, C, supplied by $QL$
2. C is not a physical relation.

Similarly, $QL$ is a *bona fide* logic for $QM$ only if

1. for some truths of $QM$ it is necessary that they be expressed nonclassically, i.e., they be in the domain or counterdomain of a nonclassical truth-predicate $T_{QM}$ (perhaps involving 'square roots of truth' as hinted at above) supplied by the model theory of $QL$;
2. $T_{QM}$ does not denote a physical property.

---

gives a nonstandard notion of the truth values. But if, as we have already remarked, by bivalence we mean that every sentence takes the *classical* truth values, then we have it trivially that a model theory that gives a nonstandard notion of truth is nonbivalent even if every sentence is, by the lights of that account, either true or false.

To establish that $QL$ is a real or respectable candidate for logic, it suffices to find a deduction in $QM$ or a truth of $QM$ that meets these conditions. For example, suppose that a given deduction $D$ is up for scrutiny. $D$ passes the test if and only if it is provable that $D$ deploys a nonclassical, non-physical consequence relation in delivering the deductive goods intended by $D$ and that no classical relation of consequence can deliver those same goods.

### 7.5.3 Quantum Individuation

There is a large literature that bears directly on identity in $QM$.[12] Several authors argue that the intuitive idea of numerical distinctness simply does not apply to quantum objects. Paul Teller offers an interesting analogy. Suppose— adapting Teller—that you transfer from a bank in, say, Vancouver to your dollar account in a bank in London 100 dollars, and that later in the same day you transfer another hundred from Vancouver to London. In the week following, you find yourself in London and in need of some cash. You present yourself at your bank, and ask not only for a hundred dollars but the very hundred dollars that was your first deposit last week. Of course, there is no such thing for the bank to give you. The two hundred dollar sums are not numerically distinct. The familiar metaphysical distinction between qualitative and numerical or strict identity breaks down in such contexts [220, p. 115].

It is widely supposed that $QM$ presents situations that resemble our banking example, or at least resembles it enough to generate the collapse of the distinction between qualitative and numerical identity. Many writers ascribe a common cause to this collapse. Quanta, unlike classical particles, fail the principle of the indiscernibility of identicals (see e.g., [226]), which means that quanta cannot instantiate the relation of numerical identity. Again, the distinction between qualitative and numerical identity topples in the quantum domain.

The fact (or the appearance) of the damage done this distinction by quantum objects presents the would-be quantum logician with a twofold task. His negative task is to show that the loss of strict identity carries implications for any model for quantum discourse that preclude classical workings-up of those properties in which $QM$ has a legitimate *logical* interest—for example, validity as a desired characteristic of quantum deductions. But the interested logician also has a positive task. He must describe very carefully the sorts of thing quantum models are, and he must do so in such a way as to show that how they are—especially in their model theoretically nonclassical details—is how $QM$ requires them to be. It would be an easy thing to rig models whose basic entities are electronic movements of sums of money. Such could not be classical models, of course; the collapse of identity would see to that. But

---

[12]See, for example, [47].

## 7.5. The breakdown of bivalence; or ex superpondendo quolibet?

neither could they be quantum models, even when these electronic entities were treated with considerable abstraction.

The would-be quantum logician is thus faced with a possible problem. Given the present state of our knowledge of the quantum domain, he may be able to perform his negative task with precise and accurate reference to the quantum realities that bring identity to heel; but he might also find it very difficult to find in those quantum details what it is that requires us to jig quantum model theory in the required ways, that is, in ways that both honour the physical imperatives and yet provide the wherewithal to account for something recognizable as logical properties. It is easy to see that the negative task is more easily performed than the positive. Showing the inapplicability of classical models requires no more than giving up on numerical identity. Anyone satisfied that the physics overturns the indiscernibility principle can say with perfect accuracy that his rejection of classical models flows directly from how the *physics* of the quantum world goes. But in offering this, that, or the other nonclassical model as a model for quantum discourse, it is not enough that, in so choosing, the would-be logician honours the physics; for he must also 'honour the logic'. To do this latter thing it is essential that, in his proferred model theory for quantum discourse, he not merely redescribe QM in a new formalism, as Birkhoff and von Neumann did. What the quantum logician wants (or should do) is not an analysis of physical states, but rather an analysis of logical properties of discourse about physical states. He wants, that is to say, an account of *quantum validity* and *quantum truth*.

In discharging his negative and positive responsibilities, it is essential that the quantum logician not fall into the trap of taking every peculiarity or downright oddity of the quantum domain as logically significant, as a second thought experiment, also due to Teller, will show [220, pp. 114–116]. Imagine two quantitatively identical particles roaming about in a closed box, whose right and left sides are of equal volume. Suppose also that the particles are independent in their motion and small enough to avoid collision. Where at a given time would we find these particles? Intuitively, there are four equiprobable possibilities: they are both on the right side; they are both on the left side; one is on the right side and the other on the left side; or vice versa. However, as Teller observes, there are situations galore in which in quantum contexts these are simply the wrong numbers. The probabilities, instead, are identical for *three* possibilities, not four: Both particles are on the right; both are on the left; and one on each side. One way of capturing the difference between the intuitively expected options and the experimentally indicated options is to say that quantum setups such as this one don't obey classical statistics, and obey instead something we dignify as *quantum statistics*.

Imagine now a logician who reasons as follows: Since the physics of such setups is queer enough to defeat classical statistics and to honour instead quantum statistics, the physics in question is *very* queer indeed. So it will require a purpose-built logic of its own.

Unless we are ready to plead that mathematics just is logic, at least in part, this is a mistake. The mathematics involved amply attests to the queerness of quantum physics. But queerness is not what counts. What counts is that in the quantum setup it is impossible to discern the distinction between the third and fourth options which classical statistics is obliged to posit. In the quantum setup, there is no discernible difference between these same particles exchanging these positions. Not everything that explains this indiscernibility is logically significant. But if it is explained by the fact or apparent fact that there *is* no numerical distinctness between the two particles, then they cannot be the individuals required by classical models. That, of course, would make the indiscernibility logically significant.

It is possible, but far from perfectly obvious, that quantum sentences owe their nonbivalence directly to the fact that QM's basic entities lack the property of numberability.[13] Teller makes an interesting case for saying that what unnumberable objects lack is the haecceititic 'property' of *thisness*. If this is right, there is no quantum body that is this body, hence no situation in which this quantum body differs from that quantum body. Equally, there is no quantum body to which, for any, this is identical to it. This gives unnumberability, right enough. But does it give nonbivalence? It would seem not. If it did, bivalence would then imply numberability. But (reverting now to Teller's bank example), it would seem that the sentences that record the deposits and withdrawals of that example are straightforwardly bivalent without its being the case that for some clump of a hundred dollars it is this clump that was transferred from the chequing account to, say, the Water Company's account. If the Teller example is a good enough analogue of quantum unnumberability, we have a case from supposing that nonbivalence and unnumberability are logically independent properties in quantum contexts.

Still, we are not entirely home-free. We admit to some lingering doubts. We strongly suspect that if the view that particles can be continuously existent entities with continuous trajectories could be formalized in just the right way, it would lead to a Bell Inequality—one that would almost certainly be violated by actual quantum predictions.

### 7.5.4 Modal Interpretations: Is Quantum Logic a Modal Logic?

One of the most interesting lines of investigation is the modal viewpoint advocated by Bub [44], and first put forward by van Fraassen [224]. It is that the state vector does not actually describe a putative reality, but a possibility. This solves one of the central interpretive puzzles. Consider Schrödinger's

---

[13]Numberability is not to be confused with denumerability, which is a necessary but not sufficient condition of it. Items count as numberable when they can be identified and *reidentified* in experimental settings.

## 7.5. The breakdown of bivalence; or ex superpondendo quolibet?

cat, which exists in a superposition of states before we open the box and look at it. No real cat can be simultaneously alive and dead. It is very hard to interpret the state vector for the cat realistically. However, the possibilities for incompatible outcomes can easily co-exist. It is therefore very natural to think of quantum mechanics as a calculus of the evolution of *possibilia*. And quantum logic must therefore be a species of modal logic. And, in fact, quite a lot of work has already been done to interpret quantum logic as a modal logic. (For review, see [49].)[14]

On the modal view, we can interpret kets as possible input states—states whose possibility is consistent with the way we know the system was prepared, while bras are possible output states. The mysterious extra step in the QM algorithm is therefore a move from possibility to probability, a distinction that is entirely collapsed in the classical, Boolean picture.

It may be that Bub is on the right track in insisting that this insight has to be taken very seriously. However, much work done on the modal interpretation has possibly been side-tracked into the pursuit of a red herring. It focuses on the problem of finding a way of assigning a so-called determinate variable, a quantity that can be presumed to be definite, and thus represent the closest approach we can make to a classical realism, throughout the course of a physical investigation—*despite* the modality of quantum talk.

This work has culminated in a recent 'uniqueness' theorem by Jeffrey Bub and Rob Clifton (see [44]). It shows precisely *how definite* one can be in the face of quantum indeterminacy. It is always possible to assign some observable as 'determinate' in the course of a physical investigation. But, at the same time, we find ourselves right back where Schrödinger warned us we would be: it is, in general, impossible to make *all* the variables pertaining to a given system determinate at once. We can move quantum indeterminacy around, but we can't make it go away.

The modal interpretation therefore poses a philosophical challenge: if our very best physical theory (best in the sense of having a great predictive power over the widest range of phenomena) can do no better than describe the world in terms of *possibilia* and *probabilia*, if the very notion of something that can *be* is at best a large-scale approximation and at worst a mathematical contradiction, then perhaps we have to simply give up Einstein's hope of finding a theory that can successfully map one to one with the deepest 'elements of physical reality', whatever those elements might be. Perhaps physical theory in the last analysis is simply a highly sophisticated *descriptive schema*, or an elaborate form of applied mathematics. Perhaps some will say that it is not so much that QM obeys or expresses a modal logic, but that quantum mechanics *is* a quantitative modal logic in the spirit of the original QL of Birkhoff and von Neumann [31].

---

[14] And perhaps this is a response to Quine: if he is going to include quantum logic as an interesting deviant logic, he had best include modal logics as well.

The apparent collapse of physical theory as a means for describing what *is* does not imply that there is no such thing as physical reality; we are not advocating some species of idealism, solipsism, or social constructivism here. We merely suggest that (essentially because of non-commutativity) that we cannot hope to faithfully *map* that reality all at once. The notion of the incompletability of physical theory is entirely consistent with the notion of a larger reality that can be partially or wholly independent of human consciousness and observation. We really do not think that the Great Nebula in Andromeda has been shimmering in its glory for billions of years precisely because some anthropoids on a minor planet in a neighbouring galaxy finally noticed its existence (although we are certainly prepared to suppose that human astronomers may have interacted in interesting ways with the wave functions of a few photons from that vast Galaxy).

We said at the beginning 'It depends on what you mean by "logic".' We also said that a logic cannot be a *physical* system; that, in effect, the models of a logical language shouldn't be confused with the ontology of a physical language. If this is right, the modal suggestion presently under review will suggest not a logic, but rather a modal ontology for QM. It depends on what you mean by 'logic.'

### 7.5.5 Quantum Paradoxes

It is proposed by those, among others, who favour the quantum logical interpretation of QM, that a further way in which to attempt to motivate a purpose-built nonclassical logic for QM would be to show that the so-called paradoxes of QM are solvable if classical logic is replaced by a suitable nonclassical logic. For this to have any real chance of being brought off, it must be demonstrated that at least the following four conditions are met:

1. classical logic has an irreducible role in the generation of the quantum paradoxes;
2. displacement of those classical principles that abet the paradoxes by quantum logical principles meets two important conditions:
    a) the paradoxes disappear
    b) no damage is done to the physical integrity of QM;
3. it is independently ascertainable that the principles of a putative quantum logic are logical principles, and not just principles of QM dressed up in a new formalism; and
4. the quantum paradoxes must give genuinely logical offence rather than just being queer.

## 7.5. The breakdown of bivalence; or ex superpondendo quolibet?

This is all very problematic. If, as condition (4) requires, quantum paradoxes must be genuinely illogical, it is necessary to ask 'By the standards of what logic?' If we were to decide that the relevant standards are those of classical logic, then, if (4) is satisfied, the $QM$ paradoxes are classical contradictions or logical falsehoods. But, since the classical rules are provably consistent and sound, the fault must be that of $QM$, not of classical logic. On the other hand, if the paradoxes violate the standards of some other logic, it would have to be shown *independently* that this logic is a better bet for $QM$ than classical logic. So it cannot be a sufficient motivation of quantum logic merely that conditions (1) to (4) are discharged.

Here is one such possibility. If $QM$ sentences are nonbivalent, then, as we have said, classical validity utterly fails to serve the logical purpose of distinguishing in a principled way between valid and invalid quantum deductions. There is an important similarity between this situation and the $QM$ paradoxes. From the point of view of classical logic, every quantum deduction is valid, and, from that same point of view, every sentence of the language of $QM$ is true. Just as classical logic can be said to have nothing to offer the quantum theorist with regard to his interest marking the difference between validity and invalidity, neither does it offer anything valuable as regards the $QM$ theorist's interest in the distinction between truth and falsehood.

Suppose now that it comes to pass that in the quantum logic, $QL$, that *does* serve the theorist's interest in validity, the paradoxes are underivable, i.e., the deductions of $QM$ of which the paradoxes are their respective conclusions are invalid in $QL$. Finally, suppose that nothing else in the *physics* is deranged by this blockage in $QL$ of the quantum paradoxes. Under these conditions, not only would we have a way of blocking the paradoxes, it would be a principled way. It would be a consequence of a theory of quantum validity which is already needed because of the collapse of classical validity in quantum contexts.

Even so, this leaves the fact that the quantum paradoxes are *classical contradictions* wholly undealt with. A further step is needed. One possibility is that the quantum logician will insist that classical logic is defective, that sentences of the form ⌜Φ and ¬Φ⌝ are not always logically false in $QM$. But this overlooks the fact that the classical logical falsehoods are false under every semantic variation which they are capable of acknowledging. With this in mind, a second possibility is that the quantum logician will insist that the *metalogic* of $QL$ cannot be classical. But this turns out to be a costly solution for the quantum logician; for it denies him his argument that the nonbivalence of $QM$ occasions the collapse of classical validity in quantum contexts (which is an argument worked up in wholly classical way).

A third possibility is that the state of affairs described by our present assumptions carries only one consequence for classical logic, which is that classical logic has nothing to do with the quantum paradoxes (for recall, quantum paradoxes have no formalization in classical logic). This will be so, however, only if no paradoxical consequence of QM has a classical truth value. Supposing this to be so, the quantum logician still retains the considerable burden of showing that our present assumptions are indeed met.

### 7.5.6 Further Reflections on QL

When, as in the case of QM, conditions like these are satisfied, we shall say that the physics itself requires a nonclassical logic. This meets a fundamental constraint on a quantum logic. The physics must be such as to show that it cannot be served by a classical logic with regard to the basic logical properties (such as validity) in which it has a nontrivial stake.

It is one thing to say that a scientific theory such as QM cannot have a classical logic. It is another thing to say in appropriate detail what kind of non-classical theory it does or must have. Two things stand out as basic necessities. A quantum logic must display models in which it is ascertainable in a principled way that the 'right' sentences came out classically non-truth-valued, and it must develop a theory of nonclassical validity such that the valid deduction of QM are valid according to the model's account of validity, and its invalid deductions are invalid in the same way. In this we *may come to see* that the deductions of QM are intrinsically mathematical (e.g., set theoretic). This being so, the model theory would have no chance of characterizing a concept of validity that applied in a principled way to the valid and non-valid deductions of QM, *unless* it made validity intrinsically mathematical in the model. We could then say that, whereas there is a principled reason to distinguish mathematics from classical logic, the opposite is true of quantum logic and mathematics. The sixty-four dollar question, of course, is what such a notion of validity would look like, and—flowing from it—what is it about the *physics* that makes it so?

Here is a possibility that seems to us interesting enough to introduce now. Given that it is a requirement on any system that aspires to the name of quantum logic that it produce an account of quantum validity, a standard enough way of producing this *kind* of analysis is via a description of the consequence relation. In [80], Engesser and Gabbay propose that for each ray of a Hilbert space $H$ it is possible to associate one-to-one a non-monotonic consequence relation. This enables us to conceive of the projectors in $H$ as revision operators of a certain kind. It can then be shown that the lattice of closed subspaces of $H$ is a natural generalization of the classical notion of a Lindenbaum algebra. It also emerges that the quantum consequence relations reflect, to a rather surprising extent, their metatheory at the object level. The logic of this approach involves a tight partnership between non-monotonic logic and Hilbert space theory. Without here judging the success of this approach in any detail, we can say that the Engesser-Gabbay account meets our two main criteria. It gives an account of quantum validity and it

## 7.5. The breakdown of bivalence; or ex superpondendo quolibet?

does so in a way that is motivated by and enabled by peculiarities of quantum physics. So whether ultimately a success in all its details or not, this is the right *kind* of approach.

Much is made of the sheer conceptual difficulty of QM, by its queerness, as we were saying earlier on. Some would go further, with harsher verdicts such as incoherence. Often the failure of Existential Instantiation is taken as evidence of these difficulties. This is a mistake. If someone reports a dream in which there were some flowers in a vase on a table but, for no colour, reported that the flowers were that colour, then the flowers of his dream would have been coloured but of no particular colour. (To say that, the dreamer would have overcome this indeterminacy had he been more attentive simply misjudges what it is to report a dream.) Dreams are utterly common experiences, concerning which something like the failure of Existential Instantiation is also common. Then, too, the mathematically-minded seem to be reasonably at home with the $\omega$-inconsistency of first order number theory, in which for some property $\Phi$ it is provable that some number lacks $\Phi$ even though each individual number has it.

There are still further examples from quite ordinary English to which EI seems rather obviously inapplicable. One whole class of these is mass terms, such as 'snow', which take the quantifier and yet have no instances. So 'Some snow fell overnight' is perfectly all right, but there is no name that names *a* snow, hence no candidate for an instantiation of this quantification. This is not to say that quantification over quantum states is quantification of mass terms. But if it is not, what is it, pray?

It is also true that, from 'Some snow fell overnight', there must be inferrable something like 'This snow fell overnight'. This is interesting. 'Snow' is a mass term, but it also takes indexicals. Indexicals particularize occurrences of snow without naming them. This matters in two ways. One is that EI doesn't instantiate to indexicals. The other is that, even if it did, it would give us nonclassical quantification, since indexicals have no occurrence in classical logic.

### 7.5.7 Complementarity

One of the most important tasks of the logician is to take the measure of complementarity, considered as a property of physical states prior to the collapse of the wave function. It does little good to for the logician-theorist to consult his 'intuitions' about what is and what is not real negation. What counts logically is the bearing that such complementarities have on the truth values of the formulae that describe them. Here are some possibilities to consider.

1. Complementary states contradict one another. In that case, they are fit candidates for a dialethic logic.

2. Complementary states don't contradict one another, even though one at most is realizable. In that case, we might take the states as representing two different but logically incompatible physical possibilities, one of which and only one is made actual by measurement. Again, this might indicate the suitability of a modal logic, in which $\ulcorner M\Phi \urcorner$ and $\ulcorner M\neg\Phi \urcorner$ can both be true (or have a designated value) and yet $\Phi$ and $\ulcorner \neg\Phi \urcorner$ must have opposite or conflicting truth values.

We keep saying that the fundamental question for the logician is whether the statements of $QM$ take the classical truth values. If so, this works an enormous simplification into the question of the extent, if any, to which $QM$ requires or deserves a $QL$. If not, then $QM$ is straightaway a many-valued logic. The trouble is that there are more many-valued logics than one can shake a stick at. Which, then, is the one that $QM$ demands to have? A related difficulty is sorting out which of these values to designate and which to contradesignate. A further problem is that a logic with an even number of truth values tends to operate classically,[15] whereas a logic with an odd number of truth values can make it hard to get negation (or complementarity) right. (See [183, pp. 89–90].)

### 7.5.8 Convention T and Quantum Computation

Consider again our putative set, $\mathbf{I}_{qm}$, of $QM$ sentences which fail to have a classical truth value. Informally, the lesson that we are invited to learn from $\mathbf{I}_{qm}$ is not that its sentences *say nothing* (which would be why interrogative sentences lack truth values), but rather that they say nothing *determinate*. Ordinary English has lots of such sentences; e.g.,

'Bill is somewhat angry'
'Sue is rather tall'
'Harry is kind of angry'

Notice, however, that in each of these cases, indeterminacy is no bar to bivalence; for each of these sentences satisfies Convention T. So what is it about the $\mathbf{I}_{qm}$ sentences that is unlike this? What is it that requires us to code up the quantum indeterminacies in the *metalanguage*?

There has been much ado of late about the peculiarities of quantum calculation (e.g., [60, 154]). This might lead us to suppose that since calculating is a kind of reasoning, and since logic is the science of reasoning, logic must take these quantum peculiarities into account in a principled way.

One of the fascinating consequences of quantum computation is that we have to give up the idea that we should look for the kind of definiteness of

---

[15] More precisely, if $L$ is a many-valued Kleene-regular logic with equal numbers of designated and contradesignated values, then $L$ is isomorphic to classical logic.

## 7.5. The breakdown of bivalence; or ex superpondendo quolibet?

result that Descartes insisted upon. The results will often be merely probable—although if the circuit designer knows what she is doing, she can arrange phase factors such that the circuit will almost certainly compute the answer we want. As Deutsch *et al.* say,

> The basic idea of quantum computation is to use quantum interference to amplify the correct outcomes and to suppress the incorrect outcomes of computations. [60]

Furthermore, quantum computations, if mapped into sequences of parallel classical computations, would be intractably complex; the human mind must give up all hope of being able to simply follow and thereby check all the steps of the calculation. The price we pay for the greater computational power of a quantum computer is the near-total loss of any sort of Cartesian 'clear and distinct' grasp of why the result is what it is.

Despite these difficulties, we are drawn to Deutsch's argument that this must change our whole picture of how computation, indeed all reasoning, works. In particular, we think that this carries the implication (which will not make everyone happy) that *all logicians, especially those interested in computation, decidability, and similar meta-issues, must learn quantum mechanics*. This seems almost too much to ask of the chronically-overworked logician. But we don't see how one could get around this. Consider, for instance, the fact that Deutsch [58] has apparently succeeded in *proving* the Church-Turing thesis (subject to some very natural constraints) in terms of a generalized quantum Turing machine. How can anyone from now on discuss such things as completeness or provability without taking this into account?

Closely following from the last point is that it may be more helpful to think of quantum logical operations in terms of linear operators (represented by matrices), rather than as a problem in lattice theory. The lattice theory vein may well be played out, for now at least. One sees this possibility from the construction of the square root of 'not' as a certain kind of matrix (representing the transformations of a state in a Mach-Zehnder interferometer) [154]. The theory of quantum logical circuits seems to represent a natural generalization of classical Boolean circuit theory; the quantum theory can represent all of the Boolean logical operations that can be represented by the classical theory of logic gates, but it can also represent other operations (such as $\sqrt{NOT}$) that have no classical Boolean meaning. There is, therefore, a clear sense in which Boolean logic can be embedded in a more general non-Boolean theory; the question is how we are to interpret these peculiar 'square roots' of classical concepts. If something like the modal interpretation is correct, then could we say that $\sqrt{NOT}$ is to NOT as possibility is to actuality?

### 7.5.9 Too Many Worlds?

Mention of quantum computation makes it is necessary to venture a very brief comment about the many-worlds interpretation of *QM*, even though Abner Shimony has sagely warned us that 'discussions of the Many-Worlds interpretation tend to take up all the time allotted to them...' [203].

Having said this, we note that Deutsch has put forward a very challenging point in favour of the Many-Worlds theory, or 'multiverse' theory as he calls it. Quantum computers can sometimes perform calculations very much faster than any possible classical computer, and the way they do this, in effect, is that there is a separate amplitude for each possible state of the circuit and the computation is carried out in all of these Schrödinger-cat circuit-states at once; one has, in effect, massive parallelism. Now, Deutsch says that the fact that such a computer can produce a result, and even out-perform a classical computer, shows that all these parallel computations must be actually taking place *somewhere*; and if they are not taking place in our space-time, they must be taking place in real parallel space-times.

Deutsch, in other words bites the ontological bullet posed by Schrödinger's cat paradox. The cat really is both alive and dead. But we avoid quantum detonation because the alive and dead states are correlated to two distinct observer states, in one of which the observer sees an alive cat; the other a dead cat. These two branching states define distinct worlds which appear classical to the observers in them; there is no logical detonation within any given world, although there is an on-going ontological detonation on a colossal scale in the multiverse.

We have not seen any comment by Deutsch on the modal interpretation of *QM*, but we presume that he would not accept it; the sheer fact that quantum computation works, he would say, argues for an outright realism about state functions. Hugh Everett, founder of the MWT, was quite explicit that there is no such thing in *QM* as the transition from the possible to the actual; the wave function is all actual, always. (Everett [81, pp. 459–460]; cited in [44, p. 224]; see also papers by Everett and others in [56].)

We tend to reject any sort of modal realism—either of the Lewisian variety, or the many-worlds theory which is now so popular with quantum computationalists. It seems to us that modal realism simply fails to accurately construe possibility-talk. The entire point of possibility-talk is to be able to discuss things without ontological commitment. (There could be room, however, for reifying potentia, along Aristotelian lines, perhaps.) But Deutsch argues that the many-worlds (or multiverse) theory is the only conceivable explanation of how quantum computers can carry out computations that are vastly more complex than any classical Turing-machine-equivalent computer can do in the same time. Any sort of logical or mathematical operation is something that has to take place on a physical device, not in Plato's heaven. Any critic of the multiverse theory, Deutsch insists [59, Ch. 9], must provide an alternate

## 7.6. The Unity of Science, Again

*physical* explanation for the power of quantum computation; *where*, pray tell, does all that computation actually take place?

There are, perhaps, alternative explanations. In a Bohm-de Broglie pilot-wave model, for instance, we suspect that one could write a consistent story according to which the computations are carried out within the pilot wave itself. (Deutsch [59] rejects this possibility, for unclear reasons.) Another candidate location for quantum computation is the quantum vacuum itself, which probably contains quite enough complexity to account for all the computations a quantum computer can perform, without having to move to alternate space-times. But much work remains to articulate these possibilities in detail.

### 7.5.10 The Promise of Quantum Computation

Certainly, we must concede that quantum computation is a particular challenge for modal interpretations of *QM*; certainly, also, regardless of what interpretation proves to be the most effective in the long run, we are in for some fairly radical ontological readjustments.

Quantum computation is an interesting idea, but care needs to be taken. There are at least two respects in which this is so.

> *Respect number 1*. Mainstream classical logic makes no claim whatever to be a science of actual, everyday reasoning [21, 124, 205]. If quantum peculiarities do enter the reasoning picture, no logic need or should take account of it. *Or* we should change our notion of logic across the board. That is, we should insist that *anything* deserving of the name of logic is required to say something about at least certain aspects of the operation of reasoners or cognitive systems. (See Gabbay and Woods [92].) In which case, there is nothing special about *QM* in necessitating a logic of this kind.
>
> *Respect number 2*. 'The calculations are different'. This could mean that *QM*'s *mathematics* is nonclassical; in which case, it is indeed nonclassical. Or it could mean that there is a certain kind of reasoning whose description must have a *QM* component. If so, then *QM* and cognitive science come together fruitfully. But this has no impact on *logic* unless we are already pledged to the idea that logic is a description of the reasoning behaviour of cognitive agents or cognitive systems, or some such thing.

### 7.6 The Unity of Science, Again

What, then, does this come to? As we warned at the beginning, we would not be able to establish many firm conclusions in this exploratory paper. On the one hand, we might note that the pluralisms inherent in trying to say just what logic (any logic) really *is* tends to undermine a Cartesian tree-of-knowledge model of the unity of science. If there are many logics, with different motivations and different structures, then they might not map into each other with sufficient lack of ambiguity to constitute a genuine root-system for Descartes' tree. On the other hand, we have noted that there is considerable evidence (especially through recent work on quantum computation) that Boolean reasoning can be embedded in a broader quantal structure, so perhaps unity can be salvaged after all. This unity would come, if it comes at all, at a price: the conclusions of a quantal computation are inherently probabilistic, and the steps of most quantum computations are so intractably complex as to be utterly unsurveyable by the human mind. Quantum logic must therefore fail to satisfy two of the conditions that Descartes insisted are essential for any discipline to be called a science: certainty and surveyability.

Despite all of these large difficulties, it seems certain that could Descartes be brought back to our time he would have been thrilled and fascinated by the tremendous predictive power of quantum mechanics—a power we cannot deny even though we still have no satisfying explanation of the grounds of its possibility.[16]

---

[16] An early version of this chapter was presented to the New York Logic Group in February 1999. For incisive and helpful comments we thank Jonathan Adler, Arnold Koslow, Rohit Parikh and Alex Orenstein. A revised version was read at the University of Alberta the following March, and additional valuable advice was forthcoming from Bernard Linsky and David Sharp, for which our thanks. The present version reflects the fruitful stimulation provided by participants in Kent Peacock's course on Deviant Logic in Lethbridge in the Fall of 2000, and John Woods' Group on Quantum Logic at the University of Groningen in the Spring of 2001. Our thanks to David Atkinson and Jan Willem Romeyn. A special word of gratitude to our colleague, Peter Alward, for helpful advice. We thank the Social Sciences and Humanities Research Council of Canada, the Engineering and Physical Sciences Research Council of the United Kingdom, and Professor Christopher Nicol, Dean of Arts and Science of the University of Lethbridge, for financial support.

# Chapter 8

# Temporal Presentness and the Dynamics of Spacetime[1]

The purpose of this paper is to pick up the threads of a debate about the ontology of becoming in spacetime that was triggered by a provocative article published by Nicholas Maxwell [140]. This debate is itself merely a recent episode in a long dialogue that goes back at least as far as the time of Parmenides and Heraclitus [197]. Here is the question around which this debate is centred: is change or becoming the distinguishing feature of the natural or physical world, as suggested obscurely by Heraclitus and argued at length by Aristotle? (See [72, 91], and Aristotle's *Physics*, in, e.g. [143].) Or is our usual uncritical belief in the reality of change the product of some sort of perceptual illusion or intellectual error, as believed by Parmenides and a small host of recent authors such as Gödel [97] and Julian Barbour [20]?

I will not be able to solve the whole of this momentous problem here. However, I intend both to set aside a few unwarranted assumptions, which have for a long time dogged our thinking about the puzzle of becoming, and to assemble some tools which should aid in finding a solution to it. In particular, I will argue that we can do much better than is usually supposed in identifying structures that can both 'live' within Minkowski spacetime and represent objective becoming. I shall also discuss whether such structures would necessarily contradict the Principle of Relativity, and finally consider the impact of quantum mechanics on the problem of becoming.

---

[1] First published in D. Dieks (ed.), *The Ontology of Spacetime*. (Philosophy and Foundations of Physics, Vol. 1). Amsterdam: Elsevier, 2006, pp. 247–261. My thanks to Elsevier for permission to reproduce this paper in *Quantum Heresies*.

This paper is dedicated with affection and respect to the memory of Rob Clifton—although without any presumption that he would have endorsed the views presented here!

## 8.1 Probabilism and Spacetime Structure

Maxwell's major claim was that probabilism contradicts the special theory of relativity. 'Probabilism', says Maxwell [140, p. 23] 'is the thesis that the universe is such that, at any instant [whatever that might mean], there is only one past but many alternative possible futures'. Maxwell argues that probabilism derives its strongest support from quantum mechanics, but we can introduce the notion by recalling a famous discussion by Aristotle about the truth conditions of a proposition.

Aristotle invited us to consider the following statement: 'There will be a sea battle tomorrow'. (See *de Interpretatione*, Chapter 9, in (e.g.) [143, pp. 45–48].) He used this as a counter-example to the claim that all propositions have a truth value, since he took it to be self-evident that a proposition about what may happen tomorrow has no truth value on the day in which it is uttered. (Tomorrow's battle might well be highly probable today, but Aristotle believed that no matter how probable the battle is, there are many factors that are, in principle at least, free to act *today* to change what happens tomorrow; for instance, the naval commanders could decide at the last minute not to fight after all, or a sudden storm could blow up and prevent the battle.) Thus, in this view, while the present consists of coexistent or co-actual realities, and the past is settled but no longer actual, the future is ontologically open. What is to become is merely a possibility, which in itself has no being outside the minds of those who conceive of it—though there is room in such views, as both Aristotle himself and Maxwell indicate in different ways, for reification of propensities or potentialities so long as they are conceived to act in the *present*.

The Newtonian picture differs from the Aristotelian in that Newtonian mechanics conceived of physical processes as entirely governed by deterministic dynamical laws.[2] This meant that at any given time there was only one possible future; or, if there seemed to be many, it would be only due to our ignorance of the details of the physical world at that given time. Still, one can in a Newtonian universe uphold an ontological distinction between present and future, even though, because of determinism, the distinction is moot [197].

Special relativity calls into question the possibility of ontological distinctions between past, present, and future, because of the relativity of optical simultaneity [151]—that is, simultaneity defined in terms of equality of time coordinates constructed according to the procedures set out by Einstein [217]. Suppose Alice and Bob are two inertial observers moving toward each other.

---

[2]Richard Arthur (private communication) has cautioned me to choose my words carefully here, since Newton himself believed that God could intervene from time to time in order to pat the planets back into their proper orbits, as it were, should their motion become chaotic. The notion that Newton's laws, expressed in terms of differential equations, are sufficient to determine the future of the physical world for all time solidified only with the work of the great mechanicians of the 18th century. This line of thought culminated in the famous quip of Laplace (when asked by Napoleon what role God played in his celestial mechanics) that he had no need of that 'hypothesis' [22].

## 8.1. Probabilism and Spacetime Structure

Let $O$ and $O'$ be events on Bob's and Alice's worldlines respectively such that $O$, $O'$ are simultaneous in Bob's coordinates. Then we can easily see from Minkowski diagrams that the hyperplane of simultaneity in Alice's coordinates that passes through $O'$ wlll intersect Bob's worldline at some event-point $E$ which is later than $O$ (let us say it is a day later) in terms of proper time along Bob's worldline. Therefore, events that are optically simultaneous in Bob's system will not necessarily be optically simultaneous in Alice's, and vice versa. So if objective means invariant (and it is hard to see what else it could mean in relativistic terms), there is no objective way of partitioning spacetime by means of a hyperplane of simultaneity, and thus no way to ground a global ontological distinction between past and future.

Now, $E$ is tomorrow with respect to $O$ but today with respect to $O'$. However, $O'$ is today with respect to $O$; therefore, if the relation "today with respect to" is transitive then we end up with the uncomfortable result that $O$ and $E$ are today with respect to each other!

Of course, I am playing on an ambiguity. If 'today' means 'at the same date or time' then transitivity does not apply, since such judgements are valid only within a given coordinate system. However, if 'today' means something like ontologically coexistent, co-occurrent, co-present, or co-actual, we have a tougher problem, for whether or not something exists, and thus whether or not two events coexist or co-occur, can hardly be relative to a mere choice of viewpoint or coordinate system [171]. This follows from the common conception of such notions as marking an ontological distinction. (Perhaps this common conception of coexistence is wrong, but I have no idea what a sensible alternative would be.) In fact, by the usual conception, coexistence ought to define equivalence classes: whatever exists coexists with itself; if $e_1$ coexists with $e_2$, then $e_2$ coexists with $e_1$; and if $e_1$ coexists with $e_2$, and $e_2$ coexists with $e_3$, then surely $e_1$ coexists with respect to $e_3$. Therefore, if events that are at the same time in some coordinate system or other are deemed to coexist, then by transitivity all events in spacetime are ontologically equivalent, and change conceived of in the Aristotelian way is an illusion.

There are at least two ways in which one could avoid this conclusion (namely, the conclusion that from the relativity of simultaneity we infer that change is unreal). First, we could adopt a notion of becoming which relativizes becoming to world-points or worldlines. This is the position supported by Stein [214, 215] and Clifton and Hogarth [50]. Stein argued that all and only the points on the past cone of $O$ have become for $O$, and Clifton and Hogarth generalized this definition to worldlines. Their relativized conception of becoming has the advantage of precision but it thumbs its nose at the Aristotelian notion of change, according to which the distinction between what has become and what may become must be global.

Another approach, the one I advocate here, is to reject the assumption that two events could be coexistent if and only if their time coordinates are equal; in other words, it is to reject the usually unquestioned assumption that the time coordinate has as much metaphysical significance as is usually given to it. The new approach says that the time coordinate is merely a descriptive device, which need not necessarily be taken to track real physical or ontological changes. I call this approach 'new', but it has its roots in Aristotle's argument (*Physics B*) that time is merely a comparative scale used to keep track of motions, not motion itself.

If we want to track real physical changes (such as particle decay, physiological growth and ageing, or any other entropic process) in objects moving in a relativistic universe, the natural way to do it, as Richard Arthur [15, 16] has argued, is in terms of elapsed *proper* time. Consider the twin paradox, in which it is shown that initially identical twins who follow different paths through spacetime will, in general, be found to have aged by different amounts when they are brought together again at the end of their journeys. The physiological difference between the twins is strictly a function of their elapsed proper times. Hence, real physical changes are tied to proper time (or possibly, as we shall see, other proper quantities), not the time coordinate.

The usually unquestioned assumption that intrinsic physical change is tracked by the time coordinate is an outmoded holdover from the Newtonian worldview, where time is absolute— that is, the same (up to changes in scale) for all observers in all states of motion. It is long overdue that we move beyond this relic of bygone days, and get used to the idea that in a relativistic universe initially-standardized clocks can run at different rates depending on their acceleration history or exposure to gravitational fields.[3] It is not out of the question that two processes (either spatially distant or coincident) might well run at different rates (as judged in one frame of reference) and yet be somehow correlated or linked in some way physically. Thus, the door seems to be open to alternative notions of simultaneity that could give us more useful means to discuss non-local quantum processes, and might even allow us to define global distinctions between what has become, what is becoming, and what may become.

## 8.2 Generalizing Simultaneity

A more general notion of simultaneity is certainly required if we adopt any interpretation or extension of quantum mechanics that explicitly involves spacelike causation or influences. The details of Maxwell's theory need not concern us here, except the key point that it treats state reduction or collapse

---

[3]Of course, as a referee has pointed out to me, I have to be very careful about what I mean by saying that standardized clocks may run at different rates. In its momentarily comoving frame a clock will seem to maintain a constant rate even if it is in fact falling into a black hole. Clocks exposed to different accelerations may seem to run at different rates as judged in one frame of reference, however. Furthermore, if such clocks are brought back to rest with respect to each other they may be found to have different elapsed proper times even if they were synchronized to begin with.

as a real physical process, which must occur instantaneously. Bohm's theory does not involve state collapse, but changes in the quantum potential have to propagate faster than light, so one is still faced with essentially the same problem. Interpretations of quantum mechanics such as Bohm's or Maxwell's that entertain some sort of non-local 'connectedness' are controversial but cogent, and they need to be taken seriously. Indeed, one of their greatest weaknesses has always been that no clear way can be found of making them relativistically invariant (although de Broglie's largely neglected later version of the causal interpretation is already written in terms of four-quantities; see [54]). Examples of such theories are the causal interpretations of the Bohm/de Broglie type [32, 54] and Maxwell's 'propensiton' theory [140, 141, 142].

The problem is that 'instantaneous' (in the sense of 'occurring without time lapse') has no invariant meaning in special relativity, except in the sense in which two coincident events may be considered instantaneous with respect to each other. As pointed out by numerous authors (see especially [3, 4, 170], it is impossible to get a consistent description of quantum state reduction in spacetime if we assume that reduction occurs over hypersurfaces of constant time. We therefore need a generalized conception of instantaneity or simultaneity that could accommodate the non-locality of quantum mechanics. I will argue that such conceptions are available if we are willing, again, to drop the old Newtonian assumption that physical change must be linked to the time coordinate, and instead try to think in terms of relations between proper quantities along worldlines. I will now explore a thought experiment in this spirit.

## 8.3 Telepathic Twins?

In his science fiction novel *Time for the Stars* [107], Robert Heinlein proposed a whimsical thought experiment: what would follow if the twins in the twin paradox were telepathic? Would the twin who remains on Earth (Pat in the story) perceive his brother Tom's thoughts to be running slowly as Tom's spaceship approached the speed of light? And would Tom, conversely, perceive Pat's thoughts to be running fast? We know that at the end of the story Pat will have aged much more than Tom, but the usual view does not allow that there is any way of directly comparing their local (proper) clock rates during the voyage. But it is not entirely idle to think of what might pertain if there were such nonlocal interactions since, as noted, there is, arguably, a sort of 'telepathy' in quantum mechanics.

We set ourselves the following problem: if Pat attempts to communicate with Tom at a certain proper time $\tau$ along Pat's worldline, at what proper time $\tau'$ on Tom's worldline is the message received? We cannot tell this story without making a stipulation about how our hypothetical telepathy propagates in spacetime. Heinlein's answer was to suppose that telepathy is instantaneous in Earth's rest frame, or at least so close to instantaneous that its time-of-transmission over terrestrial distances would be undetectable. (Of course, Earth is orbiting all the time but the velocities involved are very small compared to the speed of light so we will take Earth as an approximate rest frame.) This means that Tom's and Pat's proper times (calculated from the beginning of the journey when the twins were coincident) will differ only because of their acceleration histories.

On the assumption that Pat remains on Earth throughout Tom's journey, and that Tom moves at constant velocity $\beta$, we get the familiar expression

$$\tau' = \sqrt{1 - \beta^2}\tau. \tag{8.1}$$

(This can be generalized to variable velocities.) Pat does indeed perceive his brother's thoughts to be running slow while Tom perceives Pat to be running fast.

Clifton and Hogarth [50] accurately pointed out that in my 1992 paper [161] paper I failed to make it clear that a global condition has to be imposed in order to avoid closed-loop paradoxes. (They made a similar criticism of an interesting proposal by F. A. Muller [150]). Clifton and Hogarth argued that it is necessary to specify a particular worldline (say Pat's) for which the telepathic interaction is deemed to be instantaneous, thereby defining the velocity of the interaction for all other telepaths in the universe. (F. Artzenius made essentially the same point in conversation in 1992.) More precisely, it is not so much that a certain worldline has to be privileged in this way, but that there has to be a spacelike hypersurface over which the interaction propagates superluminally; the interaction will then be instantaneous for any observer whose world-line happens to be orthogonal to that hypersurface.

The question is whether the postulation of such hypersurfaces of invariant simultaneity amounts to a violation of the Principle of Relativity. Clifton and Hogarth [50, p. 355] themselves state that this privileging of certain worldlines is 'unwarranted'. I will return to this important point, but first I want to note a very interesting feature of the Heinlein proposal.

## 8.4 Invariant Simultaneity as Equality of Action

I will show now that if we assume certain not-implausible initial conditions, the simultaneity relation Heinlein identifies can be stated elegantly in terms of equality of *action*.

Since Tom and Pat are assumed to be identical twins, we can take it that at the beginning of Tom's journey they both had the same initial energy $E_0$. At Pat's proper time $\tau$ he will possess an action $E_0\tau$. At any point in Tom's journey at which his relative velocity with respect to Pat is $\beta$, Tom will have energy as measured by Pat given by

$$E = E_0/\sqrt{1-\beta^2}. \tag{8.2}$$

Hence at such points Tom will have an action

$$E\tau' = E_0/\sqrt{1-\beta^2} \times \sqrt{1-\beta^2}\tau = E_0\tau. \tag{8.3}$$

That is, the world-points along Tom and Pat's worldlines that are simultaneous by the Heinlein criterion of 'adjusted' proper times have the same action, given plausible initial conditions. (Rietdijk [185] has also argued for a notion of invariant simultaneity defined in terms of action.) Of course, real twins on real spacecraft will exchange mass-energy with other systems during their journeys, but the story could be reformulated in terms of the very large number of identical elementary particles of which the twins are composed.

In fact, we could go farther and look at this from a cosmological point of view. If anything like the Big Bang picture is correct, in which all particles in the universe radiate from a singular initial state, the whole universe could be foliated by invariant hypersurfaces of action (perhaps possessing a rather complex topology). The interesting question is whether such action hypersurfaces could 'play a direct role as a determinant in physical processes' (as D. Dieks put it, [64, p. 456]. Later, I shall sketch an argument to show that something like this could indeed be the case; but we first turn to the very difficult question of whether any picture involving distinguished spacelike hypersurfaces such as I indicate here would be in an unacceptable conflict with the Principle of Relativity.

## 8.5  Conflicts with Relativity?

I will not be able to do justice here to the large question of the meaning of the Principle of Relativity. We can, however, say enough to rebut the charge that the kind of spacelike connectivity that I explore here is *necessarily* in conflict with relativity.

The Principle of Relativity expresses the postulate that the laws of physics take the same form in any physical frame. Special relativity follows from the assumption that the speed of light in vacuum is independent of the velocity of its source—which is, in effect, to say that it is itself a law of physics. The mathematical structure of Minkowski space and the Lorentz transformations follow from the assumption that the speed of light is an *invariant*, not an upper limit. Should the speed of light turn out to be a limit, that claim would be a theorem of the theory, not a postulate. (There are versions of relativity that take the limiting character of the speed of light as a postulate, but these theories are reconstuctions of Einstein's original theory.) The core principles of relativity do not explicitly prohibit spacelike propagation.

It is perfectly true that for any superluminal motion (even massless motions such as the searchlight beam effect which certainly do occur) there exists a state of motion in which the given superluminal process is instantaneous. This is merely a reflection of the fact that lor every spacelike worldline a frame of reference can be defined for which that worldline is one of the spatial axes.

Many authors believe that the invariant distinguishability of such frames is in conflict with the Principle of Relativity. Maxwell [140, p. 38], for instance, says that his own version of quantum theory which postulates superluminal collapse of spatially extensive 'propensitons' into very small volumes

> ...irreparably contradicts special relativity. For special relativity asserts that all inertial reference frames are physically equivalent. In only one reference frame, however, will any given probabilistic collapse of propensiton state be instantaneous; in other, relatively moving inertial reference frames the collapse will not, according to special relativity, be instantaneous (though always faster-than-light).

But surely the fact that any hypothetical superluminal propagation is instantaneous in one 'distinguished' frame does not violate the Principle of Relativity any more than the fact that any subluminal motion is associated with a distinguished frame (namely, the rest frame of the system). There is a nice near-symmetry between the subluminal and superluminal cases. Any subluminal propagation (such as a baseball flying through the air) will be at rest in one 'distinguished' frame (its local co-moving frame), but no one thinks that this violates the equivalence of reference frames. All that is required to satisfy the postulate of relativity is that in both the superluminal and subluminal cases, the description in any frame be consistent with that in any other, and this is possible so long as all such descriptions are understood as projections, as it were, into each frame of a single four-dimensional picture. There can be lots of frames of reference that can be 'distinguished' in the sense that they have some invariant characteristic. The instantaneous co-moving rest frame of any ordinary baseball is invariant in the sense that all other observers will agree on which state of motion is distinguished in this way. However, this distinction is contingent; it has to do with the acceleration history of that particular ball. The fact that there are invariant facts about the history of particular objects in spacetime does not violate the Principle of Relativity; they are privileged because of their *dynamical* history, not because of some exception to the laws of nature.

This point is difficult, so I shall repeat the essence of it: any subluminal object is at rest in one and only one frame; this frame is 'distinguished' in this way only for historical reasons (that is, only because of the history of the moving object), and its existence does not break the Principle of Relativity. Similarly, any superluminal system moves at infinite speed in one and only one frame, and this frame is also 'distinguished' only for historical reasons, and its existence does not violate the Principle of Relativity.

The equivalence of reference frames does not mean that everything looks the same in every possible state of motion—far from it. Rather, it means that the way things look in all the various possible reference frames are consistent

## 8.5. Conflicts with Relativity?

with one another in certain specific respects—namely that they respect the invariance of certain quantities such as the vacuum speed of light and, in general, the magnitudes of four-vectors such as the energy-momentum or position-time four-vectors. The only sort of phenomenon that would truly violate the Principle of Relativity (in its most general conception) would be something that depended only on the observer's position or state of motion, in such a peculiar way that it could not be seen as an aspect of some structure or process that had an equivalent description from other viewpoints. What would violate Lorentz invariance (which is not the most general sort of invariance) would not be superluminal propagation, but the breakdown of the non-dispersivity of the vacuum—a possibility that must, in fact, be taken most seriously [8, 209].

Clifton and Hogarth's worry is subtler than Maxwell's. Their austere aim was to see to what extent it is possible to define objective becoming relations in Minkowski spacetime whose 'recipe' is based 'solely on time-oriented metrical relations' [50, p. 379]. In this they took their lead from Stein, who said that any interesting becoming relation should be 'definable in terms of the geometric structure' [215, p. 149]. As Dorato puts it, in 'Stein's proof the main requirement that a becoming relation should satisfy to be regarded as objective in Minkowski spacetime is definability in terms of the geometric structure of the spacetime' [67, p. 588]. But why restrict the inquiry in this way? If one wants to investigate alternative conceptions of simultaneity that could support a global past-future distinction, the interesting question is not what *metrical* structures can *necessarily* be found in *all* time-oriented spacetimes, while assuming from the outset that there are no spacelike dynamical interactions. (To be fair to Clifton and Hogarth, it is mainly Stein who hung his hat on the latter point.) It is about what *dynamical* structures can *possibly* occur in *some* time-oriented systems, whlle *allowing* for the possibility of spacelike dynamics. The aim is to determine what is possible, not what is necessary. I decided that I would be very happy to find a class of *contingent* structures that can represent a simultaneity-like relation in spacetime so long as they had a covariant description—which both the Heinlein criterion and the action-equality criterion certainly do. But whether or not the specific suggestions explored here can be made to work, the central point is to see that covariant notions of simultaneity could be based on *dynamic* facts (facts about the spacetime distribution of matter, energy, particles, and fields) as well as purely metrical facts, because dynamical relations in spacetime are also covariant, and because simultaneity relations are relations between physical changes in actual physical systems.

The toughest problem with any sort of hypothetical superluminal connection or motion is that it may permit closed-loop paradoxes, in which events can apparently occur if and only if they do not occur! The full solution of this problem may involve thermodynamic or information-theoretic considerations that are outside the scope of special relativity. However, it is very reasonable to suppose that the frame of reference in which quantum collapses or interactions occur is somehow defined cosmologically. In cosmology, we already accept the fact that there is a cosmic rest frame defined by the cosmic background radiation (CBR). This involves no conflict with the Principle of Relativity, though, any more than does the fact that the floor of my office can in principle be used as a universal standard of rest. The CBR frame is, for reasons of cosmological history, merely the largest physical framework that we can identify. So as long as we can find a cosmological story about which frame of reference quantum 'telepathy' is instantaneous in, and so long as we can tell this story in four-dimensional Lorentz-invariant manner, there is no conflict with the Principle of Relativity.[4]

In sum, the indisputable fact that optical simultaneity is frame-dependent is simply *irrelevant* to whether there can be frame-independent conceptions of simultaneity. There could be any number of invariant simultaneity relations (many, no doubt, trivial—but not all) between spacelike separate points on worldlines so long as they are defined in terms of relations between *proper* quantities along those worldlines.

## 8.6 Covariant State Reduction Based on Phase Invariance

I will now make a quick pass at the very difficult question of finding a covariant description of state reduction—enough, I hope, to show that the usual discussions of this problem are hobbled by the same unwarranted assumption that has plagued discussions of becoming. The idea I consider here is very simple in essence, though it may turn out to be complicated in its application to concrete cases. If the sort of theory that I sketch here can be made to work, then it is not the case, *pace* Maxwell, that any sort of quantum theory involving state reduction necessarily contradicts special relativity.

Any wave packet in spacetime is a superposition of plane waves (de Broglie waves, or pure momentum states), which have the general form

$$\Psi(x,t) = a_0 e^{i(\mathbf{p}\cdot\mathbf{x}/\hbar)} \tag{8.4}$$

where $(\mathbf{x}, t)$ and $(\mathbf{p}, H)$ are the position time and momentum-energy four-vectors, respectively. Now, if a wave packet reduces, by linearity this amounts simply to the disappearance of some of the plane waves of which it is composed. If we know how an individual plane wave can blink out covariantly we know how a wave packet does it. So we begin by looking for covariant features of plane waves, and an obvious candidate is phase—intuitively, where we are in the cycle. A covariant way for a plane wave to 'blink out' is for it to disappear at the same point in its cycle for all observers. That is, we can get a covariant

---

[4] An anonymous referee asked whether I claim that 'different cosmological models may have different simultaneity properties, and may lack simultaneity relations at all?' The short answer to this question is yes, of course—although a cosmology with no interesting simultaneity relations would probably have a structure that was either chaotic or degenerate in some sense.

## 8.7. Quantum Mechanics and the Ontology of the Future

description of state reduction if we specify that if a particular component of a wave packet disappears at (say) 54° along in its cycle as a consequence of a measurement interaction, then all observers will agree that this is the case. A condition that can form the basis for a truly covariant description of state reduction, therefore, is *phase invariance*.

Now, we can relate this in an interesting way to our observation above in the telepathic twin scenario about equality of action as a simultaneity criterion. Suppose a given component of a wave packet pops out of existence at two spacetime points $(\mathbf{x}, r)$ and $(\mathbf{x}', t')$, with associated points $(\mathbf{p}, H)$ and $(\mathbf{p}', H')$ in momentum-energy space. By the equality of phase criterion, these must be related such that

$$(\mathbf{p} \cdot \mathbf{x} - Ht) = (\mathbf{p}' \cdot \mathbf{x}' - H't'). \tag{8.5}$$

But this is, again, simply equality of action.

A lot of work still needs to be done in order to make this proposal workable for complicated realistic cases, such as correlated wave packets in multiparticle systems. It is also by no means clear that foliations of spacetime in terms of the hypersurfaces of state reduction of the myriad entangled quantum systems in the universe will smooth out to something approximating a global present that would correspond to the ordinary sense of becoming perceived at the physiological level. The topology of the 'present' defined by quantum mechanics might correspond only roughly to the present as humans experience it, and there is no reason to think that the hypersurfaces over which state functions reduce are hyperplanes or that they do not have a complicated topology (connectivity). Still, the crucial point we can take away from this introductory discussion is this: if we free ourselves from the Newtonian assumption that state reduction is tied to hyperplanes of equal *time*, a covariant description of state reduction is open to us.[5]

## 8.7 Quantum Mechanics and the Ontology of the Future

I said at the beginning that the argument of this paper amounts largely to undergrowth clearance, in that what I say here is not sufficient to decide the question of becoming. It removes an obstacle to the notion of global objective becoming (namely, the assumption that the relativity of coordinate simultaneity precludes a covariant notion of global presentness), but it is still conceivable that the covariant phase surfaces identified here are simply structures within a four-dimensional plenum, with no special significance other than their interest for that small coterie of humans who entertain themselves with philosophy

---

[5]Richard Arthur (private communication) has pointed out to me that somewhat similar ideas were introduced quite some time ago by Eddington [73] and Dobbs [66], who argued that a notion of simultaneity appropriate to quantum mechanics could be defined in terms of what they called 'phase time'. As noted, Rietdijk [185] has also suggested a notion of simultaneity in terms of equality of action. I hope to explore these parallels in a future work.

of physics. Suppose there are, in fact, sets of space-like separate event-pairs that are correlated by quantum mechanics in a way that is both covariant and physically interesting. This, by itself, does not prove that there is objective becoming. Philosophically, we would be right back where we started, although perhaps with a greater appreciation of the richness of spacetime structure.

Clearly, Maxwell is right that if there is any route to an ontologically open future, it has to be through quantum physics. But even my notion of state reduction in terms of phase invariance is probably not enough to do the job Maxwell wants done; this is hardly surprising, since my theory is still semiclassical (if, for no other reason, because it assumes continuity of action). The best way to find a quantum argument for the openness of the future would probably be to appeal to deep facts about the irreconcilable inconsistencies between the non-Boolean mathematics of quantum mechanics and the classical Boolean picture. A genuinely quantum argument for the openness of the future would be parallel to other 'no-go' theorems that show certain classical (i.e., Boolean) structures to be impossible [44]; in other words, such an argument would be a Kochen-Specker paradox. One would attempt to show that given a definite assignment of physical values over some point or region (such as a phase surface) taken to be 'the present', and given the evolution of the so-defined state according to the dynamics of quantum mechanics, the assumption of definite properties in the future relative to that point or region would generate a contradiction. (By 'definite' I mean that the future would already contain answers to all of the possible experimental questions we could ask of it.) In other words, one would try to show that according to quantum mechanics, the future cannot admit of a Boolean property structure. This might not be necessary in order to establish the ontological openness of the future, but it certainly would be sufficient. I do not for a moment think that this project—to show in all generality that by quantum mechanics the future is non-Boolean—would be easy, although in a sense it has already been accomplished, if we presume that existing Kochen-Specker arguments say something about the possible futures that are open to quantum-mechanical experimenters.

One of the major interpretational problems faced by any attempt to find a non-question-begging accommodation between quantum theory and special relativity is whether any such enterprise would turn out to remove special relativity from its present status as a 'principle theory'. The working assumption of most theorists since the early days of the twentieth century has been that quantum mechanics must somehow in the end turn out to be consistent with relativity. In this spirit, we construct quantum field theories against a classical Minkowski backdrop, and we even believe that we are justified in imposing special 'patches' (such as the principle of microcausality) on the generality of quantum theory so as to avoid conflict with relativity. (See [160, 121, 168] for critiques of the generally accepted notion of 'peaceful coexistence' between relativity and quantum theory.)

## 8.7. Quantum Mechanics and the Ontology of the Future

My own view (which is very similar to the position advocated by Misner, Thorne, and Wheeler [146]) is that relativity theory as it presently stands is a classical limiting approximation to a yet-to-be-developed quantum theory of spacetime that will bear a relation to the present classical picture something like the relation between the quantum and classical theory of fluids, or classical and quantum statistical mechanics [163]. A full and proper consideration of the implications of quantum mechanics for spacetime structure will probably result in a theory that is, in effect, a sort of quantum statistical mechanics of spacetime, in which special relativity is demoted to a limit-case idealization. Nevertheless, we can come far closer than is usually supposed to accommodate many of the non-classical features of quantum mechanics (such as state reduction) within classical relativity. The key is to see that there can be alternative conceptions of simultaneity based upon *contingent* relationships between *proper* quantities along worldlines.[6]

---

[6] I thank Richard Arthur, J. R. Brown, Rob Clifton, Alex Korolev, Vesselin Petkov, Graham Solomon, and participants in the First International Conference on the Ontology of Spacetime (Concordia University, Montréal, Québec, Canada, May 11–14, 2004) for stimulating discussions. I also thank three anonymous referees for helpful comments. Financial support for this investigation came from the Social Sciences and Humanities Research Council of Canada, the University of Lethbridge, and the University of Western Ontario.

# Chapter 9

# The No-Signalling Theorems: A Nitpicking Distinction[1]

> It seems to me that it is among the most sure-footed of quantum physicists, those who have it *in their bones*, that one finds the greatest impatience with the idea that the 'foundations of quantum mechanics' might need some attention. Knowing what is right by instinct, they can become a little impatient with nitpicking distinctions between theorems and assumptions.
> 
> —John Stewart Bell [26, p. 33]

> Pronouncements by experts to the effect that something cannot be done have always annoyed me.
> 
> —Leo Szilard [184, p. 28]

## 9.1 An Occasion for Pain?

Shortly before his untimely death, John Stewart Bell remarked that his famous theorem tells us 'that maybe there must be something happening faster than light, *although it pains me even to say that much*' [emphasis added] [132, p. 90]. Bell's reaction to his own momentous discovery is puzzling: why should it have *pained* him or anyone else? Should we not be excited and fascinated by the possibility of superluminality, and want to learn as much about it as possible—instead of trying to deny its reality or minimize its importance? I'll return to this question later in this paper; first, I want to critically review the orthodox argument for what Abner Shimony has called 'peaceful coexistence' between

---

[1]This paper was written in 2009 and submitted to an essay contest run by the Foundational Questions Institute (FQXi) on the question of fundamental limiting results in physics. It didn't win a prize, but it ended up circulating on the Internet as a sort of *samizdat* where it apparently attracted some attention. Jack Sarfatti proposed to include it in a collection of papers he was editing, but he kindly let me have it back for *Quantum Heresies*.

quantum mechanics and relativity [201]. The term peaceful coexistence was used by Shimony ironically[2] and was meant to suggest that while quantum mechanics apparently subscribes to a nonlocal ideology, it does not threaten the standard interpretation of special relativity because quantum mechanics does not permit the exploitation of nonlocality for *controllable* faster-than-light signalling. Thus, according to this doctrine, a compromise is possible which (like some kind of analgesic) masks the metaphysical pain occasioned in many physicists by nonlocality, even if it does not correct the underlying pathology.

There are numerous no-signalling proofs in the literature. Recently, an especially clear review of the problem has been given by Clare Hewitt-Horsmann, who claims that no-signalling (which she calls 'statistical locality') relies on 'only one prior assumption' namely that the probability distribution is given by Born's Rule,

$$\text{Prob}(x) = |\langle \Psi(x)|\Psi(x)\rangle|^2. \tag{9.1}$$

Because this is such a 'foundational part of quantum mechanics,' Hewitt-Horsmann says 'it is safe to say that the conclusion that statistical locality must be obeyed is an extremely strong one' [110, p. 886]. As a general methodological rule, one should be suspicious of mathematical rigor in physical arguments, especially when they are arguments designed to *exclude* a possibility. Rigor may indeed be a sign of the operation of a principle of great generality (such as Born's Rule). However, it can also be a sign that crucial physical factors have been ignored, or even a mere consequence of a problem having been defined in such a way as to guarantee a preconceived result. As Bertrand Russell once sardonically remarked, 'It is one of the chief merits of proofs that they instil a certain scepticism as to the result proved' (quoted in [126, p. 48]). The point is hardly that one should eschew rigor, but rather that one should ensure that one has proven what was actually to have been proven. I will argue here that despite their apparent rigor the widely accepted arguments for peaceful coexistence do not establish what most people think they establish and do not investigate the questions that actually need to be investigated.

## 9.2 The Problem

Let us illustrate the problem of signalling with the assistance of the ubiquitous experimenters Alice and Bob. We will place Alice and Bob at some distance apart, and between them there will be a source emitting pairs of entangled particles. To avoid relativistic complications we will assume that Alice, Bob, their detectors, and the particle source are all mutually at rest in an inertial frame (the 'lab' frame). Pair after pair of particles are emitted by the source and detected by Alice and Bob's apparatuses, who record their results. Alice and Bob are free to alter the angle of their detectors with each run of the apparatus.

---

[2] I have heard it said that Shimony 'did not have an ironical bone in his body', but in 1993 I asked him in conversation whether his usage was ironic and he told me that it was.

What each experimenter will record is an apparently random sequence of ups and downs, like the results of an honest coin repeatedly tossed; and yet, when they compare results afterward, they will note that certain correlations, generally sinusoidal in form, stand between their results. For example, if the particles are spin-1/2 fermions, and if Alice and Bob are measuring spin in a particular direction, then the correlation between their results will be $-\cos\theta_{AB}$, where $\theta_{AB}$ is the angle between Alice and Bob's detectors. Sinusoidal correlations like these readily violate mathematical inequalities such as those defined by Bell [25]. Itamar Pitowsky [174] showed that the Bell Inequalities are examples of 'conditions of possible experience' first written down by George Boole; these are consistency conditions between measurement results on the assumption that the results of one measurement and the way it is carried out does not influence the measurement of the other particle *at the time of measurement*. This means that there is only a vanishingly small probability that the particular sequence of results that Alice and Bob get at their respective detectors could have been encoded in the particles at the source; for some relative angles their results are too well correlated or anti-correlated for there to be any appreciable chance that they were due to local causes built into both particles when they were emitted.

If Alice and Bob are siblings they likely would resemble each other more than they tend to resemble other people chosen at random from the general population. This is due simply to the fact that they had the same parents and thus have more similar DNA than two people picked at random. Einstein, Podolsky, and Rosen [78] thought it was beyond discussion that there had to be some sort of 'quantum DNA' carried by elementary particles that would cause them to obey the correlations predicted by quantum mechanics. Since the work of Bell in 1964 [25] we know this is mathematically impossible: there is no 'DNA' that can account for the correlations of results in entangled states. Pitowsky [174] emphasized that if one insists that there be an explanation for the violation of the Bell/Boole inequalities there are very few mathematical options other than some sort of 'measurement bias'—an influence of one measurement on the outcome of the other. And given that Alice and Bob make their measurements at a spacelike separation, the influence, whatever it may be, has to operate faster than the speed of light.

Now, what will happen if Alice decides that she would like to exploit this mysterious influence to send messages in code to Bob faster than light? Suppose she tries to do this by varying her detector angle from run to run of the apparatus, hoping that this will impose a signal on Bob's local results. It won't work as Alice hoped, for both she and Bob will continue to record sequences of results that look entirely random. However, what Alice can indeed do—and this is a most interesting accomplishment in itself—is encode a message in the *correlations*, for the correlations, as noted, are a function of relative detector angle. This phenomenon is the basis for quantum cryptography, which is likely

## 9.3. The 'Proofs'

the most theoretically secure form of encryption; because both experimenters' local results are random the message cannot be decoded from one set of results alone, but each set of results serves as a key in combination with the other.

Alice is still not satisfied, however, and now she tries to *force* her particles to go either up or down in her detector. She could likely do this by interposing additional electromagnetic fields in just the right way. But she still won't be able to signal to Bob, for she will discover that she has destroyed the nonlocality: if Alice forces her particles to go one way or the other, not only will Bob's local results stay random, but the correlations between her results and Bob's will obey a Bell Inequality.

Alice's inability to control her local results without washing out the nonlocal correlations seems to be just a technical problem; surely, Alice might think, if she could simply interact with her particles more *gently* or if there were some way to make the nonlocal connection between the particles *stronger*, then she ought to be able to influence Bob's local statistics. The authors of the no-signalling proofs insist that Alice's problems are not merely technical; instead, they say, there are deep reasons of principle why Alice, no matter how carefully she may interact with her particles, cannot hope to influence Bob's local statistics.

### 9.3 The 'Proofs'

Many papers have been published setting forth alleged proofs that there is nothing Alice can do to influence Bob's local statistics, and there is not space here to review them all. (See [160, 121].) They fall into two broad categories, those that use the tools of non-relativistic quantum mechanics, and those within local quantum field theory.

#### 9.3.1 Non-Relativistic No-Signalling Proofs

We'll look at non-relativistic no-signalling arguments first, since this is the type of proof cited by Hewitt-Horsman [110]. There are many algebraic variants of these proofs but they depend upon essentially the same physical assumptions. Hewitt-Horsman is correct that these arguments use key elements of the basic formalism of quantum mechanics, such as the Born Rule. However, they also depend upon a crucial physical assumption that many authors, apparently including Hewitt-Horsman, think is so natural that it does not even need to be acknowledged as a special assumption. Let $\mathcal{O}_{AB}$ be the operator representing the effect of Alice's measurement procedure upon the Hilbert space of the combined entangled system (that is, the tensor product space representing Bob's distant particle as well as Alice's). Let $\mathcal{O}_A$ be the operator representing Alice's measurement in the subspace of her particle, and let $\mathbb{1}_B$ be the identity operator in Bob's subspace. The crucial *physical* assumption that drives the non-relativistic no-signalling arguments is that Alice's measurement operation acts only trivially on Bob's subspace:

$$\mathcal{O}_{AB} = \mathcal{O}_A \otimes \mathbb{1}_B. \tag{9.2}$$

With this assumption in hand, Bob's local statistics remain the same regardless of what choice of measurement parameters Alice makes when interacting with her particle. It is fairly straightforward to demonstrate this result, although some no-signalling papers accomplish the task by means of some truly impressive algebraic machinery. Machinery notwithstanding, what is going on in these arguments is very simple: one *assumes* that Alice does not have a physical effect on Bob's side of the system, and then shows that a *confirmation* of this assumption can be extracted from the quantum mechanical formalism. Viewed uncharitably, such no-signalling arguments amount to little more than trivial consistency checks of the formalism, for all they say is that an operator that is *assumed* to not act in a subspace does not change the statistics in that subspace. Such arguments are completely powerless to tell us whether anything that Alice can do to her particle does *in fact* have a superluminal physical effect on Bob's particle. But surely, *that* is what we really need to find out.

It is possible to view such no-signalling arguments in a slightly more positive light, for one can say they do at least demonstrate that Alice could not influence Bob's local statistics *without* the aid of some sort of superluminal dynamics. We can't get controllable signalling in quantum mechanics without actually expending some free energy on the receiving device any more than we can with any other kind of signalling; one could say, then, that the conventional no-signalling arguments also amount to a confirmation of the Second Law of Thermodynamics in the sense that no transmission of information can be accomplished without the expenditure of free energy. But again, the standard no-signalling arguments do not *prove* that there is no such superluminal dynamics, but instead *assume* that proposition.

A few papers attempt to establish no-signalling in non-relativistic quantum systems by directly assuming that the Hamiltonian of the combined system of experimenters and particles is local [202]. This means that the total Hamiltonian of the combined entangled state together with Alice and Bob's detectors is simply the sum of the Hamiltonian on Alice's side and the Hamiltonian on Bob's side:

$$\mathcal{H}_{AB} = \mathcal{H}_A + \mathcal{H}_B. \tag{9.3}$$

The authors of such proofs thereby take it that the Hamiltonians of multiparticle systems are never entangled even if the states of the system, expressed in terms of other observables on the system, are entangled—for entangled states of any observable, including energy, in general cannot be represented as a simple sum of local properties of individual particles.

This line of argument at least has the merit of not being quite so obviously question-begging, in that it makes explicit its assumptions about the dynamics

## 9.3. The 'Proofs'

of the system. But it also rests upon essentially the same unproven assumption as the algebraic approaches described above, for there is no proof that in general all of the energy states of an entangled system are local. Indeed, there are good reasons to think that energy in quantum systems is nonlocal, or at least has a nonlocal component. To see this, one need only think of the energy of an atomic orbital, which cannot be said to be localized until a portion of it is emitted in an atomic transition. Bohm's quantum potential is an explicitly nonlocal form of energy, and it can be shown to be entangled for entangled states [52]. Energy-entangled states appear in recent studies of nonlocal interferometry [88, 128]. The requirements of symmetrization based on the fact that all particles obey either Bose-Einstein or Fermi-Dirac statistics also point to terms in the Hamiltonians of multi-particle systems that do not break down neatly into localizable parts (see Chapter 11). There is also a thermodynamic argument for the nonlocality of energy in entangled states: if a number of particles interact and thereby become nonlocally correlated, the entropy of the ensemble decreases (equivalently, its mutual information increases) and this is only possible if there is energy associated with the mutual information of the system above and beyond the local energies of the particles in it. Finally, lurking behind modern theoretical physics is the puzzle of the nonlocality of gravitational energy in general relativity, which is a consequence of the Equivalence Principle [146].[3] It remains to be seen whether the nonlocality of gravitational energy has anything to do with quantum mechanics, but it gives further support to the idea that nonlocal energy must be taken seriously. In view of such considerations, there is no basis for assuming without argument that the energy of entangled states is entirely local to the particles of which it is composed, and thus no basis for a no-signalling proof on this assumption—except, possibly, when fluctuations in the system are such that its *effective* Hamiltonian has the form (9.3).

### 9.3.2 Field-Theoretic Proofs

The other major strategy used in no-signalling proofs is to appeal to a principle of local quantum field theory (LQFT) called microcausality or (in some books) local commutativity. This is a postulate that all observables acting at a spacelike separation commute, even if they are observables (such as position and momentum) that would not commute if they were acting on the same system locally. It is fairly straightforward to arrive at a no-signalling result given microcausality [70]. Most, but not all, authors of such proofs are careful to assert that all they really meant to prove is that within LQFT microcausality is equivalent to no-signalling. The possibility certainly exists of a nonlocal

---

[3] As Misner, Thorne, and Wheeler explain (§20.4), the gravitational field itself has energy—gravitation gravitates. But by the Equivalence Principle, a gravitational field can always be transformed away locally. Therefore the energy of a gravitational field configuration cannot, in general, be localized in spacetime, at least in an invariant way.

quantum field theory either in which microcausality could be derived without the expedient of bare postulation or in which one would find circumstances in which it was violated. But the historical fact remains that microcausality was *written into* LQFT by its founders (such as Pauli) precisely in order to preempt predictions of signalling. Microcausality can therefore be thought of as a sort of security patch, downloaded, as it were, into the structure of field theory in order to prevent conflict with the orthodox interpretation of relativity, and any presumption that it provides for a completely general prohibition on signalling is question-begging [160, 147].

### 9.3.3 The Dissenters

The literature on the signalling problem is huge, and I can't hope to do justice to it here, even its heretical branches. As far as I know, the first author to publish doubts about the conventional wisdom regarding signalling was P.J. Bussey [45], who in 1987 suggested that the standard no-signalling proofs depend upon 'ad hoc' assumptions. I published a short review of the problem in 1992 [160] in which I outlined a taxonomy of the various methods that have been used to demonstrate no-signalling, and argued that they are all question-begging. A longer and more detailed treatment was published by J B. Kennedy in 1995 [121], and in 1998 Peter Mittelstaedt published much the same conclusions as Kennedy and myself about the circularity of the local field theoretic arguments [147]. Similar worries are expressed in a recent paper by Steve Weinstein [232].

### 9.3.4 A Historical Perspective

I have been describing the conventional approach to the signalling problem as if it were a methodological error, and it is, but it is helpful to see it in the context of the history of modern physics. This is also somewhat fairer to those who have advocated peaceful coexistence, for the approach they have taken, although *now* clearly outmoded, was reasonable given the challenges and priorities faced by physicists in the early years of quantum mechanics and quantum field theory.

In the very early years of quantum mechanics, even before Heisenberg enunciated his uncertainty relations in 1927, physicists such as Max Born speculated that the very notion of a classical spacetime would break down in the face of quantum discontinuities. The question opened by a few far-seeing physicists, even at this time, was whether ways could be found of constructing spacetime *from* quantum mechanics. As it became increasingly apparent that in some sense all physics is quantum physics, it began to seem natural to suppose that the whole relativistic theory of spacetime might be merely a classical approximation or limiting case of a deeper quantum theory of spacetime—a quantum theory of gravity. The relation between the theory of relativity and quantum gravity might be something like the relation between the classical and quantum theory of liquids. It soon became apparent, however, that constructing a quantum theory of gravitation or spacetime was just too difficult, especially when, in the 1930s and 1940s, physicists were faced with the more immediate crisis of the infinities of quantum electrodynamics and the burgeoning 'particle zoo.' Physicists found it necessary to adopt a much more conservative approach. They accepted Einstein's view that special relativity is a 'principle theory'—a background into which other theories should fit. Add to this a general suspicion, probably endemic to physicists all the way back to the time of Newton, of the notion of action at a distance, and it seemed eminently reasonable to the framers of the brash new theory of quantum mechanics to assume that relativity is logically prior to it and that it should therefore not contradict relativity. As they attempted to axiomatize quantum mechanics and the field theory that was growing out of it, they deliberately restricted the generality of quantum theory by imposing the postulate of microcausality and (even in the face of entanglement) the assumption that spacelike separation guaranteed dynamic separability. This approach was reinforced by the dominance of the Copenhagen interpretation of quantum mechanics, which held that the classical level of description is (in some obscure sense) independent of the quantum level.

This conservative approach, in which quantum processes are taken to occur against a classical, locally-Minkowski background, allowed for the development of very powerful and predictively effective quantum field theories. However, as Lee Smolin and other proponents of quantum gravity have argued [210], the conservative approach is no longer open to us since the task now is to show how to construct spacetime out of quantum mechanics—not shoehorn quantum mechanics into spacetime. The problem of peaceful coexistence therefore bears on very current and contentious debates about how to construct quantum gravity in a background-independent way, and how much of the classical picture of spacetime will be left when that large task is accomplished. I do not take lightly the task of constructing a genuinely nonlocal quantum field theory that would actually work and would contain present local quantum theory and relativity as limiting cases. There is no reason to suppose that when this large task is accomplished, however, that the familiar, almost comforting, causal structure of Minkowski space will be anything more than a (frequently useful) approximation. There can no longer be any justification for assuming *without argument* that the predictions of quantum mechanics must not conflict with relativity.

## 9.4 Where the Investigation of Signalling Might Go

Even if practical superluminal communication as such is never feasible, controllable nonlocality may have other possible applications, and I shall briefly mention two that are not as far-fetched as they might immediately seem. First, it has not been appreciated that a quantum computer would amount to a superluminal communication device in the sense that both have to do the same thing: extract information from an entangled state without collapsing the state. As with Alice's communicator, reasonable approaches to explore would include the use of protective, or non-demolition measurements, and finding ways of pumping up the coupling strength of the nonlocal interaction. One can imagine that this could also have applications to the search for high $T_c$ superconductors. There, the barrier has been that quantum coherence is disrupted by thermal randomness, and again the solution could be to find a way—conceivably *via* some sort of resonance phenomenon—to strengthen the nonlocal interaction.[4]

Aharonov *et al.* published a signalling scheme in 2004 based on the notion that protective measurements could allow a way of extracting information from an entangled state without collapsing it [1]. Their scheme would only allow for signalling under limited conditions but it is quite immune to the assumptions used in the standard no-signalling arguments. If anything like what Aharonov and his colleagues propose could be made to work, then nonlocality is normally uncontrollable only because the nonlocal dynamics of entangled states are very weak and thereby easily perturbed by standard measurement procedures. Perhaps Alice was right after all: the key to signalling would be either to create very robust entangled states (perhaps by using a large number of phase-coherent particles as in a Bose-Einstein condensate) or (as in Aharonov *et al.*'s scheme) by using a very gentle measurement interaction. Every effort should be made to find out whether it is actually possible to build an apparatus such as that envisioned by Aharonov *et al.*

## 9.5 Causal Paradoxes and the 'Spirit of Relativity'

Part of the metaphysical pain occasioned in many physicists by nonlocality stems from the fact that it seems to violate something called the 'spirit of relativity.' I have never seen a precise explanation of the scientific meaning of this phrase, and it seems to be not much more than a vague prejudice against talk of spacelike physics.

Bell himself had more specific worries about the causal paradoxes that would apparently arise if superluminal effects could be controlled [27]. It is easy to show that if Alice and Bob can send signals at arbitrary velocities then causal paradoxes can be set up. The causal paradoxes of superluminality are a genuine problem to which I do not have a complete answer. We can say enough, however, to show that worries about causation should not be sufficient to lead us to rule the possibility of superluminal effects out of court *ab initio*.

There are two kinds of causal paradoxes that are connected with superluminality, *one-way* and *two-way* or *closed-loop* paradoxes. In a one-way paradox, Alice sends a superluminal signal to Bob. In some frames of reference

---

[4] I have since learned that Jack Sarfatti has proposed something along these lines, based on the far-seeing ideas of H. Fröhlich [89].

Bob receives the signal at an earlier time coordinate than when Alice launches it. The 'paradox' is that this conflicts with our familiar sense that causation always runs forward in time. In a two-way paradox, Bob sends a response back to Alice in such a way that she receives it at an earlier proper time on her worldline than when she sent her message. This seems to open the door to outright *logical* paradox, because presumably Bob could send a message that would negate Alice's initial transmission.

Whatever causation may be, it is clearly something that goes along particle worldlines. For causal connections inside and on the light cone, the direction of causation is the same for all worldlines, and with a suitable choice of conventions it can be made the same as the direction of time in all Lorentz frames. For causal connections outside the light cone, if any, the direction of causation may differ from the direction of time in some Lorentz frames. Bell thought this was unacceptable [27], but I submit that this is merely an odd effect; one-way paradoxes are not logical, but merely involve a conflict with essentially Newtonian (and thus outmoded) intuitions about causation.

Now let us suppose that there is some way in which Alice and Bob can exchange superluminal messages *via* a spatially-extensive entangled state. Bell himself was well aware that we can avoid closed-loop paradoxes if the velocity of the messages, although superluminal, has an upper limit such that Bob's return message to Alice always hits Alice's worldline at a later proper time than when she sent her initial message. Bell was deeply troubled by the notion that all nonlocal quantum interactions might have a maximum velocity, since he feared it would imply that there is a 'preferred frame' whose existence would violate the Principle of Relativity.

The idea that all particles in the universe are entangled in a completely consistent way is not unreasonable, given that something like the Big Bang theory is probably true. But this does not imply a violation of the Principle of Relativity any more than does the existence of the cosmic background radiation (CBR) rest frame. That is the state of motion in which there is no Doppler shift in the cosmic background radiation. It defines a sort of *de facto* standard of rest for the whole universe but it does not violate the Principle of Relativity in any way since the CBR rest frame is defined by cosmological history, not by some violation of frame-equivalence in fundamental law. It is well known that history can break fundamental symmetries. There is almost certainly something similar going on in the case of quantum nonlocality. Quantum nonlocality should not be an occasion for metaphysical or logical pain, but it is still going to take some getting used to.

## 9.6 The Limits of the Possible

The quest to define the limits of the physically possible is, of course, a legitimate and indeed necessary scientific enterprise. But we have to take care that we really have surveyed all relevant possibilities. The history of science is littered with the wreckage of failed impossibility 'proofs,' and Bell has warned us that 'what is proved by impossibility proofs is lack of imagination' [24, p. 167]. Bell was not talking specifically about the signalling problem when he wrote these words, but they apply to it. It seems highly likely that a few things really are just impossible, but perhaps not as many as one thinks in a quantum world, where 'impossible' often means nothing more than 'highly improbable' or 'usually highly improbable.' The problem of quantum signalling is of interest not only in itself, but also as a case study in the larger problem of determining when an apparent limit in nature is a genuine limit or merely the result of an attempt to define an awkward phenomenon out of existence. I claim that the latter is precisely what has happened around the signalling problem. As Bell pointedly remarked, nature is telling us that something is going faster than light in quantum mechanically entangled systems, and to date there is *no* proof either that Bell was wrong about this or that such superluminal effects could not be controlled in ways that so far we can only sketchily imagine. If nonlocality *can* be controlled we need to learn as much as we can about how to do it, *soon*. If the doctrine of peaceful coexistence is correct after all and nonlocality *cannot* be controlled, we need to prove this from the first principles of a theory of quantum gravity, when they are finally available, and not merely build it into physical theory as an assumption.[5]

---

[5] The author thanks Richard Arthur, Bryson Brown, James Robert Brown, Sheldon Chow, Rob Clifton, Robert DiSalle, P. H. Eberhard, Christopher Fuchs, Brian S. Hepburn, J. B. Kennedy Jr., Jordan Maclay, Wayne Myrvold, Cody Perrin, Itamar Pitowsky, Abner Shimony, and Sharon Simmers for helpful advice, discussion, or assistance. None of these people are responsible for any misconceptions that may have found their way into this paper. Thanks are due also to the University of Lethbridge and the Social Sciences and Humanities Research Council of Canada for financial support, and the Perimeter Institute for support and hospitality.

## Chapter 10

# Would Superluminal Influences Violate the Principle of Relativity?[1]

**Abstract**  It continues to be alleged that superluminal influences of any sort would be inconsistent with special relativity for the following three reasons: (i) they would imply the existence of a 'distinguished' frame; (ii) they would allow the detection of absolute motion; and (iii) they would violate the relativity of simultaneity. This paper shows that the first two objections rest upon very elementary misunderstandings of Minkowski geometry and on lingering Newtonian intuitions about instantaneity. The third objection has a basis, but rather than invalidating the notion of faster-than-light influences it points the way to more general conceptions of simultaneity that could allow for quantum nonlocality in a natural way.

### 10.1  Alleged troubles with superluminal effects and influences

There are at least two good reasons to take seriously the possibility of superluminal influences. First, they are arguably though controversially implicated in the violations of locality found in quantum mechanics.[2] Second, it is not at all clear whether special relativity as it is usually formulated actually *excludes* superluminal influences or simply *fails to describe them properly*.[3] To some

---

[1] This was first published as, 'Would Superluminal Influences Violate the Principle of Relativity?', *Lato Sensu: revue de la Societé de philosophie des sciences* 1(1), 2014: https://sites.uclouvain.be/latosensu/index.php/latosensu/article/view/33. I am grateful to Alexandre Guay for permission to reprint it here.

[2] See, e. g., Maudlin [138] for a defence of this view.

[3] In support of the latter possibility I can only cite the large but admittedly inconclusive body of literature exploring the possibility of tachyons, superluminal frames, and extended relativity. It is not possible to do a comprehensive review of this literature here. The modern era of tachyon theory began in the 1960s, and papers from that era by G. Feinberg [83] and O.-M. Bilaniuk and E. C. G. Sudarshan [30] are widely cited; see also [155]. E. Recami insightfully advocated the significance of tachyons in several publications; see his [180] for comprehensive review. A neglected paper of 1986 by R. I. Sutherland and J. R. Shepanski [216] is an important

knowledgeable observers these two claims will seem obvious, to others they will seem to be 'not even wrong.' I will not attempt a detailed explication or advocacy of them in this paper, although it will become clear where my sympathies lie. The major purpose of this note is two-fold. First, it will attend to a job of undergrowth clearance, which is to defend the notion of superluminality against certain too-common misconceptions which stem from misunderstandings of Minkowski geometry and from lingering Newtonian intuitions about simultaneity. Second, it will sketch a notion of simultaneity which (properly developed) could allow for quantum-mechanical superluminal influences in a natural way. This paper is propaedeutic to a larger project being undertaken by this author that is aimed at defining generalized conceptions of simultaneity which would be adequate to the fact that we live in a quantum universe.

Some of the misunderstandings I will criticize here were dealt with rather clearly by Frank Arntzenius [13] over twenty years ago. However, they continue to appear in the professional literature, and so it seems necessary to respond to them yet again. Let's begin with Barry Dainton, since the particular problems he cites will be useful talking-points for my discussion. Dainton, in his *Time and Space* [53, p. 339], begins by quoting J. R. Lucas [131, p. 9–10], who said,

> if some superluminal velocity of transmission of causal influence were discovered, we should be able to distinguish frames of reference, and say which were at rest absolutely and which were moving.

Dainton (p. 339) agrees, saying,

> [a]nd in this he [Lucas] is surely right. Were we to discover that a truly instantaneous connection exists between objects at different places in space, then assuming the connection has some detectable effects, not only would the notion of absolute simultaneity have a real application, but we would have a way of determining which frames of reference are at absolute rest and which are not: *it is only with respect to frames truly* [sic] *at rest that the relative changes would occur at precisely the same time.* [Emphasis added.]

---

milestone: their approach is different than the orthodox treatment of tachyons given by most authors. The orthodox approach is to substitute the condition $v > c$ into the usual Lorentz transformations; this gives an imaginary Lorentz factor $1/\sqrt{1-v^2/c^2}$ leading to many difficulties of interpretation. Sutherland and Shepanski show that by re-deriving Lorentz-like transformations for the superluminal case (rather than merely substituting the condition $v > c$ into the subluminal transformations) one arrives at a Lorentz factor $1/\sqrt{v^2/c^2 - 1}$ which makes all proper quantities real-valued for superluminal frames. M. Fayngold's review monograph [82] on superluminal physics is very useful, but it does not take account of Sutherland and Shepanski's important innovation. Very recently, J. M. Hill and B. J. Cox [112], and R. S. Vieira [227] have developed 'extended' versions of special relativity that use the same real-valued Lorentz factor as Sutherland and Shepanski's for $v > c$. These approaches merit further study and development.

## 10.1. Alleged troubles with superluminal effects and influences

Adán Cabello, a distinguished researcher in quantum information theory, has worries about instantaneity similar to Dainton's. In *Nature* Cabello reviewed recent findings on quantum-mechanical correlations, and expressed his objection to instantaneous influences in quantum mechanics as follows:

> ...the decision of what test is performed in one location cannot influence the outcome of the test performed in the other location, unless there is an instantaneous influence of the two tests on each other. ... But this is too high a price to pay, *because it is impossible to fit instantaneous influences into any theory in which such influences travel at a finite speed* [emphasis added] [46, p. 456].

Views like these have been held by other notable authors. Wesley Salmon, for instance, argued that

> [a]rbitrarily fast signals yield absolute simultaneity of the strongest sort; the presence of the relativity of simultaneity in special relativity hinges crucially upon the existence of a finite upper speed limit on the propagation of causal processes and signals [196, p. 122].

Nicholas Maxwell [140, p. 38] seems to suggest that the *mere existence* of a superluminal effect would conflict with the Principle of Relativity. He cites his own interpretation of quantum mechanics, which postulates the superluminal collapse of spatially extended 'propensitons' which, he argues, would explain quantum correlations. Maxwell insists that his own theory

> irreparably contradicts special relativity. For special relativity asserts that all inertial reference frames are physically equivalent. In only one reference frame, however, will any given probabilistic collapse of propensiton state be instantaneous; in other, relatively moving frames the collapse will not, according to special relativity, be instantaneous (though always faster-than-light).

From these remarks we can tease out four closely-related charges against superluminality. Before stating them, though, it will be helpful to settle on terminology:

- A superluminal *effect* will be any physical process that involves the faster-than-light propagation of a geometric locus such as the intersection point between a beam of light and a background, without presuming that this involves the transmission of any sort of influence or information faster than light. A widely-discussed example is the searchlight-beam effect [188, 232]: a beam of light from a rotating point source will track across a distant screen faster than light if the screen is at a sufficient distance. Another example of a superluminal effect would be a string of flashbulbs or firecrackers set to go off simultaneously in a given inertial frame.

In all other inertial frames the sequence of flashes or detonations will propagate superluminally; we'll return to the spacetime kinematics of such processes shortly. It is usually taken that there is no question of the searchlight beam effect or strings of firecrackers transmitting *influences* superluminally along their trajectories but it should not be assumed that the searchlight beam effect is unproblematic.[4]

- A superluminal *influence* would be a hypothetical superluminal process in which some sort of causation passes faster than light from one point to another distant point. I'd like to leave it as open as possible how superluminal influences, if any, would be constituted.

- A *tachyon* is a hypothetical faster-than-light particle, where we think of a particle as an entity that can be localized, at least under some circumstances. I'll take a tachyon to be a form of superluminal influence, and I will sometimes use these terms interchangeably.[5]

- I will occasionally refer to superluminal influences, superluminal effects, and tachyons collectively as forms of *superluminal propagation* when the difference between them doesn't matter.

- Some papers in this literature (e.g. [216] and references therein) speak of *superluminal reference frames*, which would be hypothetical faster-than-light Lorentzian physical systems which could be transformed *to* in some versions of superluminal kinematics.

- I'll also prefer the adjective 'invariant' ('same in all frames of reference') to 'absolute' or 'truly' because that is more in keeping with standard usage in current relativity literature, and because it avoids dubious philosophical connotations.

---

[4]Rothman [188] dismisses the possibility that the searchlight beam effect could transmit information along the trajectory of the intersection point, but Weinstein's wording [232] is more cautious, suggesting that the problem needs more investigation. H. Ardavan [12] considered a scenario in which a rotating beam of electromagnetic radiation (such as that from a pulsar) traces a superluminal locus over a conductive surface (such as a layer of plasma spread through the solar system). The beam of radiation will cause charge separation in the plasma and thereby induce electromagnetic radiation from the surface at the intersection locus. Ardavan carried out a rigorous calculation showing that if the locus orbits superluminally in a circular pattern then the induced field will diverge. Ardavan further showed [11] that the gravitational field induced by the searchlight beam effect in such scenarios will also diverge. Ardavan left it open whether these results indicate the high-field breakdown of classical electromagnetic and gravitational field theory, or some sort of otherwise-implausible prohibition on the searchlight beam effect. The important questions raised by Ardavan's work remain open.

[5] R. Sigal and A. Shamaly [207, p. 2358] state, 'we use the term tachyon to describe any propagation outside the light cone,' and this could include both of what I have called superluminal effects and influences. Sigal and Shamaly's usage is not unusual in the literature; however, I will in this paper follow my narrower usage of 'tachyon' because the three-fold distinction I sketch between different types of superluminal propagations allows me to make certain claims with less risk of misunderstanding.

## 10.2. Is there a distinguished frame?

Here are the Troubles with Superluminality with which we shall be concerned:

TS1: There is no way to reconcile instantaneous influences with 'any theory in which such influences travel at a finite speed' (Cabello).

TS2: The existence of a superluminal physical influence (such as Maxwell's propensiton collapse) would imply the existence of a distinguished frame of reference and thereby violate the Principle of Relativity (Lucas, Dainton, Maxwell).

TS3: If a superluminal influence could be used to transmit information controllably then it would be possible to detect absolute states of motion and again thereby violate the Principle of Relativity (Lucas, Dainton).

TS4: If a superluminal influence were detectable or could be used to transmit information controllably, it would allow violations of the relativity of simultaneity (Dainton, Salmon).

I will show that TS1–3 rest upon elementary but surprisingly widespread misconceptions about how superluminal motion would be represented in Minkowski geometry. As to the fourth (and much more interesting) problem, I will have to respond *guilty as charged*, but I will argue (though not as conclusively as with TS1–3) that the charge is not nearly as damaging as most people suppose, and that it may in fact open a door to interesting new physics.

### 10.2 Superluminal propagation does not imply a distinguished frame

Before we address the implications of the detectability of superluminal influences, let's review some basics of superluminal kinematics in special relativity. Consider a familiar spacetime diagram, restricted to 2-dimensional $(x, t)$ space for simplicity:

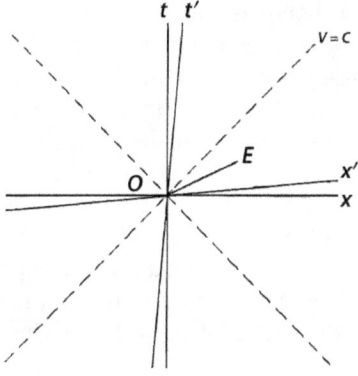

Fig. 1

We'll take the $x$ and $t$ axes to be the space and time axes respectively of the 'lab' frame $S$ and the $x'$ and $t'$ axes to be the space and time axes of another inertial frame $S'$ moving subluminally to the right. We've chosen units such that the light cone is at $45°$ with respect to the $x$ and $t$ axes, and the line $OE$ is the trajectory of something propagating with constant superluminal velocity to the right. Geometrically, what defines any form of superluminal propagation is that its spacetime trajectory is outside the light cone as shown. The line $OE$ therefore need not be the worldline of an exotic hypothetical particle, a collapsing propensiton, or the Starship *Enterprise* moving at warp speed; it could simply be a string of flashbulbs timed to go off simultaneously in some inertial frame. If the relative velocity of the moving $(x', t')$ frame steadily increases, the $x'$ and $t'$ axes rotate uniformly toward the light cone in order to preserve the invariance of the speed of light for both frames. (Of course, the proprietors of the $(x', t')$ frame are perfectly entitled to draw *their* axes as orthogonal and the axes of the lab frame as rotating away from the light cone.) Recall that the spatial hyperplanes of a Lorentz frame serve as its hyperplanes of simultaneity when simultaneity is defined according to Einstein's clock synchronization convention (see Taylor and Wheeler [217]). Any string of events along a line parallel to the $x$-axis of $S$ is simultaneous in $S$, though not in any frame moving with respect to $S$. As the $x'$-axis rotates toward the light cone, there will be exactly one relative velocity between lab and moving frames at which the spatial axis of the moving frame coincides with $OE$, and just as Maxwell says, in this frame *and this frame only* the propagation along $OE$ will be instantaneous (though it is superluminal in all frames). Indeed, if $u$ is the velocity of a superluminal propagation with respect to the lab frame, then this propagation moves infinitely fast not in a frame 'truly at rest' as Dainton has it, but in a frame moving with velocity $v = c^2/u$ with respect to the lab frame.[6]

There are thus two salient facts about instantaneity in special relativity: first, instantaneity with respect to a frame of reference is a perfectly admissible concept; second, there is no invariant concept of instantaneity if 'instantaneous' means 'traversing a distance with no lapse of coordinate time'. (The frame-dependence of instantaneity is merely the relativity of time-coordinate simultaneity in different words.) There is no question that the frame-dependence of infinite velocity clashes with Newtonian intuitions that are hard to dislodge. However, because instantaneity (or equivalently infinite velocity) is a frame-dependent concept, there is no way that any form of superluminal propagation (even though it is necessarily infinitely fast in some frame, as shown in Fig. 1) could define an absolute rest frame, a notion that cannot even be represented in the mathematics of special relativity (let alone on a spacetime diagram).

Another way to look at it is to note that any ordinary object moving at some velocity less than the speed of light defines a special frame as well,

---

[6] This follows from the Lorentz transformation for time: $\Delta t' = 0 = (\Delta t - u\Delta x/c^2)$ implies $\Delta x/\Delta t = v = c^2/u$. See Rindler [186], especially pp. 90–91.

## 10.2. Is there a distinguished frame?

namely its local co-moving rest frame. No one supposes that the fact that every subluminal object is at rest in its own private inertial frame picks out a 'privileged' frame whose existence threatens the Principle of Relativity. The local co-moving frame of a subluminal particle is determined by the contingent details of that particle's history, and is not by itself a universal law of physics. Similarly, no one need suppose that if there is so much as one instance of superluminal propagation in the universe then its existence would pose a threat to the Principle of Relativity just because its motion is instantaneous in a particular frame of reference. Again—any such frame of instantaneity would be picked out not as a matter of universal law but as a consequence of the accidents of the dynamical history which led to that particular propagation.

It is essential to grasp that while the Principle of Relativity requires that there be a covariant description of every possible physical process, it does not imply that everything looks the same in every admissible state of motion.[7] As noted, any discrete object is at rest only in its own local co-moving rest frame. Another pertinent example is the electromagnetic field; it has a covariant description (see, e. g., Misner, Thorne, and Wheeler [146, §3.4]) but this surely does not mean that any given electromagnetic field looks the same in all states of motion. For example, the field of a point charge in its own rest frame has no non-zero magnetic components, but this hardly implies that the rest frame of a charge is 'privileged' (even though when doing electromagnetic theory it is often useful to simplify a problem by finding a frame, if one can, in which some components of the field vanish). Similarly, *pace* Maxwell, the fact that any superluminal influence is infinitely fast in one but only one frame does not contradict the Principle of Relativity.

There is a subtle fact about relative velocities that is not always explicitly mentioned in books on relativity, and a failure to grasp this subtle fact may be a cause of some of the confusion about superluminal motion. In special relativity all velocities (except for the velocity of light itself) are relative, *including* zero and infinite velocity. However, it is an *invariant* fact whether or not two physical systems have a certain *relative* velocity. Thus it would be an invariant fact whether or not a certain tachyon beam is instantaneous relative to a certain inertial frame. Perhaps this is part of what has puzzled those who apparently believe that the mere existence of superluminality would imply the existence of an invariant or 'absolute' state of motion other than the motion of light itself. Dainton *et al.* possibly have confused the *invariant* fact that any superluminal propagation has infinite velocity relative to one frame (which one depends on the spacetime trajectory of the superluminal effect) with the notion (not correct) that any superluminal propagation would be invariantly infinite for *all* frames.

When Dainton speaks of 'truly' instantaneous connections his usage is ambiguous. No connection outside the light cone is instantaneous in more than one physical frame although in that frame it is 'truly' instantaneous. Which

---

[7] What I say here does not add much to the very clear argument given by F. A. Muller [149].

frame it is depends upon initial conditions and is not some law of nature. And since any instantaneous connection is *superluminal* in all frames the question of instantaneity is a red herring; the real question is what we are to make of superluminal influences.

Let's go back to Cabello's worries about Bell correlations. There is no question that if they are due to any sort of causal influence it must be superluminal, and if it is superluminal in one frame it is superluminal in all. However, that hardly implies that such superluminal influences would be instantaneous in *any* given frame. In which frames they happen to be instantaneous would depend upon the initial and boundary conditions of the experiment. Thus, there certainly is a theory that allows for influences which are instantaneous in one frame and finite (though superluminal) in all others: it is called 'special relativity.'

## 10.3 Superluminal influences would not allow detection of absolute motion

In order to address TS3, let's consider a slightly more complicated scenario. In Fig. 2, Alice and Bob are localized observers moving through spacetime. They were initially coincident at O and at that point they synchronized their local co-moving standard clocks. As the diagram suggests, they undergo varying accelerations in their careers through spacetime. If they are brought back into coincidence at a much later point it will be found that in general their elapsed proper times (given by the readings on their co-moving clocks) will differ. This is the much-debated Twin Paradox, which is based on the fact that elapsed proper time is path-dependent but invariant while coordinate time (as defined by Einstein's clock synchronization convention) is global but frame-dependent. (See Marder [133], Arthur [16], and H. R. Brown's lucid discussion of clocks as the 'waywisers' of spacetime [41, p. 95].)

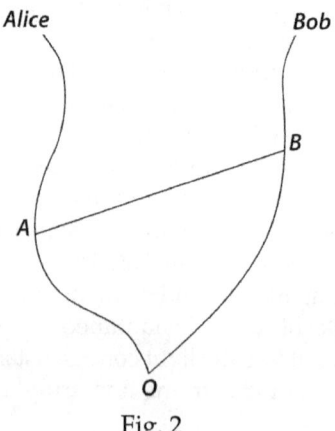

Fig. 2

## 10.3. Absolute motion?

Suppose that Alice emits a tachyon beam at $A$ which moves with constant superluminal velocity until it happens to intersect Bob's worldline at his world point $B$. I say 'happens to' since I'm not appealing here to any speculative theory that would give rules governing the motion of tachyons; for all we know, Alice's tachyon beam could have been emitted in a random direction in spacetime and the fact that it intersects Bob's worldline at $B$ could be pure chance. Nevertheless, it is invariant that the beam intersects Alice's worldline at $A$ and Bob's at $B$ and that it follows a certain trajectory through spacetime between these world points. The ordering of $A$ and $B$ with respect to a global time coordinate is frame-dependent, but the fact that these points are connected by the tachyon beam is not.

If Alice and Bob happen to be (even momentarily) at rest with respect to each other at the points $A$ and $B$, then they share a common inertial frame, which can be defined so that the line $AB$ is its spatial $x$-axis. The tachyon connecting $A$ and $B$ will be instantaneous in this frame (and, strictly speaking, in any frame related to it by mere translation). This, at the risk of repetition, is certainly an invariant fact. But if Alice and Bob are linked by a tachyon beam which is instantaneous in their mutual rest frame, that does not in the slightest degree imply that Alice and Bob are 'absolutely' at rest, as Lucas and Dainton seem to think. The invariance of a state of relative rest does not imply the existence of a globally invariant state of rest any more than does the invariance of the fact that Alice and Bob could be moving at some non-zero finite velocity $v$ with respect to each other imply that $v$ is an absolute velocity in any sense that would have interested Newton. Again, the mere fact that Alice and Bob might be connected by a tachyon beam—or for that matter a string of flashbulbs which happen to have been arranged so as to pop off simultaneously in Alice and Bob's mutual rest frame because *kinematically* these things are equivalent—surely does not by itself imply that they are at rest in any 'absolute' sense. This is despite the fact that it could be an invariant fact that they are *relatively* at rest.

Now, what about detectability? Let us imagine what some might say would be the worst case scenario, which would be that Alice can 'ping' Bob by means of a readable tachyon signal along $AB$ and Bob can bounce a readable response back to Alice along $BA$ with no lapse of proper time for her[8] between transmission and reception, and with a complete picture of Bob's local physical state at $B$ encoded in the return signal to Alice. The tachyon probe would make it as if Alice at $A$ could be momentarily coincident with Bob at $B$. Alice can therefore learn exactly as much but no more from the tachyon signal than she could if she and Bob's worldlines happen to cross at $A$ and $B$. Even with this

---

[8] I have not said anything about the elapsed proper time for the *tachyon* between $A$ and $B$. On the orthodox reading of special relativity, proper time for spacelike propagations is imaginary since $ds^2 < 0$ outside the light cone. However, in the superluminal kinematics developed by Sutherland and Shepanski [216] $ds^2 \geq 0$ for all intervals, spacelike and otherwise. It is beyond the scope of this paper to adjudicate between their view and the orthodox view. How we parameterize proper time along the tachyon's path is not relevant to our discussion here.

much information about Bob, the very most that Alice could know about Bob's velocity at $B$ is his *relative* velocity with respect to her at $A$. Why? Because that is all the information about Bob's state of motion there is to be had—Bob doesn't *have* an absolute velocity. Alice can use the tachyon beam to determine the *invariant* fact of her *relative* velocity with respect to Bob, but if she understands relativity theory she will not be confused by the fact that it is invariant whether she and Bob are relatively at rest at certain points.

Indeed, Alice need not have used tachyon beams at all to know her state of motion with respect to Bob's at $A$ and $B$, for she and Bob (when they were coincident at $O$) could have arranged in advance that they would follow acceleration schedules such that they would be relatively at rest at points $A$ and $B$. No one would dream of suggesting that the fact that they could do this would define an absolute state of rest that would violate the Principle of Relativity. There is no good reason at all to suppose that the mere fact that Alice and Bob can somehow infer that they are mutually at rest at some spacetime points or others implies the existence of an absolute or invariant state of rest, and this fact is independent of whether they are connected by a tachyon that happens to be instantaneous in their mutual rest frame, whether the 'connection has some detectable effects,' or whether Alice at $A$ and Bob at $B$ have any way at all of measuring directly or inferring each other's states of motion.

There's another way of looking at it. Suppose the point $O$ is at rest in the 'lab' frame, and suppose as before that Alice and Bob are momentarily at rest with respect to each other at points $A$ and $B$. At those points they could be moving at any velocity from zero to arbitrarily close to but not equal to $c$ with respect to the lab frame. There are therefore indefinitely many velocities with respect to the lab frame at which Alice and Bob could be at rest with respect to each other. Hence the fact that they can be at rest with respect to each other can hardly define a unique state of rest, which would surely have to be unique if it were indeed 'absolute.' Again, this is completely independent of whether or not Alice or Bob could use tachyons or any other means to tell that they were relatively at rest at $A$ and $B$.

These observations help to explicate a remark made by Arntzenius [13, pp. 229–230]):

> When W. Salmon [claims] that tachyons, if they could be used as signals, could establish absolute simultaneity, he does not indicate how one could do this. Assuming the frame-independence of the speed of light, and the frame dependence of the speed of tachyons this in fact appears to be a hopeless project: which tachyons exactly are to be used to establish absolute simultaneity?

What I am mostly doing here in my response to TS3 is to spell out in almost painful detail this point made by Arntzenius in 1990.[9] With apologies to Arntzenius, it seems that this point needs to be made again, with as much clarity as can be mustered. Again, if I may: *Any* tachyon is instantaneous with respect to *some* frame and there is no basis on which to pick one tachyon as definitive of an invariant state of rest. Conversely, for *any* inertial frame there is a trajectory which is instantaneous in that frame; which of the indefinitely many such frames do we pick as privileged?

## 10.4 Superluminal influences would not conflict with Einstein's relativity of simultaneity

It should be clear that TS1–3 can be obviated by a bit of careful thought about how spacetime diagrams work. But now we must say something about Dainton's worry (TS4) about distant clock synchronization, which raises much more interesting difficulties—and possibilities. Precisely what can Alice and Bob do with tachyons that they cannot do with light signals?

First, if a readable signal, *per impossibile* perhaps, could be imposed on a tachyon beam, then Alice and Bob could momentarily synchronize their local clocks at the points $A$ and $B$. What I mean is that if Alice can send her local clock reading at point $A$ to Bob at point $B$ then Bob could set his local clock reading at $B$ to agree with Alice's local reading at $A$. Our Newtonian intuitions prompt us to think that the distant clocks are synchronized only if they have the same reading *at the same global time coordinate*. However, this has no invariant meaning in special relativity, whereas it is invariant whether the local readings at $A$ and $B$ are equalized as described. Whether or not the local clock readings are equal at $A$ and $B$ is therefore independent of whether or not $A$ and $B$ are at the same global time coordinate in some inertial frame or other.

Distant clocks in special relativity can be synchronized using light signals but it takes a certain minimum amount of time to do that in *every* frame. The new thing that Bob and Alice could do with controllable tachyons is synchronize their distant clocks so that there exists an inertial frame in which the process takes *no* time. It could be done by picking the frame in which $AB$ is a spatial axis connecting Bob and Alice. The events $A$ and $B$ are at the same time *in this frame* and the tachyon signal will be instantaneous *in this frame*. But whether or not the clocks at $A$ and $B$ are synchronized by tachyons interchanged between $A$ and $B$ is completely unaffected by any choice of inertial frame in which the process is described.

I said that Alice and Bob could synchronize their clocks 'momentarily' because unless they happen to remain at rest with respect to each other their

---

[9] Arntzenius' paper 'Causal Paradoxes in Special Relativity' [13] is still an essential prerequisite for anyone who wishes to investigate the puzzles arising from the possibility of causal looping in special relativity. Where we can go beyond Arntzenius today is that more is known about entanglement and extended versions of quantum mechanics such as the two-state formalism; these topics, which open the door to decidedly non-classical notions of causation, are discussed briefly in later sections of the present paper.

local clocks would get out of synchrony again as they continue their careers through spacetime. On the other hand, if Alice and Bob continue to stay at rest with respect to each other then their clocks, once synchronized by tachyons at $A$ and $B$, would stay in synchrony.

The crucial point of this story is that Alice and Bob's ability to synchronize their clocks using tachyons would not violate the relativity of simultaneity defined as equality of a global time coordinate, because the latter is based upon Einstein's considerations about how one could synchronize clocks using light rays given that the speed of light is both finite and invariant. Einstein's way of defining time-coordinate simultaneity neither assumes nor requires that light signals be either the fastest or the only way of communicating between distant events; it's only about what can be accomplished with light signals.[10] Alice and Bob could have tachyon-based radios and yet still go ahead and set up a coordinate system using ordinary laser beams and Einstein's synchronization procedures (as in, e. g., Wheeler and Taylor [217]), and all the strictures identified by Einstein would continue to apply to the latter. The possibility of tachyon signals makes no difference to the relativity of time-coordinate simultaneity, for it simply would give *another way* of coordinating distant events than by means of electromagnetic signals. This point was made by G. Nerlich quite some time ago [153] but it seems that it must be made again.

Thus Salmon's statement that 'the relativity of simultaneity...hinges crucially upon the existence of a finite upper speed limit on the propagation of causal processes and signals' [196, p. 122] is simply incorrect. The relativity of time-coordinate simultaneity (where times are defined using the synchronization procedure recommended by Einstein in 1905 [74]) and indeed the entire mathematical structure of special relativity is dependent upon the assumption that the vacuum speed of light is a finite *invariant*, not necessarily a maximum. It seems clear that Einstein himself believed that $c$ is a universal speed limit, and it is also clear that many authors would *prefer* that this were the case,[11] but that assumption is not mathematically required in order to derive the Lorentz transformations. To confirm this, review Einstein's own derivation of

---

[10] The persistent belief that relativity is based upon the assumption that light is a 'first signal' [182] is arguably an instance of what John Woods [237, p. 153] has described as the *Heuristic Fallacy*:

> Let $H$ be a body of heuristics with respect to the construction of some theory $T$. Then if $P$ is a belief from $H$, which is indispensable to the construction of $T$, then the inference that $T$ is incomplete unless it sanctions the derivation of $P$ is a fallacy.

(Woods goes on (p. 154) to explain diplomatically that many fallacies are errors 'that even the attentive and intelligent are routinely disposed to make.') While the notion that $c$ is a limiting velocity certainly played a key historical role in motivating the construction of special relativity by Einstein and Poincaré, this notion is not formally used as a premise of the theory, and it is only debatably a theorem of special relativity.

[11] An important example is J. S. Bell, who said that by his theorem 'maybe there must be something happening faster than light, *although it pains me even to say that much*' [emphasis added]; [132, p. 90].

## 10.5. Alternative concepts of simultaneity

the transformations [74], or see any standard presentation of special relativity (e.g., Wheeler and Taylor [217]).

If there are, indeed, superluminal influences or connections of some sort, then there is no good reason to think that they could not peacefully coexist in parallel with Einstein's time-coordinate simultaneity.[12]

### 10.5 But superluminal influences might allow alternative concepts of simultaneity

What would superluminal influences, controllable or otherwise, add to our understanding of simultaneity? Is there any sense in speaking of superluminal influences as definitive of simultaneity-like relations on spacelike-separate events?

The problem is that even though everyone knows that simultaneity defined in terms of global a time coordinate is frame-dependent, almost everyone still wants time-coordinate simultaneity to do the same metaphysical work that absolute-time simultaneity does in Newton's universe. Newton's absolute time is the great steady heartbeat of his universe, and all physical changes in that universe are with respect to it. In Einstein's universe there are indefinitely many ways of coordinatizing events; none are metaphysically privileged though some may be preferable for practical reasons. Einstein's procedure for setting up space and time coordinates using light signals and standard measuring rods is, to be sure, very useful (in large part because it nicely reduces to the Newtonian picture in the limit of low relative velocities), but it is only one possible way of painting coordinates onto events; general covariance tells us that no coordinatization of events is privileged in any physical or metaphysical sense [190].[13] It is therefore not automatically given that any physical connectivity or equivalence between spacelike separate events must be described in reference to hyperplanes of constant time coordinate.

This, by the way, is the blind spot that has dogged discussions of the problem of finding a covariant description of quantum state reduction. Even the best-informed authors in this literature (e. g., Aharonov and Albert [3, 4]) assume that wave function collapse has to occur over hypersurfaces of constant time coordinate, which leads to the immediate conclusion that there is no covariant description of the process, if it is a physical process at all.[14] If one

---

[12] In this paper I have entirely skirted the large and subtle literature on the conventionality of simultaneity, because that problem is about what can be accomplished with light signals—an important question that is orthogonal to my interest here, which is to explore what could be accomplished with other sorts of signals than light. For an up-to-date review of the conventionality of simultaneity, see [41, pp. 95–105].)

[13] In many relativistic cosmologies, such as Robertson-Walker universes, there can be a global time, but it is *history-dependent* and does not conflict with general covariance. See, e.g., [231].

[14] According to Aharonov and Albert,

[i]n the nonrelativistic case a measurement is taken to set initial conditions for the propagator over the equal-time hypersurface of the measurement event... In

were to seek a covariant description of state reduction, one would want to see if this can be done in terms of covariant properties of the wave function.[15] An obvious candidate is *phase*: it is far more natural to think of wave functions as reducing over hypersurfaces of constant phase, and this automatically gives a covariant picture; given appropriate initial conditions, it may also be possible to describe state reduction in terms of constant *action* [185, 164]. These proposals require much technical development but, from the spacetime point of view advocated in this paper, the conventional assumption that state reduction is linked to hypersurfaces of constant time coordinate seems to be among the *least* promising approaches to the problem.

Returning to the problem of simultaneity, consider Fig. 2, and again suppose there is some sort of connection or influence outside the light cone between points $A$ and $B$. This would most likely be quantum mechanical in its basis, but to see the point I want to make we need not worry about the precise nature or origin of this connection; whether or not there are such influences or connections is an empirical question which cannot be settled on an *a priori* basis from the postulates of special relativity as they presently stand. Whatever the details of the dynamics may be, the *kinematics* of such connections is clear in the following respect: the connection between $A$ and $B$ is *factual* in the sense that all observers in all states of motion will agree that it is *those* two points, $A$ and $B$, which are connected in this particular way; the fact that these points are connected is relativistically invariant. As we have seen, $A$ and $B$ will be at the same time in one and only one frame, which (again) is 'distinguished' only by its dynamical history and not by some law of nature. In all other frames $A$ and $B$ will be at different time coordinates, and so whether or not two spacetime events are connected in this peculiar invariant but history-dependent way has nothing to do with whether or not they are at the same time in some Lorentz frame.

---

> the relativistic case, however, different observers will in general have different definitions of this hypersurface... different observers may derive different sets of probabilities. [3, p. 3322]

They go on to explain that there is, after all, a consistent way of predicting the probabilities of local measurement results, with the aid of microcausality, but 'a description of the physical system in terms of its observables simply cannot consistently be written down' [3, p. 3324]. But if state reduction is superluminal, which it must be, then for the elementary kinematic reasons explained in this paper there is only one frame in which it could reset probabilities over an equal-time hypersurface. Therefore, it is just a mistake to suppose that every observer would describe the reduction process as instantaneous.

[15] It is important to say what sort of wave function we are discussing when we talk of the problem of finding a covariant description of wave function collapse. The wave function is not *necessarily* an object living in configuration space. A wave function in general is simply the projection of the state function into a continuous representative [51, Ch. II, §E], which could be configuration space, ordinary spacetime, or momentum-energy space. What I am talking about here, and what most of this literature concerns itself with, is the de Broglie wave packet, which is a projection of the state function into Minkowski space; see Dirac [65, §30] for a succinct review of the de Broglie wave.

## 10.5. Alternative concepts of simultaneity

I would now like to suggest that if such connections do exist it is meaningful to say that they define a kind of simultaneity relation between $A$ and $B$—though obviously not the sort of simultaneity defined by Einstein, which is based on equality of a global time coordinate. A full treatment of this question is beyond the scope of this paper, but I'll try to say enough to show where this inquiry could go.

The key is that the modern usage of the term 'simultaneity' equivocates on two distinct senses of the term. According to Max Jammer [118], the etymological root of 'simultaneity'

> is, of course, the Latin 'simul,' which in turn derives from the Sanskrit 'sem' (or 'sema'), meaning 'together,' both in the sense 'together in space' and 'together in time' [118, p. 11].

The *Oxford Latin Dictionary* [222] tells us that the Latin *simul* has two distinct senses: two events may be *simul* if they occur at the same time, but events may also be judged *simul* if they are in some way *together* or *in joint process*—that is, part of some larger or more extensive coherent whole. Our events $A$ and $B$ are *simul* in the second sense in all frames of reference, but *simul* in the first sense in only one. The notion of simultaneity as joint process is an epistemically more primitive sense of simultaneity than simultaneity in terms of time coordinate, since judgements of time are built up from judgements of coincidence (localized joint process) between clock readings and localized events. In a Newtonian universe it is natural to assume that events in joint process are at the same absolute time, but this does not follow in an Einsteinian universe.[16]

In orthodox relativity the notion of invariant joint process is accepted so long as the events are coincident. In Einstein's words,

> We assume the possibility of verifying 'simultaneity' for events immediately proximate in space, or—to speak more precisely—for immediate proximity or coincidence in space-time, without giving a definition of this fundamental concept [75, p. 115].

---

[16] A small number of authors have explored the notion that there are distinct senses of simultaneity. Adolph Grünbaum [100, p. 203] defined what he called *topological* simultaneity: events simultaneous in this sense are those that cannot be connected causally. Since he thought that any sort of spacelike causal connections are excluded by relativity theory, all events spacelike separate from $A$ are topologically simultaneous with respect to it. Whether or not events are topologically simultaneous is an invariant distinction. Brent Mundy [151] similarly defined what he called *causal* simultaneity as the absence of any possible causal connection, but unlike Grünbaum he argued that relativity does not logically exclude the possibility of spacelike causal connections; therefore, on Mundy's view, the sets of causally simultaneous events might not comprise the whole region outside the light cone. The synchronization of distant clocks according to Einstein's clock synchronization convention was called by Mundy *optical* simultaneity. Mundy argued that the presentations of relativity by Grünbaum and Reichenbach [182] are reconstructions, based on the unnecessarily strong assumption that light is a 'first signal,' which distort the meaning of the theory and drastically limit its scope.

But even in his earliest writings on the theory of relativity Einstein was well aware that the notion of the coincidence of two presumably point-like events is neither mathematically nor physically clear:

> We shall not here discuss the inexactitude which lurks in the concept of simultaneity of two events at approximately the same place, which can only be removed by an abstraction [74, p. 39].

Up to now I have been largely concerned with pointing out the respects in which superluminal influences are consistent with relativistic kinematics as presently understood. We now reach a boundary beyond which one must consider ways in which relativity needs to be expanded to take account of quantum mechanics. Physics can no longer avoid addressing the 'lurking inexactitude' cited by Einstein.

In classical relativity the ambiguity in the notion of infinitesimal closeness is simply ignored; spacetime is taken to be built up out of point-like events and if these are spacelike separate they are presumed to be causally disjoint (except insofar as they can be linked by backwards and forwards light cones). Therefore, from the point of view of quantum mechanics the concept of an event in classical relativity is ambiguous in two respects. First, the physical meaning of coincidence or infinitesimal closeness is unclear. This is partially because of the Uncertainty Relations; also, some current approaches to quantum gravity (e.g., [7]) open up the possibility that space and time may be discrete at the Planck scale. If spacetime is discrete then even events separated by one quantum of length are spacelike separate and, by the classical criteria, could not be considered coincident. Second, and most pertinent to the theme of this paper, is the vexing question of whether events outside each other's light cones are causally disjoint. No one doubts that any collection of events can be associated by convention in an essentially arbitrary way; the question is whether it makes any sense to speak of *distant* events as being in 'joint process' in a causal or dynamical way that is somehow demanded by the physics of the situation.

There is increasing evidence that quantum mechanics shows that distant particles, especially if they are entangled, may be nonseparable or form or partake in a unity in surprising ways. It may therefore be sensible to generalize the conception of an event to allow for events and states that are extended throughout spacetime in an invariant way.

A dramatic example of the inseparability of spatially extended quantum states appears in a recent experiment by K. C. Lee *et al.* [128]. These experimenters used a complicated interferometric apparatus in which two 3 mm diamond chips separated by 30 cm were put into entangled phonon states (phonons are quanta of vibrations) and then 'pinged' by an ultra-high frequency laser. The key point for our discussion here is that the diamond chips were demonstrably put into a *single* quantum state despite their spatial

## 10.5. Alternative concepts of simultaneity

separation. As Lisa Grossman explains,

> [t]o show that the diamonds were truly entangled, the researchers hit them with a second laser pulse just 350 femtoseconds after the first. The second pulse picked up the energy the first pulse left behind, and reached the detector as an extra-energetic photon. If the system were classical, the second photon should pick up extra energy only half the time—only if it happened to hit the diamond where the energy was deposited in the first place. But in 200 trillion trials, the team found that the second photon picked up extra energy every time. That means that the energy was not localized in one diamond or the other, but that they shared the same vibrational state [99].

It is as if quantum mechanics simply does not know or care that the two diamond chips are 30 cm apart. Lee *et al.* do not attempt a covariant description of their nonlocal energy states but their result is an example of the sort of scenario we discuss here: at certain proper times along their world-lines, the two diamond chips share a certain common energy state. Whatever the detailed spacetime description may be (this remains to be worked out) it has to be an invariant fact that *those* points on their world-lines are linked in *that* particular invariant and nonseparable manner. Most important, the single nonlocal energy state shared by the two distinct diamond chips is demonstrably not reducible to two local energy states possessed by the two chips. That's an important part of what it means to say that the state is entangled: it is not separable into distinct and localizable sub-states. To be sure, the diamond chips have other physical properties which are localizable in the normal way, but their non-separable, spatially-extended energy state seems to be a very natural candidate for an entity that is *simul* in the second sense. One cannot avoid speaking of it as being in 'joint process' because it cannot even be analyzed into distinct localized parts.

It is quite likely that such alternative notions of simultaneity as suggested here—invariant but history-dependent—would violate some people's intuitions about a vaguely-defined 'Spirit of Relativity,' but it is not obvious that they are not allowed by the mathematical structure of relativity and they seem to be demanded by quantum physics. While relativity is far more amenable to superluminal influences that has been generally supposed, ultimately it is classical relativity that must adapt itself to the quantum [48, 163].

To summarize: if we grant that there could be invariant connections between spacelike separate events, likely quantum mechanical in their basis, then it is reasonable to call it a kind of simultaneity relation because it answers to the notion of distant events as being part of a single process. Quantum mechanics *prima facie* demands that we disambiguate the two key senses of simultaneity that have been conflated since the time of Newton.

## 10.6 Are 'causal' accounts of quantum mechanics consistent with the Principle of Relativity?

An anonymous referee for this paper made a very helpful observation:

> [T]here are theories that are phenomenologically compatible with special relativity in which superluminal propagation does pick out a preferred frame. Bohmian mechanics (also referred to as 'pilot-wave' theory or de Broglie-Bohm theory) has a preferred frame of reference. Perhaps theories like these are feeding the intuitions of those making claims akin to TS2...

This is quite likely right. For instance, Maudlin [138] argues that Bell's Theorem could force us to concede that there is a special frame which is preferred although *undetectably* so. Thus one must ask whether any theory that attempts to underpin quantum statistics by means of nonlocal dynamics is *necessarily* in conflict with Lorentz invariance. Or to turn the question around, can there be a *covariant* theory of nonlocal dynamics?

Bohm's 'hidden variable' theory of 1952 [35, 52] is Galilean invariant because Bohm never intended it to be otherwise; his aim was to show that non-relativistic wave mechanics could be underpinned by a causal (though unavoidably superluminal) dynamics in which particles apparently have definite trajectories. Hence it is reasonable to investigate whether a relativistic generalization of Bohm's theory is possible. Bohm himself apparently thought not: he and Basil Hiley state that 'it would be extremely surprising to obtain a Lorentz invariant theory of particles that were connected nonlocally' [32, p. 282]. They consider two spacelike separate particles $A$ and $B$, 'both at rest in the laboratory frame' at worldpoints $a$ and $b$ respectively, and then remark,

> [i]f there is a nonlocal connection of the kind implied by our guidance condition, then it follows that, for example, points $a$ and $b$ instantaneously affect each other. But if the theory is covariant, there should be similar instantaneous connections in every Lorentz frame.

Their accompanying figure shows connections from $a$ to other points on $B$'s worldline. Although their language is unclear, Bohm and Hiley do seem to grasp that each possible spacelike connection between $a$ and the points along the worldline of $B$ would be instantaneous in one and only one Lorentz frame; there is no covariant sense in which *all* are instantaneous. However, they go on to say that from the fact that there could be instantaneous connections between $a$ and earlier points on $A$'s own worldline via points on $B$'s worldline, it would be possible to set up a typical closed-loop causal paradox in which an influence from $a$ could interfere with $A$'s own history at an earlier worldpoint along $A$'s worldline in such a way as to prevent the influence from being emitted at $a$.

## 10.6. 'Causal' accounts of quantum mechanics

Closed causal loops are a genuine problem for superluminal theories, but the risk of a closed causal loop has nothing to do with whether or not the connections are instantaneous in some frame or other, for that is a frame-dependent concept. To this extent, Bohm and Hiley suffer from confusions about instantaneity similar to those I have criticized elsewhere in this paper. Rather, the risk of closed-loop paradox has to do with the invariant fact that points in spacetime can sometimes be connected in a closed loop by means of the presumed superluminal influences; the problem, if any, arises from the fact that the influences would be superluminal (and thus outside the light cones of both $A$ and $B$), not that they would be instantaneous. So the question is whether any putative superluminal theories should be rejected *just because* they may open up the possibility of closed causal loops. I'll return to this point below.

While Bohm's theory is the best-developed causal alternative to conventional quantum mechanics, it is not the only possible such theory. Late in his life Louis de Broglie was inspired by Bohm to revisit his own early attempts at a causal version of quantum mechanics [54, 55]. De Broglie's late causal theory, though incomplete in many respects (for instance, it applies only to spin-0 particles), is fully Lorentz-covariant. Bohm and Hiley themselves were not comfortable with theories like de Broglie's later approach (see [32, p. 238]) because such theories imply that any particle interacts *via* the four-dimensional wave field with other particles both past and future throughout spacetime. Bohm and Hiley seem to have thought that this was simply too strong a violation of classical intuitions or expectations about causality. This is why they rejected the possibility of covariant pictures of nonlocality (such as de Broglie's), *not* because such theories are technically out of the question.

The need to revise our intuitions about causality could be the price to be paid for any causal interpretation of quantum mechanics that satisfies the Principle of Relativity. In particular, a four-dimensional picture of the wave field could be the answer to worries about paradoxical closed causal loops: if such loops are mediated by a genuinely covariant quantum field then it simply would not be possible to write a description of a self-contradictory loop in the language of the theory, any more than any other sort of quantum state vector can be validly written in manifestly contradictory terms. That is, while there may well be amplitudes for past-future-past loops, each possible amplitude could only be for sequences of events (more precisely, measurement outcomes) that are mutually consistent. Thus, while such a theory such as de Broglie's would certainly do violence to classical intuitions (prejudices?) about the proper order of cause and effect it is quite likely that it would *not* allow for outright logical paradoxes of the kind that worried Bohm and Hiley.

A similar picture arises in the two-vector formalism studied by Yakir Aharonov and collaborators [2]. Their theory is not explicitly a causal interpretation of quantum mechanics, but it also considers amplitudes from both the past and the future. It could be worthwhile to investigate parallels between de Broglie's Lorentz covariant causal theory and the two-vector formalism. Although there are closed loops in the two-vector formalism, there is no risk of paradox for the reason outlined above: no single looped amplitude is, in itself, inconsistent. Like the possible states of Schrödinger's cat, the possible classical outcomes may well be inconsistent with each other, but each possible outcome set is internally consistent—*and only one is ever observed*. In versions of quantum mechanics that allow for future-to-past amplitudes, the mystery of causal looping is therefore subsumed into the larger mystery of understanding the relation between the quantum mechanical descriptions of physics in terms of amplitudes and the outcomes that are actually observed. These possibilities require much further study, but enough is known now to show that one should not *automatically* reject a version of quantum mechanics because it allows for causal loops.[17]

There is a larger question: Lorentz invariance itself fails to satisfy the Principle of Relativity in a certain crucial respect, since the Lorentz transformations are divergent at a critical velocity (the velocity of light in vacuum). Sutherland and Shepanski [216] point to this as the key factor hindering the extension of the principle of relativity to all relative velocities, since it makes it impossible to cover all of spacetime, both inside and outside the light cone, with a single group of continuous transformations. It is thus impossible to transform *to* a frame moving with velocity $c$ and this fact arguably violates the presumption of the equivalence of all frames. It is conceivable that a deeper theory which avoids this problem (possibly by allowing for quantum effects which would suppress the divergence at velocities very close to $c$) will obey some invariance principle more general than Lorentz invariance. Let us call such a to-be-written principle *Planck covariance*. Presumably it would would reduce to Lorentz invariance in suitable limits just as Lorentz-covariant theories reduce to Galilean theories in the limit of low relative velocities.

I have indulged in some reasonably well-founded speculations in this section. However, what is not speculative is that (as the example of de Broglie's theory shows) it is not necessarily the case that any account of quantum mechanics in terms of some more general physical principles would demand the return to Galilean covariance and a preferred frame; rather, the move to a fully quantized theory of relativity will probably take us even farther from Galilean covariance than does special relativity.

---

[17] There is a large literature exploring the puzzle of closed causal loops that could arise given the possibility of time travel or backwards causation (not necessarily in the context of quantum mechanics). Some notable papers in this genre include [13, 38, 208]. The upshot of these investigations is that it is by no means *obvious* that a physical theory should be automatically excluded because it allows for the possibility of causal looping.

## 10.7 Summary—and what must lie ahead

A lot more needs to be said before anyone has any business being entirely comfortable with the notion of superluminal influences, quantum mechanical or otherwise.[18] But a necessary prerequisite to the analysis of any of the substantial problems with superluminality is to grasp the kinematics of propagation outside the light cone.

The following points are elementary even though they have been persistently misunderstood by professionals working in this field:

- Trajectories outside the light cone have a natural description in the kinematics of special relativity.

- Infinite velocity (equivalently, instantaneity) is a frame-dependent concept, and thus any form of superluminal propagation is instantaneous in one and only one frame.

- The mere existence of some form of superluminal propagation, even if it is controllable, does not imply the existence, much less the detectability, of any suppositious absolute state of motion.

It is perhaps less immediately obvious, but still clear enough, that the possibility of distant clock synchronization *via* superluminal influences does not invalidate the frame-dependence of time-coordinate simultaneity—because the latter is simply not about what one could do with superluminal signals. And finally it is arguable, though not conclusively at this stage, that the increasing evidence of dynamic inseparability in a wide variety of quantum mechanical

---

[18] Further problems with superluminality include but are not necessarily limited to the following:

- The temporal order of spacelike separate events is frame-dependent; this may require the abandonment of causal order as a global invariant.
- With some combinations of relative velocities, superluminal trajectories can form closed causal loops, apparently allowing for logical paradoxes.
- Rest mass diverges at $v = c$, apparently precluding the acceleration of massive bodies through the speed of light.
- There are problems with reconciling superluminal motion with local quantum field theory as it is presently understood.
- In some but not all versions of superluminal or 'extended' relativity proper quantities are imaginary.
- It is widely though controversially held that quantum mechanical entanglement cannot be exploited for controllable superluminal signalling. (For the orthodox view of quantum signalling, see, e.g., [71, 202]. For critical responses to this orthodoxy, see [160, 121, 147]).
- The existence of space-like influences or connections demands a rethinking of the postulate of microcausality which is one of the building blocks of local quantum field theory.

There are candidate responses to all of these problems but they require discussion that would go far beyond the issues considered in this paper, which are prerequisites for those discussions.

experiments (such as the recent dramatic results by Lee *et al.* [128]) points to the cogency of notions of invariant simultaneity-like relations between spacelike separate entities (or portions of entities) that are much in the spirit of the ancient notion of simultaneity as a kind of jointness, wholeness, or coherence of possibly spatially-extensive events. The task remaining is to articulate these possibilities in a precise and testable way.[19]

---

[19] I am grateful to the following people for valuable discussion or advice about this paper or the topics of which it treats: Richard Arthur, Bryson Brown, Adán Cabello, Sheldon Chow, Robert Clifton, Saurya Das, Brian Hepburn, Alexander Korolev, Pamela Lindsay, Nicholas Maxwell, David McDonald, Fred Muller, Vesselin Petkov, Ricardo S. Vieira, and two anonymous referees for this journal. I am especially grateful to J. R. Brown for guidance in the early stages of this research. Needless to say (but it must be said), none of these individuals are responsible for any errors on my part in the present work, and it should not be presumed that they accept my views. For financial support I thank the Universities of Toronto, Western Ontario, and Lethbridge, and the Social Sciences and Humanities Research Council of Canada. Thanks also to Evan Peacock for the figures.

Chapter 11

# The Truth is (Still) Out There: Quantum Signalling and the Dynamics of Multiparticle Systems[1]

Kent A. Peacock & Brian S. Hepburn[2]

**Abstract** The abundant experimental confirmation of Bell's Theorem has made a compelling case for the nonlocality of quantum mechanics, in the precise sense that quantum phenomena exhibit correlations between spacelike separate measurements that are inconsistent with any common cause explanation. Nevertheless, many authors state that this odd nonlocality could not involve any controllable superluminal transmission of momentum-energy, signals, or information, since there are several proofs in the literature apparently showing that the expectation value of any observable at one location in a phase-entangled multi-particle system cannot be affected by any choice of measurement strategy employed on some other spacelike-separate part of the system. We show that most or all no-signalling proofs published to date are question-begging, in that they depend upon assumptions about the locality of the dynamics of the measurement process that are the very points that need to be established in the first place. In this paper, we undertake a critical examination of no-signalling proofs by Bohm and Hiley [32] and Shimony [202], which illustrate the problem in an especially striking way, and we outline a *reductio* argument showing that the dynamics of entangled states cannot be local in the sense assumed by these authors.

---

[1] This is an updated version of 'Begging the Signalling Question: Quantum Signalling and the Dynamics of Multiparticle Systems', by Kent A. Peacock and Brian S. Hepburn, in M. Bryson Brown and John Woods (eds.), *Logical Consequences: Rival Approaches and New Studies in Exact Philosophy: Logic, Mathematics, and Science*, Vol. II. (Series in Logic and Cognitive Systems.) Oxford: Hermes Science Publishers, 2000, pp. 279–292. Preprint at https://arxiv.org/abs/quant-ph/9906036.

[2] Department of Philosophy, Wichita State University, Wichita, Kansas, U.S.A.

## 11.1 Introduction

Let us imagine a typical EPR (Einstein-Podolsky-Rosen) experimental scenario, in which a centrally-located source is sending out pair after pair of correlated particles, which we shall label $A$ and $B$, in opposite directions [78, 34]. At equal distances from the source we shall suppose that there are two detectors, $D_A$ and $D_B$, at rest with respect to the source. (We make these stipulations to evade the considerable complications entailed by relative motions of source and detectors.) At $D_A$ and $D_B$ sit Agents Mulder and Scully respectively, patiently writing down the results of each run of the apparatus. Mulder is holding his detector at a constant angle, while Scully varies her detector angle from time to time, hoping to send a message to her partner.

We know that the results recorded by Mulder and Scully will be correlated. If the particles are fermions of spin 1/2, and if we are recording spin up or down in a particular direction, then the correlation will be given by $-\cos\theta_{AB}$, where $\theta_{AB}$ is the relative angle between the two detectors. We know that this correlation violates a Bell Inequality [32, p. 140–147], and we know that this means that the particular results our two agents get could not have been encoded in the particles when they left the source [174]. But we also know that Scully's attempts to communicate with Mulder directly will be thwarted, for no matter what manipulations she performs on her detector, all that either she or Mulder will record will be an apparently *random* sequence of ups and downs. Only when the two sequences of results are compared at a later time, will it be seen that correlations stand between them, satisfying the above formula.

The best that Scully can do is impose a signal upon the *correlations* by varying her detector angle; and indeed, this would make possible, in principle at least, the most theoretically perfect encryption scheme that one could imagine. Either agent's string of random results would serve as the unique key for the other, and eavesdropping could be detected by a tendency of the results to *obey* a Bell Inequality (since eavesdropping destroys the correlations) [130]. But there does not seem to be any way that Scully can send a message that shows up in Mulder's local statistics. If all she does is adjust her detector angle, Mulder just continues to see what looks like random noise. If, on the other hand, Scully interposes some magnets or other devices to force the particles to go through her detector in a particular direction, she will discover later on, after the results are compared, that not only does Mulder continue to receive random noise, but that she has also washed out the correlations.

The relativistic prohibition against superluminal signalling thus seems to be protected. However, Mulder is still puzzled, because he is swayed by Tim Maudlin's very persuasive arguments that the violation of the Bell Inequalities in experiments such as this can only be accounted for by the assumption that there is some sort of superluminal causation, in apparent violation of the theory of relativity [137]. Mulder is well aware that if there were something

## 11.2. Can We Explain the Correlations?

Scully could do that would preserve the correlation between their results, but at the same time allow her to control which way her particles go, then this would not only threaten causal paradoxes, but would allow him and Scully to synchronize their watches instantaneously and thereby violate Einstein's relativity of simultaneity. But he quite fails to see why this might not, in principle at least, be possible. Finally, in utter frustration, Mulder concludes that there is a hidden conspiracy between quantum mechanics and relativity, such that relativity will always appear to be obeyed even when it is being covertly violated.

The ever-sensible Scully will assure Mulder that things are just as they should be, since numerous authors have published proofs demonstrating, or supposedly demonstrating, that no-controllable-signalling is a completely general property of quantum mechanics [70, 71, 202, 93, 19, 120]. However, Mulder, never content merely to accept the authority of experts, reads some of this literature, and begins to develop suspicions about the logical pedigree of the widely-cited proofs it contains. In this paper, we will put two especially pertinent examples of no-signalling proofs under the microscope, and show that Mulder's worries are justified.

### 11.2 Can We Explain the Correlations?

To place the discussion of signalling in context, we will consider two strongly contrasting approaches to the following question: How can we explain correlations between spacelike-separate events, when recourse to a common cause is ruled out?

1. 'Don't ask'. One notes that we already have an empirically adequate set of algorithms for predicting observable correlations, and combines this fact with the warning of Bohr [36] that to ask for a spatio-temporal account of the interactions between correlated particles is to ask an experimentally ill-posed question. As David Mermin puts it,

   > My own view on EPR which keeps changing—I offer this month's version—is that barring some unexpected and entirely revolutionary new developments, it is indeed a foolish question to demand an explanation for the correlations beyond that offered by the quantum theory. This explanation states that they are the way they are because that's what the calculation gives. [144, p. 202]

   This very Humean view has it that there is no basis for belief in 'hidden powers' or 'necessary connexions' between events. The price we have to pay for the huge predictive effectiveness of quantum mechanics, is, in effect, to give up the hope of understanding the actual basis of physical phenomena.

2. One accepts that if there is any sensible explanation of the correlations at all, then it must involve some sort of direct (and therefore superluminal) causal interaction between the distant particles. Tim Maudlin puts it bluntly:

> Bell concluded that violations of the inequality demonstrate that the world is not locally causal, i.e., that these phenomena cannot be reproduced by any theory which postulates only locally defined physical states which cannot influence states at space-like separation... Philosophers of physics have been wont to question this conclusion... Bell was, however, quite correct in his analysis. Statistics such as those displayed by the photons [in an EPR scenario] cannot be reliably reproduced by any system in which the response of each particle is unaffected by the nature of the measurement carried out on its distant twin. The photons remain "in communication" no matter how great the spatial separation between them. Instead of trying to deny these non-local (i.e., superluminal) influences, we should begin to study the role such influences must play in generating the phenomena. [136, p. 405]

We take the notion of studying 'the role such influences must play in generating the phenomena', to mean that we should find out what features of a theory of superluminal influences would be *necessary* in order to reproduce the observed behavior. As we shall see below, there is one class of candidate theories—the causal interpretations of quantum mechanics proposed by Louis de Broglie and David Bohm—that are apparently *sufficient* to account for the observed phenomena. However, we still do not know how much choice we have in adopting such theories.

These are only two of the many attempted interpretations of QM, some of which are of great subtlety and ingenuity. However, it is not too much of an exaggeration to say that most interpretations of QM are aimed at finding some way of *accepting* the nonlocality implied by Bell's Theorem—which, as noted above, is essentially a negative result, amounting to the elimination of common-cause explanations of quantum correlations—*without* going as far as alternative 2 contemplates; that is, without swallowing the idea that one particle *literally* exerts an instantaneous influence on its distant partner. Hence, it is useful to focus on these two views, since they represent two extremes of thought on the problem.

Note carefully that a supporter of position 1 (above) could say that there is a *non sequitur* in Maudlin's argument: from the fact that no local explanation is available, it does not follow that some other sort of explanation is possible. It might well be that there is no explanation at all; in other words, that the Bell-Inequality-violating correlations of QM are simply basic, raw data that are the *starting points* for any full development of physics, not something that could be explained by any deeper physical theory. (This has been proposed, for instance, by Fine [86] and Pitowsky [174].) A defender of position 2, therefore, will ideally have to show that there are other motivations for considering non-local causation, apart from the fact that it would furnish a *prima facie* explanation for the correlations. And, indeed, supporters of the Bohm-de Broglie alternatives do have some grounds to claim that their theories are broadly motivated by the mathematical structure of wave mechanics.

The 'don't ask' option is widely endorsed, especially by many working physicists. It does have the advantage that it tends to keep one out of trouble, and this has some survival value in today's scientific ethos, according to which it is impermissible to be perceived to have made a mistake.[3] Furthermore, option 2 has been long regarded by many as outside serious discussion both because it leads to possible conflicts with relativity, and because of a deeply-felt instinct that physics should be local. Einstein himself dismissed the notion of nonlocal causation as "spooky action at a distance".

An important difference between answers 1 and 2, is that according to the latter, there is *new physics* to be uncovered; while according to 1 there is no reason to suppose that the present formulation is not as good a theory as we are going to get. According to 1, nonlocality would not be something one understands, but something to which one adjusts. Interpreting QM would be a typical case of what Wittgenstein famously called 'letting the fly out of the fly-bottle'—seeing that if only we think about a problem the right way, there is no problem at all. It must be said that this position, while logically open given our present state of knowledge, is most uninteresting, since it virtually guarantees that our understanding will not move much beyond its present state.

## 11.3 Causal Interpretations of QM

Despite long-standing prejudices against taking the idea of superluminal or nonlocal causation seriously, there is increasing recognition that the causal interpretations inspired by the theories of David Bohm [35] and Louis de Broglie [54, 55] are among the best contenders to provide a deeper explanation, if not a generalization, of QM. The central feature of such theories is that they countenance some sort of direct dynamic interaction between correlated particles.[4] Bohm's theory (which is much more widely studied) can be considered to be a non-relativistic approximation to the relativistic theory of de Broglie. In Bohm's

---

[3] At the risk of over-stating the obvious, we believe that this aspect of the contemporary scientific ethos is counter-productive.

[4] There is a recent variant of Bohm's theory known as 'Bohmian Mechanics', in which particle motions are supposed to be correlated by a sort of pre-established harmony. We will not consider that here, save to note that it is subject to the same objections to any theory with a local Hamiltonian, that we raise in the next section. For a superbly perspicuous overview of the various flavours of the causal interpretation, see [52].

theory, interactions between particles are mediated by a mysterious potential having the form

$$Q = \frac{\hbar^2}{2m} \frac{\nabla^2 R}{R} \qquad (11.1)$$

where $m$ is the particle mass, $R$ is the amplitude of the wave function

$$\Psi = R \exp(iS/\hbar) \qquad (11.2)$$

and $S$ is the action of the system. In the case of phase-entangled multiparticle systems, the quantum potential for the system cannot, in general, be written merely as the sum of the quantum potentials for the individual particles. Rather, it is a global property of the system as a whole. (See [52, p. 62–63].) The quantum potential contributes to the total mass-energy of a multi-particle system, and, when differentiated with respect to distance, defines a force—literally, a sort of action at a distance—that Bohm frequently argued would be a natural way to account for the correlations between distant particles.

There are many questions to be asked about the best way to interpret and develop the insights of Bohr and de Broglie. The crucial point to grasp, though, is that the quantum potential $Q$ is by no means an arbitrary construct, but something that can be derived straightforwardly from certain basic assumptions of wave mechanics. (See [35, 52, 54], or many other sources.) Option 2 is, therefore, to be taken very seriously, both because (as Maudlin insists) it seems, *prima facie* at least, to be demanded by the observed failure of the Bell Inequalities, and also because something like the theories of de Broglie or Bohm have been implicit in the mathematical structure of quantum theory from the outset. But this makes the question of signalling especially acute, as we shall see.

## 11.4 Bohm and Hiley on Signalling

In their *Undivided Universe* [32, Chapter 7], David Bohm and Basil Hiley attempt to address the problem of superluminal signalling in quantum mechanics. Our claim will be that their argument is question-begging, since, as we shall see, they rule out of consideration from the beginning the very possibility they most need to examine—*especially* given their stated commitment to causal interpretations of QM.

The charge of circularity has already been leveled against a large class of no-signalling proofs within non-relativistic quantum mechanics and local quantum field theory by J. B. Kennedy [121], and also by one of us [160, 163]. The value in studying this particular argument by Bohm and Hiley is that they express in a remarkably clear form the fallacy that is typical of virtually all the no-signalling arguments with which we are familiar. We say this in all due respect for these authors, who have made great contributions to physical

## 11.4. Bohm and Hiley on Signalling

science. (It is, in particular, a disgrace that Bohm, like J. S. Bell, was not awarded the Nobel Prize in Physics.) Our claim is not that they have been especially careless, but that, given the long-standing commitment of science to locality, theirs is a remarkably easy mistake to make.

In discussing various possible interpretations of the EPR experiment, they remark,

> ...it seems very reasonable to suggest that $A$ and $B$ [the spacelike separate particles] are directly connected, though in a way that is perhaps not yet known. [32, p. 139]

This is essentially a variant of alternative 2, above, and it is, indeed, the central claim of causal accounts of QM such as the theories of Bohm and de Broglie. The ultimate problem, of course, is to elucidate the nature of the 'connection' between the particles.

However, they then set out to immediately scotch any fears that such hypothetical direct connections, whatever they might look like in detail, could be used to signal superluminally. Their argument is given in wave-mechanical terms; what follows here is their derivation re-expressed in the more perspicuous Dirac notation.

We shall suppose that 'an external system [measurement device] with coordinate $y$ is allowed to interact with the spin of particle $A$.' The initial state vector for a system of two spin-coupled particles $A$ and $B$, and a measuring apparatus with coordinate $y$, will be

$$|\psi_0\rangle = |\phi_0^y\rangle \frac{1}{\sqrt{2}}[|+_\alpha^A\rangle|-_\beta^B\rangle - |-_\alpha^A\rangle|+_\beta^B\rangle] \qquad (11.3)$$

where the superscripts $A, B, y$ indicate the Hilbert spaces for particle $A$, particle $B$, and the measuring apparatus, respectively. The subscripts $\alpha$ and $\beta$ indicate the spin direction for which the $|+\rangle, |-\rangle$ is a basis set, and the ket $|\phi_0^y\rangle$ represents the initial wave function for the measuring device. (The ket products are to be understood as direct products, although we have dropped the usual $\otimes$ notation).

An interaction between the measuring device and the spin of particle $A$ is then 'carried out'. The immediate question is how we should represent this.

Here is the key passage:

> The most general possible result of this interaction will be represented by a unitary transformation on the subsystem consisting of $y$ and $A$, because, *by hypothesis* [our emphasis], we are assuming our interaction does not directly disturb $B$. If it did then this would not constitute sending a signal from $A$ to $B$, but would just be a direct disturbance of $B$ by its interaction with $y$. [32, p. 139]

Bohm and Hiley then go on to show that given this assumption there is no change in the expectation value of the spin operator for particle B as a consequence of the measurement made on A. We will comment, below, on the cogency of the reasoning expressed in this passage. First, though, we summarize the calculation.

We represent such a unitary transformation by the operator $U^{A,y}_{\alpha,\alpha'}$ where the superscripts indicate that this operator only works on the Hilbert spaces of the apparatus and particle A and the subscripts show that it performs the operation of rotating the initial basis states of A from the direction $\alpha$ to $\alpha'$. The state of the system then becomes

$$U^{A,y}_{\alpha,\alpha'}|\psi_0\rangle = \frac{1}{\sqrt{2}}|U^{A,y}_{\alpha,\alpha'}\phi_0^y\rangle[|+^A_{\alpha'}\rangle|-^B_\beta\rangle - |-^A_{\alpha'}\rangle|+^B_\beta\rangle]. \qquad (11.4)$$

By assumption, the basis kets of B are unaffected by this transformation. Bohm and Hiley then go on to show, unsurprisingly, that given this assumption there is no change in $\langle \sigma_{\beta'} \rangle$, the new expectation value of the spin operator (in direction $\beta$) for particle B as a consequence of the measurement made on A. We write

$$\begin{aligned}
\langle \sigma^{B'}_\beta \rangle &= \langle U^{A,y}_{\alpha,\alpha'}\psi_0|\sigma^B_\beta|U^{A,y}_{\alpha,\alpha'}\psi_0\rangle \\
&= \frac{1}{2}\langle U^{A,y}_{\alpha,\alpha'}\phi_0^y|U^{A,y}_{\alpha,\alpha'}\phi_0^y\rangle \\
&\quad [\langle+^A_{\alpha'}|\langle-^B_\beta| - \langle-^A_{\alpha'}|\langle+^B_\beta|] \\
&\quad \sigma^B_\beta[|+^A_{\alpha'}\rangle|-^B_\beta\rangle - |-^A_{\alpha'}\rangle|+^B_\beta\rangle]
\end{aligned} \qquad (11.5)$$

Since the orthonormality of the states is retained under a unitary transformation, and since $\sigma^B_\beta$ operates on particle B alone (as if it 'passes through' the A-kets), this gives

$$\frac{1}{2}[\langle-^B_\beta|\sigma^B_\beta|-^B_\beta\rangle - \langle+^B_\beta|\sigma^B_\beta|+^B_\beta\rangle] = \langle \sigma^B_\beta \rangle. \qquad (11.6)$$

To sum up: since *ex hypothesi* the unitary transformation only operates on the Hilbert spaces of the measuring device and particle A, the expectation value for the spin of particle B is the same before and after the interaction.

Several comments come to mind. First, this whole line of reasoning is very odd, since the authors only a few lines above on the same page readily concede that A and B may be 'directly connected', and it is hard to see how, if this were so, something done to A might not produce a 'direct disturbance' of B. (Presumably, 'direct' means 'nonlocal', at least in the sense of being instantaneous, or not involving only retarded reactions.) Bohm and Hiley therefore seem to contradict themselves; they insist on the plausibility of a direct connection between the particles, but then describe the situation in a way that excludes that very possibility.

## 11.4. Bohm and Hiley on Signalling

Does their proof amount to anything more than an illustration of the truism that an operator that doesn't operate on a wave-function doesn't change the wave-function? (Kennedy [121] argues that virtually all no-signalling arguments within nonrelativistic quantum mechanics boil down to this unexceptionable claim, at least mathematically.) That would not seem to be especially illuminating.

Here is a more charitable reading: even though proofs of this sort cannot show that there is no direct causal interaction between left and right particles, they do show that there is no inconsistency in the formalism of quantum mechanics, such that we would get evidence of a superluminal causal interaction if we *assume* there is none. (That would indeed be an inconsistency in the formalism of the theory.) One cannot beat the house merely by some sort of statistical trickery.

It was, no doubt, a salutary exercise to have shown this, but the use of such a calculation in support of a general no-signalling claim is completely question-begging. This is because it is very hard to see how any sort of signal from $A$ to $B$ would not require the disturbance of $B$ by $A$, albeit in some fashion 'that is perhaps not yet known'.

This point requires special emphasis. It is a basic result of information theory that any form of information transmission requires the expenditure of free energy. The reason is that to encode information in a physical structure (for instance, to do something that causes a measurement device to display some definite outcome) is to lower the entropy of that structure. There are many ways in which this can be accomplished, but all require the doing of some work on that structure. Transmission of information from $A$ to $B$ without direct disturbance—*whether controllable or not*—would be a violation of the Second Law of Thermodynamics, since one would have achieved an energetically free reduction in entropy. Therefore, to suppose that one could signal without 'direct interaction' is to misunderstand the nature of signalling in general.

In other words, the most that the no-signalling argument by Bohm and Hiley really shows—and this is true of all the no-signalling arguments we cite above, and most in the literature[5] —is that the quantum mechanical measurement process cannot be used to violate the Second Law of Thermodynamics. One cannot signal by sheer sympathetic magic; that is, *without* actually, physically interacting with the receiver. However, these arguments utterly fail to

---

[5] A. Valentini has a highly original treatment of the signalling problem in his own version of Bohmian Mechanics [223]. Valentini, following Bohm and Vigier [33], treats the equation $P(x) = |\Psi(x)|^2$, which he dubs the 'quantum equilibrium' condition, not as a mathematical identity, as it is in the standard abstract formulation of quantum mechanics, but as a thermodynamic average which could have been violated in the early universe. Valentini shows that, in his theory, no-signalling holds so long as quantum equilibrium holds. Whether or not Valentini's approach is sound, it is less obviously question-begging than the usual no-signalling arguments. However, all presently extant versions of Bohmian Mechanics assume a local Hamiltonian for the multi-particle system, and are thus open to objections we raise in the next section.

show whether or not there *exists* a direct interaction between the distant particles, even though this is precisely the point that is at issue. It is not relativity that is protected by the no-signalling arguments, but thermodynamics.

## 11.5  Nonlocality of Multiparticle Dynamics

It will be instructive to take a closer look at the widely-cited no-signalling argument by Abner Shimony [202], which (by using the Hamiltonian formalism) explicitly considers the dynamics of entangled states.

Shimony invites us to consider an EPR scenario with correlated particles $A$ and $B$. We want to write the Hamiltonian for this system, in the case that a measurement device $D_B$ acts on $B$. Shimony assumes that this total Hamiltonian can be written in the form

$$H_{\text{tot}} = H_A \otimes \mathbb{1}_B + H_{DB} \otimes \mathbb{1}_A, \tag{11.7}$$

where $H_A$ is the Hamiltonian of particle $A$, $\mathbb{1}_A$ is the identity operator on $\mathcal{A}$, the Hilbert space for $A$ (and similarly for $\mathbb{1}_B$), and $H_{DB}$ is the Hamiltonian of the combined system of $D_B$ and particle $B$. Adopting a Hamiltonion of this form amounts to assuming dynamic locality at *two* levels:

**S1** It assumes that $D_B$ interacts only with $B$;

**S2** It assumes that the combined system of $D_B$ and $B$ does not interact with $A$.

These assumptions do seem to be perfectly reasonable given normal classical intuitions about how particles interact, since we would assume that once the particles are sufficiently far apart, any immediate reactions between them would drop rapidly to zero. (There could be retarded interactions, of course, but here we are only concerned with what happens at some definite time in the lab frame of reference.) However, in the context of this investigation, we are not entitled to rely upon such classical intuitions, because the *entire point* is to see whether or not classical notions of causality are sound in the face of quantum mechanics.

In any case, given Eq. 11.7, one can show (by series expansion) that the time evolution operator for the total system factorizes:

$$\begin{align}U(t) &= e^{iH_{\text{tot}}t} \tag{11.8}\\ &= e^{iH_A t} \otimes e^{iH_{DB}t}. \tag{11.9}\end{align}$$

Shimony then sets out to calculate the expectation value of some operator $G$ acting on particle $A$ alone, given this action of $D_B$ on $B$. If any such measurement carried out on $B$ can influence the expectation value of any observable measurable on $A$, then Scully can, indeed, signal to Mulder, by varying the parameters of the apparatus $D_B$.

## 11.5. Nonlocality of Multiparticle Dynamics

We first need an expression for the total system state. Let $|a_i\rangle$ be basis states for $\mathcal{H}_A$ and $|b_i\rangle$ be basis states for the Hilbert space $\mathcal{H}_B$ of particle B. The assumption that $D_B$ acts dynamically on B alone implies that we can represent the effect of $D_B$ on the total system in terms of operators acting strictly on a Hilbert space $\mathcal{H}_{B'} = \mathcal{H}_{D_B} \otimes \mathcal{H}_B$, where $\mathcal{H}_{D_B}$ is the Hilbert space of the measurement apparatus. Writing the basis states of $\mathcal{H}_{B'}$ as $|b_i'\rangle$, the state of the total system (apparatus plus entangled particles A and B), at time $t_0$, can be written as

$$|\psi(t_0)\rangle = \sum c_i |b_i' a_i\rangle. \tag{11.10}$$

Clearly this is not, in general, factorizable—even though we are assuming that its time evolution is!

After a time $t$ the system has evolved to a state

$$|\psi(t)\rangle = U(t - t_0)|\psi(t_0)\rangle. \tag{11.11}$$

As with Bohm and Hiley's calculation, we are assuming that the measurement interaction with $D_B$ does not collapse (i.e., project) the state, but evolves it in a unitary way.

To calculate $\langle G \rangle$, we observe that $G$'s action on the global system can be represented by $G_{tot} = G \otimes \mathbb{1}_B$. Then we get

$$\begin{aligned}
\langle G_{tot} \rangle &= \langle \Psi(t) | G \otimes \mathbb{1}_B | \Psi(t) \rangle \\
&= \langle \Psi(t_0) | U^\dagger(t - t_0)(G \otimes \mathbb{1}_B) U(t - t_0) | \Psi(t_0) \rangle \\
&= \langle \Psi(t_0) | (e^{-iH_A(t-t_0)} \otimes e^{-iH_{DB}(t-t_0)})(G \otimes \mathbb{1}_B) \\
&\quad (e^{iH_A(t-t_0)} \otimes e^{iH_{DB}(t-t_0)}) | \Psi(t_0) \rangle \\
&= \langle \Psi(t_0) | (e^{-iH_A(t-t_0)} G e^{iH_A(t-t_0)}) \\
&\quad (e^{-iH_{DB}(t-t_0)} \mathbb{1}_B e^{iH_{DB}(t-t_0)}) | \Psi(t_0) \rangle \\
&= \langle \Psi(t) | G | \Psi(t) \rangle \\
&= \langle G \rangle
\end{aligned} \tag{11.12}$$

In the end, $\langle G \rangle$ shows no dependency on whatever may have been done on particle B. In sum: since A and B are presumed causally independent, a measurement on B cannot influence the statistics of measurements on A. This is, of course, just a more general version of the argument of Bohm and Hiley.

Abner Shimony himself was well aware of the relevance of the dynamics for the signalling problem. Elsewhere, he states,

> ... quantum mechanical predictions concerning ensembles of pairs of particles do not violate Parameter Independence [no-signalling], provided that nonlocality is not explicitly built into the interaction Hamiltonian of the particle pair. [203, p. 191]

Evidently, Shimony did not believe that there was any physical justification for considering explicitly nonlocal Hamiltonians. However, we need only look a few pages ahead in Bohm and Hiley's book to see that there is.

## 11.6 Symmetrization and Nonlocality

In a section of *The Undivided Universe* entitled 'Symmetry and antisymmetry as an EPR correlation', [32, pp. 153–157] Bohm and Hiley point out that wave functions of multi-particle systems may be symmetric or antisymmetric. Particles belonging to systems with symmetric wave functions exist in identical states, and accordingly obey Bose-Einstein statistics, while particles with antisymmetric wave functions obey Fermi-Dirac statistics, and must obey the exclusion principle.

Suppose our particles $A$ and $B$ are bosons. We wish to measure some operator $O_A$ on particle $A$. There will have to be a corresponding operator $O_B$ acting on $B$, since $A$ and $B$ must obey identical statistics. Therefore, as Bohm and Hiley explain ([32, p. 153–154]), in order to maintain the symmetry of the Hamiltonian between the two particles, we must write the Hamiltonian of the measurement interaction as

$$H_I^S = \lambda(O_A + O_B)\frac{\partial}{\partial y} \qquad (11.13)$$

This obviously violates assumption S1 above, because of the dependence upon $O_B$, and thus renders Eq. 11.7 entirely inapplicable. It also, again obviously, contradicts the behavior of the unitary transformation used by Bohm and Hiley only a few pages earlier in their own book. We note, also (a point not explicitly mentioned by Bohm and Hiley), that, as far as we know, *all* particles are either bosons or fermions, and must therefore obey symmetrization conditions. The best we can say, therefore, is that the whole treatment of signalling typified by the Bohm-Hiley and Shimony proofs could only be applicable in cases in which these symmetrization conditions can be ignored.

Observe that one has to use the nonlocal Hamiltonian of Eq. 11.13 *whether or not* one accepts a causal interpretation of QM. As Bohm and Hiley carefully note, we have to use a symmetrized Hamiltonian like this if we want to get the right predictions for Bose particles, and that fact is quite independent of whatever interpretation of QM one chooses. Hence, the question of signalling is, in the last analysis, just as unavoidable for Option 1 as for Option 2.

Nothing we have said here shows that systems with nonlocal Hamiltonians such as Eq. 11.13 could, indeed, be used for controllable signalling. However, proofs of the type offered by Shimony, or Bohm and Hiley, are clearly powerless to show that they cannot.

## 11.7 The Hamiltonian for Entangled Particles Cannot Be Additive

Up to this point, the gist of our argument has been to claim that it is question-begging to *defend* peaceful coexistence by means of a premise (localized dynamics for entangled states) that is *based upon* a prior assumption of peaceful coexistence. However, a staunch defender of peaceful coexistence could reply that the critique cuts both ways. Might it not said to be question-begging in *favour* of nonlocal signalling to arbitrarily insert cross-terms in the Hamiltonian, since that would guarantee at least the in-principle possibility of controllable signalling?

One of us (K.P.) happened to have a conversation with Abner Shimony in 1993. When Shimony was asked why he did not allow for the possibility of cross-terms in the Hamiltonian, Shimony replied in a shocked voice, 'But then you could violate Parameter Independence [no-signalling]!' Shimony was a thinker who did not have difficulty distinguishing premises from conclusions. However, he simply took it as beyond discussion that relativistic causality was not to be violated; therefore, the burden of proof was on those who would claim otherwise. For there is indeed a question of burden of proof: are there any compelling physical or mathematical reasons to suppose that the Hamiltonians of entangled states are themselves entangled, *independently* of one's view of the relationship between relativity and quantum mechanics? It can't be merely a question of taste or philosophical preference.

In this paper we will not attempt to present a complete theory of the dynamics of entangled states, though components of such a theory are widely available in the literature (especially the literature on quantum information theory). Instead, we will present a straightforward *reductio* argument that *prima facie* undermines the claim that one can associate a Hamiltonian in an unambiguous way with each of the particles belonging to an entangled state. If this line of reasoning is correct (and we are aware that it requires further investigation), it shows that any no-signalling argument such as Shimony's that depends upon an additive or localized Hamiltonian such as Eq. (11.7) cannot apply to entangled states.

It is well known that subsystems of a tensor product (entangled) state cannot be pure states:

> It can be shown... that an interaction between the two systems transforms an initial state which is a product into one which is no longer a product: any interaction between two systems therefore introduces, in general, correlations between them. ... This question is very important since, in general, every physical system has interacted with others in the past ... *it is not possible to associate a state vector* $|\phi(1)\rangle$ *[a pure state] with system (1) alone* [emphasis added]. [51, p. 293]

Now suppose, as did Shimony, that it is possible to associate a Hamiltonian $H_1$ with particle 1 that is presumed to be a member of an entangled state. The question is what we can mean by such an association. Clearly, given the calculation that he carried out, Shimony was willing to treat the Hamiltonian associated with an entangled particle as if it were a Hamiltonian that can be associated with a particle in a quantum-mechanically unambiguous way. What does that imply? The Hamiltonian is an observable, and every observable associated with a state $|\psi\rangle$ has a set of eigenstates which define a basis for $|\psi\rangle$. Therefore, the most straightforward reading of the claim that a particle 'has' a Hamiltonian is that the particle has a state that can be written as an expansion of the form

$$|\phi(1)\rangle = \sum_i e_i |e_i\rangle \qquad (11.14)$$

where $\{|e_i\rangle\}$ are the energy eigenstates of particle 1 with respect to $H_1$.

*Any expression of this form is a pure state.* However, because 1 is taken to be a member of an entangled state, it cannot, by itself, itself be represented as a pure state. Hence, there cannot exist a Hamiltonian that can be associated with 1 in this way. Conversely, if a particle has a state that can be written in the form of Eq. 11.14, then it cannot be entangled.

These facts imply that the Hamiltonian for an entangled state cannot in general be written as a tensor product of trivially extended Hamiltonians for the individual particles as in Eq. 11.7—because there is no such entity as a single Hamiltonian for each of the particles in an entangled state. The Hamiltonians for entangled particles cannot be additive since it is not possible to define a 'pure' Hamiltonian for each particle.

It is well known, however, that the Hamiltonians for *product* states are additive. This strongly suggests that attempts to demonstrate no-signalling on the basis of the assumption that the Hamiltonian for the system is additive amount merely to trivial demonstrations of no-signalling for product states. Insofar as it depends upon the dynamics of the multiparticle system, the question of signalling in entangled states remains open.[6]

Cohen-Tannoudji et al. also observe as follows:

> Just as with vectors, there exist operators in $\mathscr{E}$ [a tensor product space] which are not tensor products of an operator of $\mathscr{E}_1$ and an operator of $\mathscr{E}_2$ [the subpaces]. [51, p. 157]

---

[6]The other major strategy that has been used to demonstrate no-signalling is to appeal to microcausality, the assumption that any measurement operations done at a spacelike separation will commute. Microcausality-based no-signalling proofs are critiqued elsewhere in this volume; see also [147]. The problem with the microcausality defense of peaceful coexistence is that it, again, depends upon the prior assumption of peaceful coexistence; microcausality was installed as a postulate of local quantum field theory by authors such as Pauli precisely in order to forestall conflicts with relativity [157]. An adequate reconsideration of microcausality demands a broadening of the concept of simultaneity, and some suggestions are sketched elsewhere in this volume.

## 11.7. The Hamiltonian for Entangled Particles Cannot Be Additive

We should expect to find that just as the individual particles belonging to an entangled state can be represented only by mixed states, the Hamiltonians for individual particles in entangled states would have to be written in mixed form—as classical probability distributions over a range of possible Hamiltonians for each particle. This indicates that it is a poor choice of words to describe the particles as 'individual'. It also indicates that a theory of *mixed operators* is required in order to properly describe the dynamics of entangled particles (a theory that does not yet seem to have been developed in detail).

If we are correct that the energy operators for entangled particles must be mixed, that would be a manifestation of the spooky action that Einstein dreaded: the energy states for particle 1 would, in effect, be classical probability distributions over the measurement choices made on particle 2. Again, this by itself does not guarantee that *controllable* signalling is possible, for the *outcomes* on particle 2 (and thus particle 1) might still be random. However, it does suggest that whether or not it is possible to control the local results on particle 2 without breaking the nonlocal connection is essentially an engineering question—likely a very difficult engineering question, but not a question of fundamental principle.

In this paper we have made no attempt to determine the *magnitude* of the nonlocal energy that would be associated with entangled states; this is a major problem that remains to be solved. It is odd, in particular, that neither Bohm himself nor anyone else who has worked on his theory has attempted to determine quantitatively how much energy the quantum potential actually contributes to the total energy of a system of particles.[7]

It could be that the nonlocal contributions to system energy are so small as to be negligible in most or all practical circumstances. But the Shimonian reading of the dynamics of entangled states demands that any nonlocal contribution to the system energy be *exactly* zero; usually or nearly zero is not good enough. If we are right about the existence of cross-terms in the Hamiltonian for entangled states, then any successful argument for peaceful coexistence has to be of a very different sort than the arguments (such as Bohm and Hiley's, and Shimony's) that appeal to dynamic locality. Such an argument might turn on a claim that any terms in the wavefunctions that could allow for signalling are phase-incoherent. But the nonlocal terms would have to *always* wash out; no exceptions allowed, or else peaceful coexistence would again turn out to be something that depends upon mere practical difficulty and not principle.

Finally, we draw attention to the remark by Cohen-Tannoudji *et al.* in the passage quoted above: '... in general, every physical system has interacted with others in the past.' If taken seriously, this implies that every particle in the universe is entangled and therefore cannot be described, in full accuracy, as a pure state (though of course that is a useful approximation for many

---

[7] At least, we have been unable to find any published evidence of such work, after a fairly diligent literature search. If we are wrong about this we welcome correction.

practical purposes). Entanglement therefore has cosmological implications, which remain to be fully determined.

## 11.8  Nonlocal Energy: It's Everywhere

There is a curious inconsistency in Bohm's thought. On the one hand, he, more than any other physicist, drew attention to the feature of quantum mechanics that he called 'unbroken wholeness'—a pervasive connectedness of all physical phenomena that manifests itself in entanglement and the quantum potential. And yet on the other hand, even Bohm could not permit himself to imagine that the facts he had discovered about quantum mechanics could be allowed to challenge his beloved theory of relativity. As we have shown in this paper, this ambivalence led to a glaring inconsistency in his treatment of the signalling problem. Bohm, in particular, never seriously examined one of the most obvious implications of his own theory—that if particles are affected by the quantum potential, then the quantum potential must be affected by particles, which opens up the possibility of *controllable* nonlocal effects (not merely signalling). As noted, Abner Shimony correctly pointed out that the question of whether or not some sort of nonlocal interaction is needed to explain the Bell-violating correlations, and whether or not such interactions would be controllable, are logically separate questions.

In our view the really important fact to which Bohm drew attention is the nonlocality of quantum dynamics. The questions of whether or not Bohm's approach permits of an 'ontological' interpretation, or whether 'particles can be particles,' are red herrings. What really needs to be better understood are the dynamics of interference and entanglement phenomena; surely, by now, it is clear that no one is entitled to attempt to settle the question by simply *assuming* from the get-go that these are local.

The notion of nonlocal energy is, admittedly, difficult to grasp. One might be inclined to think that according to a causal interpretation of quantum mechanics, there must be some sort of superluminal transmission of a localized pulse of mass-energy between the remote particles. However, if we ask whether energy is being shuttled superluminally between $A$ and $B$, by tachyons perhaps, we miss the point. Some such description might be useful in some contexts. However, the real point is that some, at least, of the mass-energy pertaining to quantum systems is *nonlocal*, a *global* property of a multi-particle system. It might even be less confusing to refer to such globalized energy as *a*local, rather than nonlocal. The category of localization does not apply to it, until the system partakes in an interaction which leads to emission or absorption of a localized particle.

The multiparticle system as a whole will have a spectrum of possible energy states, and the energy is not any place in particular at all; it is just a general property of the system, that may make itself manifest in a variety of ways. This is analogous to the way in which the energy of an electron orbital

## 11.8. Nonlocal Energy: It's Everywhere

in an atom is a global property of the orbital as a whole; it is not localized until part of it is released when the orbital undergoes a transition and emits a photon.

In the end, we can safely say to Agent Mulder that there is no hidden conspiracy, but merely a confusion. Except for systems in which the Hamiltonian approximates to a local form, as in Eq. 11.7, we still simply do not know whether one can violate relativity (as it is presently understood) by means of some sort of controllable nonlocal effect in entangled multiparticle states. The truth is still out there.[8]

---

[8] This work was supported by the Social Sciences and Humanities Research Council of Canada and the University of Lethbridge. K. P. thanks James Robert Brown for valuable discussions and guidance in the early stages of this research.

# Envoi: The Work To Be Done

I'll conclude with a few words about what directions I suspect physics, and the philosophy of physics, have to go in order to resolve the problems pointed to in this book.

1. There is no more immediately pressing question in theoretical physics than to get clear, once and for all, on the correct dynamics of entangled states. The failure to face this problem has hobbled physics since the 1930s. The main thing that has prevented this problem from being addressed by those with the technical ability to address it has been philosophical prejudice against the notion of dynamic nonlocality. There is, indeed, a kind of cognitive dissonance in modern physics: while foundational authors continue to claim that quantum mechanics is 'kinematically nonlocal' (because of Bell's Theorem) but 'dynamically local' (because Hamiltonians should always be additive to protect relativity), it is routinely taken in quantum information theory that the general Hamiltonian for entangled states contains cross-terms (see, e.g., [68]). A coherent picture is needed. Resolving this bit of unfinished business is an essential prerequisite to any hope of progress in virtually any branch of modern physics in which quantum mechanics plays a role.

2. This volume is compiled during a fraught time in which the survival of our species likely depends in important part upon finding means of releasing and manipulating energy that do not destroy our planetary habitat [103, 10]. It is necessary to take very seriously the possibility that nonlocal dynamics can be exploited technologically. The failure of the attempt to establish, without the use of special pleading, a completely general no-controllable-signalling result in quantum mechanics opens the door to the possibility, however remote, that nonlocality could be controlled in ways that we can now only sketchily imagine. This possibility will seem far-fetched to some, but it needs to be thoroughly and open-mindedly investigated and not merely assumed out of existence.

3. In this book I have not attempted to predict how quantum signalling might actually be made to work, if it could. For now, I'll say simply this: It

does not seem to be widely appreciated that the requirement for nonlocal signalling is essentially the same as that for quantum computing—one must somehow extract information from a quantum state without collapsing the state. At first glance this might seem to be an impossible demand. But a hint as to how to do the impossible can be extracted from a remark by Basil Hiley and David Peat:

> [I]t is well known that when we go to low enough temperatures, bulk matter behaves very differently. Currents flow without dissipation in superconductivity, superfluids flow without viscosity, etc., but as the temperature rises, the distant correlations necessary for non-dissipation break up and the particles no longer flow without resistance. If we regard these long-range correlations as stemming from quantum non-locality, then they seem to be very fragile and can be broken quite easily, simply by raising the temperature. In fact it is this fragility that makes it impossible to send signals in EPR situations. This is another way of explaining why a conflict with relativity is by no means necessary. [111, pp. 15–16]

However, if it is *merely* fragility that hampers quantum signalling (and conceivably other forms of locally controlled nonlocality), then a conflict with relativity is inevitable. For it is certainly conceivable that the fragility of the nonlocal connections could be overcome either by interacting with entangled states *very* gently (as in quantum non-demolition) or by exploiting some sort of amplification or resonance to *strengthen* the nonlocal connection. Of course, I do not have a detailed blueprint for anything like this in my briefcase, but it seems increasingly likely that achieving quantum signalling and possibly other forms of controlled nonlocality (such as quantum computing and high-temperature superconductivity) is essentially an engineering problem.

4. I have already cited a statement by Abner Shimony that quantum nonlocality gives us reason to refine 'the concept of an event' [203, p. 182]. I am not aware that Shimony ever expanded upon what he could have meant by this pregnant remark. Orthodox relativity, as conceived by Einstein, pictures spacetime as built up of point-events, defined operationally by coincidences between two identifiable local events such as, for example, the tick of a clock and the emission of a photon. Einstein himself was well aware that there is an ambiguity built into the very notion of point-coincidence, which is only exacerbated by the indeterminacy relations of quantum mechanics. This ambiguity needs to be resolved, and that must be part of 'refining' the concept of an event. But there is another possibility that needs to be explored: arguably one way in which we

could refine or generalize the concept of an event is to think of events as *multiple* or *multilocal*. (Redhead, following David Lewis, has suggested something along these lines; see Chapter 5.) When we interact with one member of an $n$-tuple of entangled particles, there must be not one but $n$ localization or actualization events, which may well be at a spacelike separation but which can be thought of as a single multilocal process. Then we must come to understand spacetime as built up not of single event-points, but of multiples of such relatively or approximately localized event-points. The $n$-tuples of such points must be related invariantly, and so this demands a generalization of our concepts of simultaneity, possibly along the lines I have suggested in several of my papers—that is, one conceives of a notion of simultaneity as 'joint process' rather than 'at the same time coordinate' (see §10.5). These sketchy ideas, both the notion of multilocality and expanded notions of simultaneity, need much further development.

5. Closely tied to the previous point is the need to critically review the concept of microcausality (also called local commutativity). This is the postulate of local quantum field theory that observables at a spacelike separation always commute, even if they are operations (such as the measurement of position and momentum in the same direction) that would not commute locally. Kennedy, Mittelstaedt, and I have all argued independently that no-signalling 'proofs' based on microcausality are question-begging, since this postulate was inserted *by hand* into quantum field theory precisely in order to forestall conflicts with the orthodox view of relativistic causality [160, 121, 147]. While it is trivial to show that distant operations on systems of localized particles (product states) must commute, it seems very reasonable to suppose that operations on spatially extended or multilocal quantum systems would not necessarily behave so nicely. The question of commutativity of distant operations, again, demands a rethinking and generalization of our notions of simultaneity— another important piece of the work in progress.

6. I have also not directly discussed at any length the measurement problem of quantum mechanics, even though it lurks behind all of the issues treated in these papers. From the early days of quantum mechanics it was obvious that one possible explanation for the way that measurement can 'steer' (Schrödinger's term) distant particles into one definite state or another is that measurement manifests or triggers some sort of action at a distance or nonlocal dynamics. But all of the founders of quantum mechanics (with the possible exception of de Broglie) disparaged this solution—indeed, they rejected it with horror and distaste—and since then the many attempts to solve the measurement problem could be described as an increasingly desperate series of attempts to try every

conceivable possibility other than the one that has always been the most obvious. My conjecture (and at this point it is only a conjecture) is that the most obvious approach to the measurement problem will turn out to be the correct approach: measurement involves the reweighting of probabilities due to nonlocal interactions. But a lot of work remains to be done in order to turn this conjecture into a testable theory.

7. In the early 1990s I was privileged to share an office with Itamar Pitowsky, when he was a visiting professor at the University of Western Ontario. Pitowsky combined a penetrating understanding of the mathematics of Bell's Theorem (his [174] is indispensible) with strongly conservative views about the relationship between relativity and quantum mechanics. When I raised with him the possibility of nonlocal dynamics in quantum systems he replied that if there were such a thing then the physical world would be deeply irrational. Although we did not pursue the conversation further, I am sure he was referring to the closed-loop causal anomalies that apparently would arise in special relativity if controllable superluminal interactions were possible. (So long as one has certain combinations of relative velocities, if Bob sends a tachyon to Alice, she can return a tachyon to Bob that blocks his transmission, creating a logical contradiction.) An adequate treatment of causal anomalies would require another book, but I will provide just a hint as to where a proper investigation might lead: although it would be possible to write a quantum state with backwards-in-time amplitudes so as to define a closed causal loop (after all, this is just what happens in a Feynman diagram), the mathematics of quantum mechanics does not allow one to write a state that is self-contradictory. Quantum states are defined in terms of conservation laws (such as spin or charge) and are always internally self-consistent even if two distinct pure states (such as the state for the alive cat and the dead cat) may be inconsistent. Granting this, one might still ask what is to stop two distinct entangled states from having contradictory observable outcomes, even if each are internally consistent. The answer to this could be cosmological. If the universe as a whole is a single, vast entangled state, a giant EPR apparatus in effect—precisely as the Big Bang cosmology suggests it must be—then there are no contradictory quantum loops. (This does not necessarily argue in favour of the block universe; quite the contrary, since quantum mechanics does not allow for the global Booleanity that would be definitive of the block hypothesis.) Much more needs to be said; in particular, it remains to be explained why there would be no contradictory measurement *outcomes* in a nonlocal universe. Pitowsky's judgement on matters quantum mechanical deserves a great deal of respect, but I am of the view that the risk of paradox is not a sufficient reason to abandon the investigation of nonlocal dynamics in quantum mechanics. Rather, I think that the evidence for nonlocal dynamics is strong enough that we

need to be prepared to rethink our notions of causality. This is another large piece of unfinished business.

8. As shown in Chapter 4, it is possible to derive Lorentz-like transformations for superluminal frames that are devoid of imaginary quantities, so long as one explicitly allows for the possibility that one or more of the frames are superluminal. Most authors who have studied tachyons merely substitute the condition $v > c$ into the usual Lorentz transformations (which are well-confirmed for the subluminal case). Unsurprisingly, this leads to an unphysical picture. The issue, again, is circularity: the derivation of the usual transformations takes *both* frames to be subluminal, so by uncritically applying the usual transformations to superluminal frames we are implicity treating them as if they were subluminal. So another major task is thoroughly to revisit the treatment of faster-than-light motion in special relativity. This could be very important in particle physics, since it could put the whole question of the physicality of tachyons in a new light.

9. Philosophers of physics may well decide that everything I have said in this volume is rubbish. However, even if they reject every specific point I've raised, they would do well to heed this plea from physicist Carlo Rovelli:

> Due to the conceptual vastness of the problematic involved, the generality and accuracy of philosophical thinking and its capacity to clarify conceptual premises are probably necessary to help physics out of a situation in which we have learned so much about the world, but no longer know what matter, time, space, and causality are. As a physicist involved in this effort, I wish the philosophers who are interested in the scientific description of the world would not confine themselves to commenting and polishing the present fragmentary physical theories, but would take the risk of trying to look ahead. [189, p. 182].

Lee Smolin has also called for philosophical engagement in the problems faced by modern physics [210]. There is a certain irony in this: while philosophers of physics defer to the superior wisdom of the physicists, some of our most distinguished physicists are begging the philosophers for help with the apparently intractable conceptual problems they face. Smolin and Rovelli are right: the job of philosophers of science is not merely to be cheerleaders for eminent scientists, but, by means of criticism and conceptual innovation, to aid in the solution of the deep problems still besetting science. Philosophers who wish to contribute to the advancement of science must, of course, make themselves deeply conversant in the details and technicalities of the sciences they are interested in. (A shining model in this regard is Abner Shimony himself, who earned doctorates in both philosophy and physics.) But they must not be unduly deferential to the physicists, who sometimes have little training in logic or the history of science, and little time or incentive to take intellectual risks or to imaginatively place their research in larger context. Philosophy has both a critical and a creative component, and conceptual analysis, creative vision, and a certain amount of sheer heresy—which John C. Polanyi called 'the lifeblood of science' [176]—are all going to be needed in order to see physics through its present impasse.

# Acknowledgements

There are many people to thank, especially since this volume covers the larger part of my professional career so far, at least those phases of it concerned with space, time, and the quantum. I have preserved the statements of acknowledgement published originally with these papers (though I converted all of them to footnotes at the end of each paper). In addition, some global acknowledgements are needed. As noted in the Preface, John Woods invited me to submit a proposal to College Publications for a collection of my quantum papers. I owe thanks to John not only for this honour but for the very existence of my academic career, since he and other members of the Department of Philosophy at the University of Lethbridge saw fit to rescue me from the prospect of unemployment back in 1996. Thanks also to Dov Gabbay for accepting the proposal, and Jane Spurr for essential assistance during the production of this book. The book was formatted with LaTeX (using the memoir class and mathpazo package), and I am very grateful to the large LaTeX community whose volunteer labour over many years has made these and other wonderful tools available. I am very grateful as well to James Robert Brown for allowing and encouraging me to pursue an unconventional line of inquiry in my PhD dissertation, and for his generous encouragement and assistance throughout my career since then. Thanks to my son, Evan Peacock, for the cover illustration and figures. For indispensible support I am indebted to the Universities of Toronto, Western Ontario, and Lethbridge (my present academic home), and the Social Sciences and Humanities Council of Canada. Thanks to the Perimeter Institute for hospitality (in a visit in 2008) and to several of its members for valuable discussions. For conversations, advice, or debate about the topics of this book, or assistance with the work reported in it, I am honoured to thank Richard T.A. Arthur, John L. Bell, M. Bryson Brown, Jed Buchwald, Rob Clifton, John G. Cramer, J.W. Crichton, Saurya Das, Bill Demopoulos, Robert DiSalle, Christopher Fuchs, Lance Grigg, William Harper, Brian Hepburn, Nick Herbert, R.I.G. Hughes, Frederick L. Jackson, Trace Jordan, J. B. Kennedy Jr., Michael Kernaghan, Alexandre Korolev, Herbert Korté, Jordan Maclay, Tim Maudlin, Nicholas Maxwell, David McDonald, Patrick McGivern, Ernan McMullen, Fred Muller, Wayne Myrvold, Jessica Oddan, Cody D. Perrin, Vesselin Petkov,

Anna Pezacki, Itamar Pitowsky, Thomas M. Robinson, John D. Ross, James Rowell, Jack Sarfatti, William Seager, Niall Shanks, Abner Shimony, Graham Solomon, James Stacey, Jesse Supina, Frank Switt, Alasdair Urquhart, Bas van Fraassen, Mark Walton, Grant A. Whatmough, and my many students at the Universities of Toronto, Western Ontario, and Lethbridge. My apologies to those whose names I may have lost track of after years of conversations, emails, and teaching. None of these fine people are in any way responsible for any errors of fact or interpretation which linger in the present work and it is not to be presumed that any of them agree or agreed with the heretical picture I advance in it.

# Bibliography

[1] Y. Aharonov, J. Anandan, J.G. Maclay, and J. Suzuki. Model for entangled states with spin-spin interaction. *Physical Review A*, 70:052114, 2004. 134

[2] Y. Aharonov, S. Popescu, and J. Tollaksen. A time-symmetric formulation of quantum mechanics. *Physics Today*, 27(11):27–32, November 2010. 155

[3] Yakir Aharonov and David Z. Albert. States and observables in relativistic quantum field theories. *Physical Review D*, 21(12):3316–3324, 1980. 117, 149, 150

[4] Yakir Aharonov and David Z. Albert. Can we make sense out of the measurement process in relativistic quantum mechanics? *Physical Review D*, 24(2):359–370, 1981. 117, 149

[5] David Albert and Barry Loewer. Interpreting the many-worlds interpretation. *Synthese*, 77:195–213, 1988. 67

[6] Miguel Alcubierre. The warp drive: Hyper-fast travel within general relativity. *Classical and Quantum Gravity*, 11(5):73–77, 1994. 56

[7] A. Ali, S. Das, and E.C. Vagenas. Discreteness of space from the Generalized Uncertainty Principle. *Physics Letters B*, 678:497–499, 2009. 152

[8] G. Amelino-Camelia, J. Ellis, N.E. Mavromatos, D.V. Nanopoulos, and S. Sarkar. Tests of quantum gravity from observations of $\gamma$-ray bursts. *Nature*, 393(6687):763–765, 1998. 121

[9] A.R. Anderson and N.D. Belnap. *Entailment: The Logic of Relevance and Necessity, Vol. I*. Princeton University Press, Princeton, 1975. 94

[10] Kevin Anderson. Duality in climate science. *Nature Geoscience*, 8:898–900, 2015. 176

[11] Houshang Ardavan. A singularity arising from the coherent generation of gravitational waves by electromagnetic waves. In W. B. Bonner, J. N. Islam, and M. A. H. MacCallum, editors, *Classical General Relativity*, pages 5–14. Cambridge University Press, 1984. 44, 140

[12] Houshang Ardavan. A speed-of-light barrier in classical electrodynamics. *Physical Review D*, 29(2):207–215, 1984. 44, 140

# Bibliography 185

[13] Frank Arntzenius. Causal paradoxes in Special Relativity. *British Journal for the Philosophy of Science*, 41:223–243, 1990. 138, 146, 147, 156

[14] Frank Arntzenius. Spacelike connections. *British Journal for the Philosophy of Science*, 45:201–217, 1994. 57

[15] Richard T.A. Arthur. Minkowski spacetime and the dimensions of the present. In Dennis Dieks, editor, *The Ontology of Spacetime*, pages 129–155. Elsevier, Amsterdam, 2006. 116

[16] Richard T.A. Arthur. Time lapse and the degeneracy of time: Gödel, proper time and becoming in relativity theory. In Dennis Dieks, editor, *The Ontology of Spacetime II*, pages 207–227. Elsevier, Amsterdam, 2008. 116, 144

[17] Henri Bacry. *Localizability and Space in Quantum Physics*, volume 308 of *Lecture Notes in Physics*. Springer-Verlag, Berlin, 1988. 45

[18] L. E. Ballentine. Resource letter IQM-2. *American Journal of Physics*, 55(9):785–792, 1987. Reprinted in L. E. Ballentine (ed.), *Foundations of Quantum Mechanics Since the Bell Inequalities* (College Park, American Association of Physics, Teachers), pp. 1–8. 42

[19] L. E. Ballentine and Jon P. Jarrett. Bell's Theorem: does quantum mechanics contradict relativity? *American Journal of Physics*, 55(8):696–701, 1987. 13, 31, 161

[20] Julian Barbour. *The End of Time*. Oxford University Press, Oxford, 2000. 113

[21] Jon Barwise. *Handbook of Mathematical Logic*. North Holland, Amsterdam, 1977. 111

[22] Eric Temple Bell. *Men of Mathematics*. Simon and Schuster, New York, 1937. 114

[23] J. L. Bell. A new approach to quantum logic. *British Journal for the Philosophy of Science*, 37:83–99, 1986. 86

[24] J. S. Bell. Speakable and unspeakable in quantum mechanics. In *Speakable and Unspeakable in Quantum Mechanics: Collected papers on quantum philosophy*, pages 169–172. Cambridge University Press, Cambridge, 1987. 90, 136

[25] J.S. Bell. On the Einstein-Podolsky-Rosen paradox. *Physics*, 1:195–200, 1964. 68, 128

[26] J.S. Bell. Against 'measurement'. *Physics World*, 3(8):33–40, 1990. 126

[27] J.S. Bell. La nouvelle cuisine. In A. Sarlemijn and P. Kroes, editors, *Between Science and Technology*, pages 97–115. Elsevier, 1990. 134, 135

[28] Greg Benford. *Cosm*. Avon Books, New York, 1998. 96

[29] C.H. Bennett and S. J. Wiesner. Communication via one- and two-particle operators on Einstein-Podolsky-Rosen states. *Physical Review Letters*, 69(20):2881–2884, 1992. 31

[30]  Olexa-Myron Bilaniuk and E. C. George Sudarshan. Particles beyond the light barrier. *Physics Today*, 22(5):43–51, 1969. 50, 55, 137

[31]  G. Birkhoff and J. von Neumann. The logic of Quantum Mechanics. *Annals of Mathematics*, 37:823–843, 1936. Reprinted in C.A. Hooker (ed.), *The Logico-Algebraic Approach to Quantum Mechanics* Vol. I, Deidel Dordrecht, pp. 1–26. 84, 86, 103

[32]  D. Bohm and B.J. Hiley. *The Undivided Universe: An Ontological Interpretation of Quantum Theory*. Routledge, London and New York, 1993. 39, 40, 41, 71, 81, 90, 117, 154, 155, 159, 160, 164, 165, 170

[33]  D. Bohm and J. P. Vigier. Model of the causal interpretation of quantum theory in terms of a fluid with irregular fluctuations. *Physical Review*, 96(1):208–216, 1954. 167

[34]  David Bohm. *Quantum Theory*. Prentice Hall, Englewood Cliffs, NJ, 1951. 68, 160

[35]  David Bohm. A suggggested interpretation of the quantum theory in terms of 'hidden variables'. *Physical Review*, 85:166–193, 1952. 154, 163, 164

[36]  Niels Bohr. Can quantum-mechanical description of reality be considered complete? *Physical Review*, 48:696–702, 1936. 29, 30, 41, 161

[37]  Dik Bouwmeester, Jian-Wei Pan, Matthew Daniel, Harald Weinfurter, and Anton Zeilinger. Observation of three-photon Greenberger-Horne-Zeilinger entanglement. *Physical Review Letters*, 82(7):1345–1349, 1999. 35

[38]  Bryson Brown. Defending backwards causation. *Canadian Journal of Philosophy*, 22(4):429–443, 1992. 156

[39]  Bryson Brown. Old quantum theory: a paraconsistent approach. In *PSA: Proceedings of the Biennial Meeting of the Philosophy of Science Association Volume*, volume 2, pages 397–411. Philosophy of Science Association, University of Chicago Press, 1992. 94

[40]  Bryson Brown. Smoke and mirrors: A few nice tricks. *Dialogue*, 38(1):123–134, 1999. 47

[41]  Harvey R. Brown. *Physical Relativity: Space-time Structure from a Dynamical Perspective*. Clarendon, Oxford, 2006. 144, 149

[42]  James Robert Brown. *The Laboratory of the Mind: Thought Experiments in the Natural Sciences*. Routledge, London, 1991. 42, 48

[43]  James Robert Brown. *Smoke and Mirrors: How Science Reflects Reality*. Routledge, London, 1994. 47, 48

[44]  Jeffrey Bub. *Interpreting the Quantum World*. Cambridge University Press, Cambridge, 1997. 89, 90, 95, 102, 103, 110, 124

[45]  P.J. Bussey. Communication and non-communication in Einstein-Rosen experiments. *Physics Letters A*, 123(1):1–3, 1987. 6, 132

[46]  A. Cabello. Correlations without parts. *Nature*, 474:456–457, 23 June 2011. 139

[47]  Elena Castellani, editor. *Interpreting Bodies: Classical and Quantum Objects in Modern Physics*. Princeton University Press, Princeton, 1009. 100

[48]  Hasok Chang and Nancy Cartwright. Causality and realism in the EPR experiment. *Erkenntnis*, 38:169–190, 1993. 28, 29, 34, 35, 43, 153

[49]  Maria Luisa Dall Chiara. Quantum logic. In D. Gabbay and F. Guenthner, editors, *Alternatives in Classical Logics*, volume III of *Handbook of Philosophical Logic*, chapter III.7, pages 427–469. D. Reidel Publishing Company, Dordrecht, 1986. 103

[50]  Robert Clifton and Mark Hogarth. The definability of objective becoming in Minkowski spacetime. *Synthese*, 103:355–387 1995. 115, 118, 121

[51]  Claude Cohen-Tannoudji, Bernard Diu, and Franck Laloë. *Quantum Mechanics, Volume I*. Wiley Interscience, New York, 1977. 150, 171, 172

[52]  James T. Cushing. *Quantum Mechanics; Historical Contingency and the Copenhagen Hegemony*. University of Chicago Press, Chicago, IL, 1994. 45, 90, 131, 154, 163, 164

[53]  B. Dainton. *Time and Space*. McGill-Queen's University Press, Montréal and Kingston, Second edition, 2010. 138

[54]  Louis de Broglie. *Non-linear Wave Mechanics: A Causal Interpretation*. Elsevier, Amsterdam, 1960. Translation by A.J. Knodel and J.C. Miller of *Une Tentative Interprétation Causale et Non Linéaire de la Méchanique Ondulatoire (La Théorie de la Double Solution)*, Paris: Gauthier-Villars, 1956. 117, 155, 163, 164

[55]  Louis de Broglie. The reinterpretation of wave mechanics. *Foundations of Physics Letters*, 1(1):5–15, 1970. 155, 163

[56]  B.S. de Witt and N. Graham, editors. *The Many-Worlds Interpretation of Quantum Mechanics*. Princeton University Press, Princeton, 1973. 110

[57]  Bernard d'Espagnat. Nonseparability and the tentative descriptions of reality. *Physics Reports*, 110(4):201–264, 1984. 12, 31

[58]  D. Deutsch. Quantum theory, the Church-Turing principle and the universal quantum computer. *Proceedings of the Royal Society of London A*, 400:97–117, 1985. 84, 109

[59]  David Deutsch. *The Fabric of Reality*. Penguin Books, London, 1997. 84, 110, 111

[60]  David Deutsch, Artur Ekert, and Rossella Lupacchini. Machines, logic, and quantum physics, 1999. http://lanl.arxiv.org/abs/math/9911150. 108, 109

[61]  Phillip K. Dick. *The World Jones Made*. A. A. Winn, New York, 1956. 20

[62]  Michael Dickson. Essay review: antidote or theory? *Studies in History and Philosophy of Modern Physics*, 27(2):229–238, 1996. 39

[63] Michael Dickson. Quantum logic is alive ∧ (it is true ∨ it is false). *Philosophy of Science*, 68 (Proceedings):S274–S287, 2001. 91, 93

[64] D. Dieks. Discussion: Special Relativity and the Flow of Time. *Philosophy of Science*, 55(3):456–460, September 1988. 15, 25, 119

[65] P.A.M. Dirac. *The Principles of Quantum Mechanics*. Clarendon Press, Oxford, fourth revised edition, 1958. 150

[66] H. A. C. Dobbs. The relation between the time of psychology and the time of physics. *British Journal for the Philosophy of Science*, 2:122–141, 1951. 123

[67] Mauro Dorato. On becoming, relativity, and nonseparability. *Philosophy of Science*, 63:585–604, 1996. 121

[68] W. Dür, G. Vidal, J.I. Cirac, N. Linden, and S. Popescu. Entanglement capabilities of nonlocal Hamiltonians. *Physical Review Letters*, 87(13):137901-1–137901-4, 2001. 176

[69] Detlef Dürr, Sheldon Goldstein, and N. Zanghì. Quantum physics without quantum philosophy. *Studies in History and Philosophy of Modern Physics*, 26(2):137–149, 1995. 82, 90

[70] P. H. Eberhard. Bell's Theorem and the different concepts of locality. *Il Nuovo Cimento B*, 46(2):392–419, August 1978. 12, 13, 31, 131, 161

[71] P. H. Eberhard and R. R. Ross. Quantum Field Theory cannot provide faster-than-light communication. *Foundations of Physics Letters*, 2(2):127–149, 1989. 12, 31, 157, 161

[72] T.M. Robinson (Ed. and Trans.). *Heraclitus: Fragments*. University of Toronto Press, Toronto, 1987. 113

[73] A.S. Eddington. *Fundamental Theory*. Cambridge University Press, Cambridge, 1953. 123

[74] Albert Einstein. Zur Elektrodynamik bewegter Körper. *Annalen der Physik*, 17:891–921, 1905. Translation by W. Perrett and G. B. Jeffrey, in *The Principle of Relativity* (Dover, New York). Page numbers refer to this edition. 43, 75, 148, 149, 152

[75] Albert Einstein. Die Grundlage der allgemeinen Relativitätstheorie. *Annalen der Physik*, 49:769–822, 1916. Translation in W. Perrett and G. B. Jeffrey (eds.), *The Principle of Relativity*, New York: Methuen, 1923, pp. 111–64; page references to this edition. 151

[76] Albert Einstein. Principles of research. In C. Seelig, editor, *Ideas and Opinions*, pages 224–227. Crown, New York, 1954. Translation by S. Bargmann. Based on an address given to the Berlin Physical Society in 1918. 46, 73

[77] Albert Einstein. What is the theory of relativity? In C. Seelig, editor, *Ideas and Opinions*, pages 227–232. Crown, New York, 1954. Translation by S. Bargmann. 42

# Bibliography

[78] Albert Einstein, Boris Podolsky, and Nathan Rosen. Can quantum-mechanical description of physical reality be considered complete? *Physical Review*, 47:777–780, 1935. Reprinted in Wheeler and Zurek, 138–141. 29, 68, 128, 160

[79] A.C. Elitzur. On some neglected thermodynamic peculiarities of quantum non-locality. *Foundations of Physics Letters*, 3(6):525–541, 1990. 34, 37, 47

[80] Kurt Engesser and Dov M. Gabbay. Quantum logic, Hilbert space, revision theory. *Artificial Intelligence*, 136(1):61–100, 2002. 106

[81] Hugh Everett. 'Relative State' formulation of Quantum Mechanics. *Physical Review*, 29(3):454–462, 1957. 110

[82] M. Fayngold. *Special Relativity and Motions Faster Than Light*. Wiley-VCH, Hoboken, NJ, 2002. 138

[83] G. Feinberg. Possibility of faster-than-light particles. *Physical Review*, 159:1089–1105, 1967. 50, 137

[84] Richard P. Feynman, Robert B. Leighton, and Matthew Sands. *The Feynman Lectures on Physics: Vol. III, Quantum Mechanics*. Addison-Wesley, Reading, MA, 1965. 88

[85] Arthur Fine. Some local models for correlation experiments. *Synthese*, 50:279–294, 1982. 34

[86] Arthur Fine. Do correlations need to be explained? In J.T. Cushing and E. McMullin, editors, *Philosophical Consequences of Quantum Theory: Reflections on Bell's Theorem*, pages 175–194. University of Notre Dame Press, Notre Dame, IN, 1989. 28, 44, 163

[87] Gordon R. Fleming. Lorentz invariant state reduction, and localization. In A. Fine and J. Leplin, editors, *PSA 1988: Proceedings of the 1988 Biennial Meeting of the Philosophy of Science Association, Vol. II*, pages 112–126. Philosophy of Science Association, East Lansing, MI, 1989. 32

[88] J. D. Franson. Nonlocal interferometry: Beyond Bell's Inequality. arXiv.org/abs/1707.0475, 2007. 131

[89] Herbert Fröhlich. Long-range coherence and energy storage in biological systems. *International Journal of Quantum Chemistry*, 2(5):641–649, 1968. 134

[90] K. Fujiwara. Is the light velocity in vacuum really a constant? Possible breakdown of the linear $\omega - k$ relation at extremely high frequencies. *Foundations of Physics*, 10(3/4):309–331, 1980. 44

[91] D.J. Furley. Parmenides of Elea. In P. Edwards, editor, *Encyclopedia of Philosophy, Vol. VI*, pages 47–51. The Free Press, New York, 1967. 113

[92] Dov Gabbay and John Woods. 'The new logic'. *Logic Journal of the IGPL*, 9:157–190, 2001. 111

[93] G.C. Ghirardi, A. Rimini, and T. Weber. A general argument against superluminal transmission through the quantum mechanical measurement process. *Lettere al Nuovo Cimento*, 27(10):293–298, 1980. 13, 27, 31, 38, 161

[94] G.C. Ghirardi and T. Weber. Quantum mechanics and faster than light communication: Methodological considerations. *Lettere al Nuovo Cimento*, 78 B(1):9–20, 1983. 38

[95] P. Gibbins. *Particles and Paradoxes: The Limitations of Quantum Logic*. Cambridge University Press, Cambridge, 1987. 86

[96] Louisa Gilder. *The Age of Entanglement: When Quantum Physics was Reborn*. Random House, New York, 2008. 5

[97] Kurt Gödel. A remark about the relationship between relativity theory and idealistic philosophy. In P.A. Schilpp, editor, *Albert Einstein: Philosopher-Scientist*, pages 557–562. Open Court, La Salle, IL, 1949. 113

[98] Sheldon Goldstein. Review essay: Bohmian mechanics and the quantum revolution. *Synthese*, 107:145–165, 1996. 47

[99] Lisa Grossman. Entangled diamonds blur classical-quantum divide. *New Scientist*, https://www.newscientist.com/article/dn21235-entangled-diamonds-blur-quantum-classical-divide/, 2011. 153

[100] A. Grünbaum. *Philosophical Problems of Space and Time*. D. Reidel, Dordrecht, second edition, 1973. 151

[101] Ian Hacking. *Representing and Intervening: Introductory Topics in the Philosophy of Science*. Cambridge University Press, Cambridge, 1983. 61

[102] Ian Hacking. Experimentation and scientific realism. In Jarrett Leplin, editor, *Scientific Realism*, pages 154–172. University of California Press, Berkeley, 1984. 61

[103] James Hansen. *Storms of my Grandchildren: The Truth About the Coming Climate Catastrophe and Our Last Chance to Save Humanity*. Bloomsbury, New York, 2010. 176

[104] Stephen Hawking. *Is the End in Sight for Theoretical Physics?* Cambridge University Press, Cambridge, 1980. 73

[105] William W. Hay. *Experimenting on a Small Planet: A Scholarly Entertainment*. Springer, Heidelberg, 2013. 1

[106] Robert M. Hazen. *The Story of Earth: The First 4.5 Billion Years, from Stardust to Living Planet*. Penguin Books, New York, 2012. 1

[107] Robert A. Heinlein. *Time for the Stars*. Charles Scribners Sons, New York, 1956. (Page references are to the Ballantine/Del Ray reprint, New York, 1984.). 8, 15, 17, 117

[108] Robert A. Heinlein. *Stranger in a Strange Land*. G.P. Putnam's Sons, New York, 1961. 17

[109] Nick Herbert. FLASH—A superluminal communicator based upon a new kind of quantum measurement. *Foundations of Physics*, 12(12):1171–1179, December 1982. 13

[110] Clare Hewitt-Horsman. An introduction to many worlds in quantum computation. *Foundations of Physics*, 39:869–902, 2009. 127, 129

[111] B.J. Hiley and F. David Peat. General introduction: The development of David Bohm's ideas from the plasma to the implicate order. In B.J. Hiley and F. David Peat, editors, *Quantum Implications: Essays in Honour of David Bohm*, pages 1–32. Routledge and Kegan Paul, London and New York, 1987. 177

[112] J.M. Hill and B.J. Cox. Einstein's Special Relativity beyond the speed of light. *Proceedings of the Royal Society A*, 468:4174–4192, 2012. 138

[113] John Horgan. *The End of Science: Facing the Limits of Knowledge in the Twilight of the Scientific Age*. Addison-Wesley, Reading, MA, 1996. 58

[114] Don Howard. 'Nicht sein kann was nicht sein darf', or the prehistory of EPR, 1909–1935: Einstein's early worries about the quantum mechanics of composite systems. In A.I. Miller, editor, *Sixty-Two Years of Uncertainty*, pages 61–111. Plenum Press, New York, 1990. 29

[115] F. Hoyle and J. V. Narlikar. *Action at a distance in physics and cosmology*. W. H. Freeman, San Francisco, 1974. 48

[116] R.I.G. Hughes. Quantum logic. *Scientific American*, 245(4):202–213, 1981. 92

[117] R.I.G. Hughes. *The Structure and Interpretation of Quantum Mechanics*. Harvard University Press, Cambriadge, MA, 1989. 92

[118] M. Jammer. *Concepts of Simultaneity: From Antiquity to Einstein and Beyond*. Johns Hopkins University Press, Baltimore, MD, 2006. 151

[119] Jon P. Jarrett. On the physical significance of the locality conditions in the Bell arguments. *Noûs*, 18:569–589, 1984. 5, 31

[120] Thomas F. Jordan. Quantum correlations do not transmit signals. *Physics Letters*, 94A(6,7):264, 21 March 1983. 13, 31, 161

[121] J. B. Kennedy. On the empirical foundations of the quantum no-signalling proofs. *Philosophy of Science*, 62:543–560, 1995. 6, 13, 28, 31, 70, 124, 129, 132, 157, 164, 167, 178

[122] Pierre Kerszberg. *The Invented Universe: The Einstein-de Sitter Controversy (1916–17) and the Rise of Relativistic Cosmology*. Clarendon Press, Oxford, 1989. 59

[123] Charles Kittel and Kerbert Kroemer. *Thermal Physics*. W.H. Freeman, San Francisco, Second edition, 1980. 39

[124] Stephen Kleene. *Mathematical Logic*. Johnn Wiley and Sons, New York, 1967. 111

[125] Thomas H. Kuhn. *The Structure of Scientific Revolutions*. University of Chicago Press, Chicago, Second edition, 1970. 49

[126] Imre Lakatos. *Proofs and Refutations: The Logic of Mathematical Discovery*. Cambridge University Press, Cambridge, 1976. 27, 28, 127

[127] Robert B. Laughlin. *A Different Universe: Reinventing Physics from the Bottom Down*. Basic Books, New York, 2005. 10

[128] K. C. Lee, M. R. Sprague, B. J. Sussman, J. Nunn, N. K. Langford, X.-M. Jin, T. Champion, P. Michelberger, K. F. Reim, D. England, D. Jaksch, and I. A. Walmsley. Entangling mascroscopic diamonds at room temperature. *Science*, 334:1253–1256, December 2011. 131, 152, 158

[129] David Lindley. *The End of Physics: The Myth of a Unified Theory*. Basic Books, New York, 1993. 58

[130] S. J. Lomonaco. A Quick Glance at Quantum Cryptography, https://arxiv.org/abs/quant-ph/9811056. 160

[131] J.R. Lucas. A century of time. In J. Butterfield, editor, *The Arguments of Time*, pages 1–20. Oxford University Press and the British Academy, Oxford, 1990. 138

[132] Charles Mann and Robert Crease. Interview with John S. Bell. *Omni*, pages 84+, May 1988. 126, 148

[133] L. Marder. *Time and the Space Traveller*. George Allen and Unwin, London, 1971. 21, 144

[134] Lynn Margulis. *Origin of Eukaryotic Cells*. Yale University Press, New Haven, CN, 1970. 2

[135] Lynn Margulis. *Symbiotic Planet: A New Look at Evolution*. Basic Books, New York, 1998. 2

[136] Tim Maudlin. Bell's inequality, information transmission, and prism models. In K. Okruhlik D. Hull, M. Forbes, editor, *PSA 1992 Volume One*, pages 404–417. Philosophy of Science Association, East Lansing, MI, 1992. 28, 162

[137] Tim Maudlin. *Quantum Non-Locality and Relativity*. Blackwell, Blackwell, 1994. 28, 34, 35, 37, 52, 67, 160

[138] Tim Maudlin. *Quantum Non-Locality and Relativity: Metaphysical Intimations of Modern Physics*. Blackwell, Oxford, second edition, 2002. 137, 154

[139] Tim Maudlin. Robust versus anemic: comments on *Objective Becoming*. *Philosophical Studies*, 175:1807–1814, 2018. 9

[140] Nicholas Maxwell. Are Probabilism and Special Relativity Incompatible? *Philosophy of Science*, 52:23–42, 1985. 15, 16, 113, 114, 117, 120, 139

[141] Nicholas Maxwell. Discussion: Are Probabilism and Special Relativity Compatible? *Philosophy of Science*, 55:640–645, December 1988. 15, 16, 117

[142] Nicholas Maxwell. Particle creation as the quantum condition for probabilistic events to occur. *Physics Letters A*, 187:351–355, 1994. 117

[143] Richard McKeon. *The Basic Works of Aristotle*. Random House, New York, 1941. 113, 114

[144] N. David Mermin. *Boojums all the Way Through: Communicating Science in a Prosaic Age*. Cambridge University Press, Cambridge, 1990. 161

[145] A.A. Michelson. *Light Waves and Their Uses*. University of Chicago Press, Chicago, 1903. 73, 75

[146] Charles Misner, Kip Thorne, and John Archibald Wheeler. *Gravitation*. W. H. Freeman, San Francisco, 1973. 45, 125, 131, 143

[147] P. Mittelstaedt. Can EPR-correlations be used for the transmission of superluminal signals? *Annalen der Physik*, 7:710–715, 1998. 6, 31, 132, 157, 172, 178

[148] F. A. Muller. Philosophy of physics for pedestrians. *Studies in History and Philosophy of Science*, 25(3):505–509, 1994. 29, 59

[149] F.A. Muller. On the principle of relativity. *Foundations of Physics Letters*, 5(6):591–595, 1992. 143

[150] F.A. Muller. Wordlines are growing! On ontological fatalism, temporal becoming and the special theory of relativity. Unpublished preprint, 1992. 118

[151] Brent Mundy. The Physical Content of Minkowski Geometry. *The British Journal for the Philosophy of Science*, 37(1):25–54, March 1986. 15, 43, 114, 151

[152] Thomas Nagel. *The View from Nowhere*. Oxford University Press, Oxford, 1986. 64

[153] Graham Nerlich. Special Relativity is not based on causality. *British Journal for the Philosophy of Science*, 33:361–388, 1982. 148

[154] M. A. Nielsen and I. L. Chuang. *Quantum Computation and Quantum Information*. Cambridge University Press, Cambridge, 2000. 108, 109

[155] E.C.G. Sudarshan O.-M. Bilaniuk, V.K. Deshpande. "Meta" Relativity. *American Journal of Physics*, 30(10):718–723, 1962. 137

[156] Leonard Parker. Faster-than-light inertial frames and tachyons. *Physical Review*, 188(5):2287–2292, 1969. 51

[157] Wolfgang Pauli. The connection between spin and statistics. *Physical Review*, 58:713–722, 1940. 12, 32, 70, 172

[158] T. G. Pavlopoulos. Breakdown of Lorentz invariance. *Physical Review*, 159(5):1106–1110, 1967. 44

[159] Kent A. Peacock. *Peaceful coesistence or armed truce? Quantum nonlocality and the spacetime view of the world*. PhD Dissertation, Department of Philosophy, University of Toronto, 1991. 12, 28, 31, 43

[160] Kent A. Peacock. Comment on 'Tests of signal locality and Einstein-Bell locality for multiparticle systems' by S. Roy and V. Singh. *Physical Review Letters*, 69(18):2733, 1992. 28, 31, 70, 124, 129, 132, 157, 164, 178

[161] Kent A. Peacock. A new look at simultaneity. In D. Hull, M. Forbes, and K. Okruhlik, editors, *Proceedings of the 1992 Biennial Meeting of the Philosophy of Science Association, Vol. I*, pages 542–552. Philosophy of Science Association, East Lansing, MI, 1992. 43, 118

[162] Kent A. Peacock. *Living with the Earth: An Introduction to Environmental Philosophy*. Harcourt Brace Canada, Toronto, 1996. 3

[163] Kent A. Peacock. On the edge of a paradigm shift: Quantum nonlocality and the breakdown of peaceful coexistence. *International Studies in the Philosophy of Science*, 12(2):129–150, 1998. 125, 153, 164

[164] Kent A. Peacock. Temporal presentness and the dynamics of spactime. In Dennis Dieks, editor, *The Ontology of Spactime*, chapter 13, pages 247–261. Elsevier, 2006. 150

[165] Kent A. Peacock. *The Quantum Revolution: A Historical Perspective*. Greenwood Press, Westport, CT, 2008. viii

[166] Kent A. Peacock. Symbiosis in ecology and evolution. In Kevin deLaplante, Bryson Brown, and Kent A. Peacock, editors, *Philosophy of Ecology*, pages 219–250. Elsevier, Amsterdam, 2011. 2

[167] Kent A. Peacock. A different kind of rigor: What climate scientists can learn from emergency room doctors. *Ethics, Policy, and Environment*, 21(2), 2018. 2

[168] Kent A. Peacock and Brian S. Hepburn. Begging the signalling question: Quantum signalling and the dynamics of multiparticle systems. In J. Woods and B. Brown, editors, *New Studies in Exact Philosophy: Proceedings of the 1999 Conference of the Society for Exact Philosophy*, pages 277–290. Hermes Science, Oxford, 2001. Preprint: arXiv.org/abs/quant-ph/9906036. 81, 124

[169] F. David Peat. *Infinite Potential: The Life and Times of David Bohm*. Addison-Wesley, Reading, MA, 1997. 71

[170] Roger Penrose. *The Emperor's New Mind*. Vintage, London, 1990. 117

[171] V. Petkov. Does the theory of relativity relativize existence as well? Montreal Inter-University Seminar on the History and Philosophy of Science., 2002. 115

[172] John R. Pierce. *Symbols, Signals, and Noise: The Nature and Process of Communication*. Harper and Row, New York, 1961. 38

# Bibliography 195

[173] Itamar Pitowsky. *Quantum Probability—Quantum Logic*. Springer-Verlag, Berlin, 1989. 86

[174] Itamar Pitowsky. George Boole's 'conditions of possible experience' and the quantum puzzle. *British Journal for the Philosophy of Science*, 45:95–125, 1994. 28, 29, 69, 96, 128, 160, 163, 179

[175] Plato. *Timaeus and Critias*. Penguin, Harmondsworth, 1965. Translation by Desmond Lee. 61

[176] John C. Polanyi. Heresy is the lifeblood of science. *The Globe and Mail*, page F7, November 27 2004. 181

[177] Hilary Putnam. Time and Physical Geometry. *The Journal of Philosophy*, 64:240–247, 1967. 16

[178] Hilary Putnam. The logic of quantum mechanics. In *Mathematics, Matter, and Method*, pages 174–197. Cambridge University Press, Cambridge, 1975. First published as 'Is logic empirical?' in R. Cohen and M. Wartofsky (eds.), *Boston Studies in the Philosophy of Science* 5, D. Reidel, Dordrecht, 1968. 84, 96

[179] Hilary Putnam. A philosopher looks at quantum mechanics. In *Mathematics, Matter, and Method*, pages 130–158. Cambridge University Press, Cambridge, 1975. 84, 93, 96

[180] E. Recami. Classical tachyons and possible applications. *Rivista del Nuovo Cimento*, 9(6):1–178, 1986. 137

[181] Michael Redhead. *Incompleteness, Nonlocality, and Realism: A prolegomenon to the philosophy of quantum mechanics*. Oxford University Press, Oxford, 1987. 29, 59, 70

[182] Hans Reichenbach. *The Philosophy of Space and Time*. Dover Books, New York, 1957. Translation by M. Reichenbach and J. Freund of *Philosophie der Raum-Zeit-Lehre*, 1928. 148, 151

[183] Nicholas Rescher. *Topics in Philosophical Logic*. D. Reidel, Dordrecht, 1968. 108

[184] Richard Rhodes. *The Making of the Atomic Bomb*. Touchstone (Simon and Schuster), New York, 1988. 126

[185] C.W. Rietdijk. On Nonlocal Influences. In G. Tarozzi and A. van der Merwe, editors, *Open Questions in Quantum Physics*, pages 129–151. Reidel, Dordrecht, 1985. 16, 25, 119, 123, 150

[186] Wolfgang Rindler. *Essential Relativity: Special, General, and Cosmological*. Springer-Verlag, NewYork, Revised second edition, 1979. 142

[187] Richard Rorty. Pragmatism, relativism, and irrationalism. *Proceedings and Addresses of the American Philosophical Association*, 53:719–738, 1980. Reprint in P.L. Moser and A. vander Nat (eds.), *Human Knowledge: Classical and Contemporary Approaches* (Oxford: Oxford University Press, 1987), 215. 62

[188] M. Rothman. Things that go faster than light. *Scientific American*, 203(1):142–152, 1960. 139, 140

[189] Carlo Rovelli. Halfway through the woods: Contemporary research on space and time. In John Earman and John D. Norton, editors, *The Cosmos of Science: Essays of Exploration*, pages 180–223. University of Pittsburgh Press, Pittsburgh, PA, 1997. 4, 180

[190] Carlo Rovelli. *Quantum Gravity*. Cambridge University Press, Cambridge, 2004. 149

[191] S. M. Roy and V. Singh. Response to comment by Peacock. *Physical Review Letters*, 69(18):2734, 2 November 1992. 13

[192] S. M. Roy and Virendra Singh. Hidden variable theories without non-local signalling and their experimental tests. *Physics Letters A*, 139(9):437–441, August 28 1989. P-6-30. 12, 31

[193] S. M. Roy and Virendra Singh. Tests of signal locality and Einstein-Bell locality for multiparticle systems. *Physical Review Letters*, 67(20):2761–2764, November 1991. 12

[194] Bertrand Russell. *The Principles of Mathematics*. Cambridge University Press, Cambridge, 1903. 27

[195] Carl Sagan. *The Demon-Haunted World: Science as a Candle in the Dark*. Random House, New York, 1996. 58

[196] Wesley Salmon. *Space, Time, and Motion: A Philosophical Introduction*. University of Minnesota Press, Minneapolis, MN, second edition, 1980. 139, 148

[197] Steven Savitt. Being and becoming in modern physics. In Edward N. Zalta, editor, *The Stanford Encyclopedia of Philosophy*. 2017. https://plato.stanford.edu/archives/fall2017/entries/spacetime-bebecome/. 113, 114

[198] Erwin Schrödinger. Sur la théorie de l'électron et l'interprétation de la mécanique quantique. *Annales de l'Institut H. Poincaré*, 2(4):269–310, 1932. 45

[199] Erwin Schrödinger. Die gegenwärtige Situation in der Quantenmechanik. *Naturwissenschaften*, 23:807–812, 823–828, 844–849, 1935. Translation by J.D. Trimmer in J.A. Wheeler and W. Zurek (eds.), *Quantum Theory and Measurement* (Princeton, Princeton University Press), pp. 152–167. 32, 90

[200] Silvan S. Schweber. *An Introduction to Relativistic Quantum Field Theory*. Harper & Row, New York, 1961. 12

[201] Abner Shimony. Metaphysical problems in the foundations of quantum mechanics. *International Philosophical Quarterly*, 18(1):2–17, 1978. 5, 28, 69, 127

[202] Abner Shimony. Controllable and uncontrollable non-locality. In S. Kamefuchi et al., editor, *Proceedings of the International Symposium on Foundations of Quantum Mechanics*, pages 225–230. Physical Society of Japan, Tokyo, 1983. 13, 32, 130, 157, 159, 161, 168

[203] Abner Shimony. Events and processes in the quantum world. In R. Penrose and C. J. Isham, editors, *Quantum Concepts in Space and Time*, pages 182–203. Clarendon Press, Oxford, 1986. 28, 34, 38, 110, 169, 177

[204] Abner Shimony. An exposition of Bell's Theorem. In A.I. Miller, editor, *Sixty-Two Years of Uncertainty*, pages 33–43. Plenum Press, New York, 1990. Reprinted in: A. Shimony (1993), *Search For a Naturalistic World View*, Vol. II. (Cambridge, Cambridge University Press), pp. 90–103. 28, 29

[205] J.R. Shoenfield. *Mathematical Logic*. Addison-Wesley, Reading, MA, 1967. 111

[206] Nevil Shute. *Slide Rule: The Autobiography of an Engineer*. William Morrow, New York, 1954. 63

[207] R. Sigal and A. Shamaly. Tachyon behavior in general relativity. *Phys. Rev. D*, 10(8):2358–2361, Oct 1974. 140

[208] N.J.J. Smith. Bananas enough for time travel? *British Journal for the Philosophy of Science*, 48:363–389, 1997. 156

[209] Lee Smolin. How far are we from the quantum theory of gravity?, 2003. url: https://arxiv.org/abs/hep-th/0303185. 121

[210] Lee Smolin. *The Trouble With Physics: The rise of string theory, the fall of a science, and what comes next*. Houghton Mifflin, Boston, 2006. 133, 180

[211] Lee Smolin. *Time Reborn: From the Crisis in Physics to the Future of the Universe*. Knopf Canada, Toronto, 2013. 8

[212] H.P. Stapp. Bell's Theorem and world process. *Nuovo Cimento*, 29B(2):270–276, 1975. 4

[213] H.P. Stapp. *Mind, Matter, and Quantum Mechanics*. Springer-Verlag, Berlin, 1993. 67

[214] Howard Stein. On Einstein-Minkowski Space-Time. *The Journal of Philosophy*, 65:5–23, 1968. 16, 19, 115

[215] Howard Stein. On Relativity Theory and Openness of the Future. *Philosophy of Science*, 58(2):147–167, June 1991. 15, 16, 17, 19, 25, 115, 121

[216] R.I. Sutherland and J.R. Shepanski. Superluminal reference frames and generalized Lorentz transformations. *Physical Review D*, 33:2896–2902, 1986. 50, 51, 55, 56, 137, 140, 145, 156

[217] Edwin F. Taylor and John Archibald Wheeler. *Spacetime Physics*. Freeman, San Francisco, 1966. 15, 22, 114, 142, 148, 149

[218] Paul Teller. Infinite renormalization. *Philosophy of Science*, 56(2):238–257, 1989. 61

[219] Paul Teller. Relativity, relational holism, and the Bell Inequalities. In J. T. Cushing and E. McMullin, editors, *Philosophical Consequences of Quantum Theory: Reflections on Bell's Theorem*, pages 208–221. University of Notre Dame Press, Notre Dame, IN, 1989. 42

[220] Paul Teller. Quantum mechanics and haecceities. In Elena Castellani, editor, *Interpreting Bodies: Classical and Quantum Objects in Modern Physics*, pages 114–141. Princeton University Press, Princeton, 1998. 100, 101

[221] N. Tennant. *Autologic*. Edinburgh University Press, Edinburgh, 1993. 94

[222] A. Souter et al. *Oxford Latin Dictionary*. Clarendon Press, Oxford, 1968. 151

[223] Antony Valentini. Signal-locality, uncertainty, and the subquantum $H$-theorem. I. *Physics Letters A*, 156(1):5–11, 1991. 167

[224] Bas C. van Fraassen. A modal interpretation of quantum mechanics. In Enrico G. Beltrametti and Bas C. van Fraassen, editors, *Current Issues in Quantum Logic*, pages 229–258. Plenum Press, New York, 1981. 79, 80, 102

[225] Bas C. van Fraassen. *Quantum Mechanics: An Empiricist View*. Clarendon Press, Oxford, 1991. 28

[226] Bas C. van Fraassen. The problem of indistinguishable particles. In Elena Castellani, editor, *Interpreting Bodies: Classical and Quantum Objects in Modern Physics*, pages 73–92. Princeton University Press, Princeton, 1998. 100

[227] R.S. Vieira. An introduction to the theory of tachyons ('uma introdução á teoria dos táquions'). *Revista Brasileira de Ensino de Física*, 34(3):3306–2–3306–15, 2012. Preprint (English) at https://arxiv.org/abs/1112.4187. 138

[228] Rudolph von Brown Rucker. *Geometry, Relativity, and the Fourth Dimension*. Dover, New York, 1977. 26

[229] Theordore von Karman. *Aerodynamics*. Cornell University Press, Ithaca, NY, 1954. Page numbers refer to McGraw-Hill reprint, 1963. 44

[230] Steven Weinberg. *Dreams of a Final Theory*. Pantheon Books, New York, 1992. 29

[231] Steven Weinberg. *Cosmology*. Oxford University Press, Oxford and New York, 2008. 149

[232] S. Weinstein. Superluminal signalling and relativity. *Synthèse*, 148:381–399, 2006. 132, 139, 140

[233] Hermann Weyl. *Philosophy of Mathematics and Natural Science*. Princeton University Press, Princeton, NJ, 1949. 8

[234] John A. Wheeler. Law without law. In J.A. Wheeler and W.H. Zurek, editors, *Quantum Theory and Measurement*, pages 182–213. Princeton University Press, Princeton, NJ, 1983. 41

# Bibliography

[235] Eugene Wigner. Remarks on the mind-body question. In I.J. Good, editor, *The Scientist Speculates*, pages 284–302. Heinemann, London, 1961. Reprinted in J.A. Wheeler and W. Zurek (eds.), *Quantum Theory and Measurement* (Princeton: Princeton University Press, 1983), pp. 168–181. 66

[236] M.D. Wilson, editor. *The Essential Descartes*. New American Library, New York, 1969. 83

[237] John Woods. *Paradox and Paraconsistency: Conflict Resolution in the Abstract Sciences*. Cambridge University Press, Cambridge, 2003. 97, 148

# Index

Abner Shimony, 69
absolute time, 7
Ackeret, Jakob, 44
action, 8, 124
Aharonov, Yakir, 134, 155
Albert, David, 67
Ardavan, Houshang, 44, 140
Aristotle, 8, 113
    definition of time, 116
    sea battle, 114
Arntzenius, Frank, 57, 118, 138, 146
Arthur, Richard T.A., 114, 116, 123, 144

background independence, 133
Ballentine, Leslie, 42
beables, 90
becoming
    objective, 16, 113
    temporal, 15
Bell Inequalities, 5, 102, 128, 160
Bell telephone, 4
Bell's Theorem, 4, 59, 179
    universal, 8
Bell, John Stewart, 68–69, 126, 128, 148, 162
    on impossibility, 136
Bell-Kochen-Specker Theorem, 9, 79, 90, 124
Big Bang, 119
Bilaniuk, O.-M., 137
Birkhoff, Garrett, 78, 84, 101
bivalence, breakdown, 95
block universe, 8
Bohm interpretation, 81
Bohm, David, 39, 68, 77, 154, 162, 174
Bohmian mechanics, 163

Bohr, Niels, 29, 41
boojums, 74
Boole, George, 69, 128
Boolean logic, 84
Born Rule, 87
Born's Rule, 127
Born, Max, 132
Bose-Einstein statistics, 170
Brown, H.R., 144
Brown, James Robert, 48
Brown, M. Bryson, 47
Bub, Jeffrey, 77–82, 102, 103
Bub-Clifton theorem, 79
Bussey, P.J., 6, 132

Cabello, A., 139, 144
Cartwright, N., 29
causal anomalies, 179
causal interpretation, 154–156
causal order, 23
causal paradoxes, 56, 134–135
Chang, H., 29
Church-Turing thesis, 109
circularity, 7
classical logic, 91, 92
Clifton, Rob, 78, 103, 115, 118
Cohen-Tannoudji, C., 172
common cause, 35
complementarity, 107
conjugate quantities, 65
continental drift, 1
controllable nonlocality, 5
Convention T, 108
Copenhagen interpretation, 77
cosmic background radiation, 135
Cox, J.C., 138

Crichton, J. Willison, 26
Cushing, James T., 45

Dainton, Barry, 138, 145
de Broglie, Louis, 117, 155, 162
de Broglie-Bohm pilot wave model, 111
density matrix, 12
Descartes, René, 83, 112
Deutsch, David, 84, 110
devil's advocate, 7
Dick, Philip K., 20
Dickson, Michael, 39, 91
Dieks, Dennis, 25, 119
Dingle, Herbert, 21
Dirac notation, 87
distributive law, failure of, 84
divergence at $v = c$, 156
Dobbs, H.A.C., 123

Eberhard, P., 32
Eberhard, P.H., 31
Eddington, A. S., 123
eigenstates, 87
eigenvalues, 87
Einstein, Albert, 7, 29, 43, 46, 73, 75, 96, 142, 148, 177
Einstein-Podolsky-Rosen thought experiment, 29, 68, 77, 79, 128, 160
Elitzur, Avshalom, 34, 37
energy
    nonlocal, 174
Engesser, Kurt, 106
entangled states, 6, 171
    dynamics, 176
entangled states, dynamics of, 6
Epplett, Christopher, 95
Equivalence Principle, 131
Everett, Hugh, 110
ex falso quodlibet, 95
Existential Instantiation, 107
extended relativity, 3

Fayngold, M., 138
Feinberg, G., 137
Fermi-Dirac statistics, 170
Feynman's Problem, 86–89
Feynman, Richard, 38, 60, 86
Fine, Arthur, 28, 34, 163

first order logic, 91
Forster, Marc, 7
frame of reference
    local co-moving, 120, 143
    Lorentz, 22, 135, 142
    Lorentz frame, 154
    preferred, 8
Frege, Gottlob, 91
Fröhlich, H., 134
Fujiwara, K., 44
future, openness of, 124

Gabbay, Dov, 106
Galilean covariance, 156
Gauss, K.F., 96
general covariance, 149
gentle pillow for the true believer, 80
Ghirardi, G.C., 27, 38
global warming, 2
Greenberger-Horne-Zeilinger (GHZ) state, 35
Grossman, Lisa, 153
Grünbaum, A., 151
Guarini, M., 39
Guay, Alexandre, 137
Gödel, Kurt, 74

Hacking, Ian, 61
Hamiltonian, 12, 32, 38, 130
    additive, 171
    nonlocal, 47
Hawking, Stephen, 73
Heinlein, Robert A., 8, 15, 17–19, 117
Heinlein, Virginia, 26
Heisenberg, Werner, 132
Hepburn, Brian, ix, 5, 11
Heraclitus, 113
heresy, ix, 181
Hermitian operator, 87
Heuristic Fallacy, 148
Hewitt-Horsmann, Clare, 127, 129
hidden variables, 47
Hilbert Space, 86, 106
Hiley, Basil, 39, 154, 177
Hill, J.M., 138
Hogarth, Mark, 115, 118
Horgan, John, 58

# Index

Howard, Don, 29
hyperplanes of simultaneity, 142

idealism, 64
incommensurability, 73–74
incompleteness, 74
individuation, 100
instantaneity, 137
    relativity of, 23, 117
instanteneity, 142

Jammer, Max, 151
Jarrett, Jon, 5, 31
joint process, 8

Kant, I., 96
Kennedy, J.B. Jr., 6, 31, 132, 178
Kernaghan, Michael, 24
Korolev, Alex, 24
Kuhn, Thomas, 49

Lagrangian, 24
Lakatos, Imre, 27, 28
lattice theory, 78, 89
Laughlin, Robert B., 10
Lee, K.C., 152, 158
Leibniz, G.W., 63
Lewis, David, 178
Lindenbaum algebra, 106
local quantum field theory, 12, 178
local realism, 69
Loewer, Barry, 67
logicism, 85
Lorentz frame, 150
Lorentz invariance, 46, 121, 156
Lorentz transformations, 148, 180
Lucas, J.R., 138, 145

Marder, L., 21, 144
Margulis, Lynn, 2
Maudlin, Tim, 8, 34, 37, 154, 162
Maxwell, Nicholas, 16, 113, 114, 117, 120, 124, 139
McGinn, Colin, 58
measurement problem, 41, 66
Mermin, N. David, 161
Mermin, N. David, 35
metric, 50

Michelson, A.A., 73
microcausality, 12, 32, 70, 124, 172, 178
Minkowski spacetime, 16, 133
Misner, C., 45
Mittelstaedt, P., 6, 132, 178
mixed operators, 173
mixed states, 173
modal interpretation, 80, 102
model theory, 95
Mulder, Fox, 160
Muller, F.A., 29, 59, 118, 143
multilocality, 71
multiverse interpretation, 110
Mundy, Brent, 15, 43, 151

Nagel, Thomas, 64
Nerlich, Graham, 148
Newtonian mechanics, 42
no-collapse theories, 79
no-controllable signalling
    field-theoretic proofs, 131–132
    non-relativistic proofs, 129–131
no-controllable-signalling, 31–32, 127
no-signalling arguments, circularity of, 5–6, 71
nonlocality, 86
nonrelativistic quantum mechanics, 12
Normore, Calvin, 26

observables, 65
ontological interpretation, 82

paradigm shift, 2, 10
parameter independence, 31, 171
Parker, Leonard, 51
Parmenides, 113
passion at a distance, 5
Pauli, W., 172
Pavlopoulos, T.G., 44
peaceful coexistence, 1, 5, 28, 69, 124, 127
Peat, David, 177
Pirac, P.A.M., 46
Pitowsky, Itamar, 29, 69, 96, 128, 163, 179
Planck's constant, 88
Planck, Max, 47, 90
pluralism, logical, 84

Poincaré, Henri, 148
Polanyi, John C., 181
Popper, Karl, 62
predicate logic, 94
principle vs. constructive theories, 42
Principle of Relativity, 10, 46, 55, 119, 135, 143
probabilism, 16, 114
product states, 172
Putnam, Hilary, 84

quantum chromodynamics, 60
quantum computation, 85, 134
quantum consequence relation, 99
quantum cryptography, 31, 129
quantum detonation, 95
quantum gravity, 152
quantum logic, 78, 83–94, 112
quantum potential, 41, 117, 131, 164
quantum statistics, 101

realism, 64
    vs. describability, 64
    local, 59
    nonlocal, 59, 72
Recami, E., 137
Redhead, Michael, 29, 58–76, 178
reductionism, failure of, 72
Reichenbach, H., 151
renormalization, 60
retrocausal theories of quantum mechanics, 48
Riemann, B., 96
Riemannian geometry, 96
Rietdijk, C.W., 25, 123
Rorty, Richard, 62
Rothman, M., 140
Rovelli, Carlo, 4, 180
Roy, S.M., 12
Rucker, R. von B., 26
Russell, Bertrand, 27, 91, 127

Salmon, W., 139, 146
Sarfatti, Jack, 134
Schrödinger, Erwin, 89
Schrödinger Equation, 66
Schrödinger's cat, 77, 78, 156
Schrödinger, Erwin, 32, 45, 66

Schwinger, Julian, 60
Scully, Dana, 160
searchlight-beam effect, 139
serial endosymbiosis, 1
Shamaly, A., 140
Shanks, Niall, 37
Shepanski, J.R., 50–52, 56, 137, 138, 145
Shimony, Abner, 5, 28, 110, 127, 169, 174, 177, 181
Shute, Neville, 63
Sigal, R., 140
signal locality, 12
simultaneity, 7, 15, 149–153
    absolute, 16
    causal, 151
    distant, 7
    dynamic, 24
    in terms of action, 23–25, 118
    intrinsic, 24
    invariant, 16, 19, 43, 118
    joint, 178
    joint process, 7, 151, 153
    local, 151
    optical, 15, 114–116
    relativity of, 8
    topological, 151
Singh, V., 12
singularity, 10
Smolin, Lee, 8, 133, 180
Solomon, Graham, 26
special relativity, 3
    as principle theory, 133
specious present, 8, 23
Spirit of Relativity, 134
Stalingrad, Battle of, 3
Stapp. H. P., 4
state reduction, 117, 122–123, 149–150
Stein, Howard, 16–17, 19, 115, 121
Sudarshan, E.C.G., 137
superconductivity, 134
superluminal motion, 3
superposition principle, 86
Sutherland, Roderick I., 50–52, 56, 137, 138, 145
symmetry of wave function, 170
synchronization, 142, 147
Szilard, Leo, 126

# Index

tachyon, 3, 140
telepathy, 8
Teller, Paul, 42
tenth person, 7
Theory of Everything, 72–73
thermodynamics, 39
    second law of, 13, 130
thisness in quantum mechanics, 102
Thorne, K., 45
time
    absolute, 116, 149
    elapsed proper, 22, 116
    global, 149
    phase, 123
    proper, 20, 145
    relativistic, 149
Tomonaga, S,, 60
Treiman, Sam, 96
truth
    coherence theory, 62
    correspondence theory, 62
Turing machine, 109
twin paradox, 8, 18–23, 116, 117, 144
    superluminal, 56

Uncertainty Relations, 152

vacuum as dispersive, 44, 121
van Fraaassen, Bas, 80
van Fraassen, Bas, 79, 102
van Neumann, John, 84
Vieira, R.S., 138
von Karman, Theodore, 44
von Neumann, John, 31, 66, 78, 101

Warmbrunn, Jurgen, 7
wave function collapse, 9
Weber, T., 38
Weinberg, Steven, 29
Weinstein, Steven, 132, 140
Weyl, Hermann, 8
Wheeler, John A., 41, 45, 67
Wigner, Eugene, 66, 67
Woods, John, ix, 148

www.ingramcontent.com/pod-product-compliance
Lightning Source LLC
Chambersburg PA
CBHW070739160426
43192CB00009B/1502